D0591024

LAST OF THE SUMMER WINE

THE FINEST VINTAGE

LAST OF THE SUMMER WINE

THE FINEST VINTAGE

Morris Bright & Robert Ross

Dedicated to Bill Owen MBE (1914–1999).
For true professionalism, bravery and a precious
second childhood in welly boots.

This book is published to accompany the television series
Last of the Summer Wine, which was first broadcast in 1973.
The series is written by Roy Clarke.
It has been produced and directed by James Gilbert, Bernard Thompson
and Sydney Lotterby, and is currently produced and directed by Alan J.W. Bell.

Published by BBC Worldwide Ltd,
Woodlands, 80 Wood Lane
London W12 0TT

First published 2000
Reprinted 2000
©Morris Bright and Robert Ross 2000
The moral right of the authors has been asserted.

All photographs copyright © BBC, courtesy of BBC Archive (with special thanks to
photographer Malcolm Howarth), except for page 7, courtesy of PA Photos.

All rights reserved.
No part of this book may be reproduced in any form or by any means,
without permission in writing from the publisher,
except by a reviewer who may quote brief passages in a review.

ISBN 0 563 55151 8

Commissioning Editor: Ben Dunn
Project Editor: Charlotte Heathcote
Copy Editor: Hugh Morgan
Designer: Andrew Barron & Collis Clements Associates

Set in Berkeley Oldstyle
Printed and bound in France by Imprimerie Pollina s.a.
Colour separations by Imprimerie Pollina s.a.
Jacket printed by Imprimerie Pollina s.a.

CONTENTS

INTRODUCTION

'This programme is The Mouse Trap *of television comedy.'*

JIMMY GILBERT,
FIRST PRODUCER AND DIRECTOR

Think of the all-time classic BBC situation comedies – *Fawlty Towers*, *Porridge*, *The Good Life*, even *Only Fools and Horses*. All these shows have come and gone during a time when one series, *Last of the Summer Wine*, has survived, achieving further popularity and even breaking in to the new millennium. Emerging just three years after the Beatles had broken up, *Last of the Summer Wine* was still pulling in the ratings when the fab three resurrected John Lennon's 'Free as a Bird' in 1994.

The pilot episode of *Last of the Summer Wine* was broadcast on 4 January 1973. It was the year that saw Princess Anne marry Mark Phillips at Westminster Abbey, Cliff Richard come second in the Eurovision Song Contest with 'Power to All Our Friends', Muhammad Ali beat Joe Bugner in 12 rounds in Las Vegas in the World Heavyweight Championship and Trevor MacDonald join *News at Ten*.

Its beginnings might seem an entire lifetime away but, incredibly, *Last of the Summer Wine* is still very much with us. Even more amazingly, the writer, Roy Clarke, has scripted every single episode of this ground-breaking series, and a quartet of his legendary cast – the late Bill Owen, Peter Sallis, Kathy Staff and Jane Freeman – who all appeared in the first series, were still filming some 27 years later for the year 2000 season.

Like the BritCom equivalent of the Rolling Stones, Bill Owen, Peter Sallis and their various 'third man' leaders have chugged along through a third of a century. Finally, they and the programme have reached the point of national treasures – as much a part of the British way of life as buttered scones and a cup of tea at four o'clock.

Surprisingly, critics, audiences and even the British Broadcasting

Corporation itself has often undervalued and underestimated the importance of the series. Until now.

For the first time, the full story of this classic situation comedy is revealed, from its humble beginnings as a *Comedy Playhouse* episode, through the early, influential years with Michael Bates as Blamire, the golden years with Brian Wilde's Foggy and Michael Aldridge's Seymour and into a new era with Frank Thornton. All the regular cast of comedy favourites tell their amusing anecdotes and pick their favourite *Summer Wine* episodes. We take a sneak look at how *Summer Wine* is filmed, including revealing some of the tricks of the trade that allow beloved figures such as Thora Hird to drive a car at great speed through the streets of Yorkshire, or the three old men to fall off bicycles. We look at the prolific career histories of the regular cast members both past and present, and we take you on a nostalgic stroll through the story lines for each of over 200 episodes – including Christmas Specials and the spin-off series, *First of the Summer Wine*.

So sit back and prepare to take in the bouquet as we uncork the finest vintage of British television comedy.

Cheers!

Jimmy Nail presents the Summer Wine *cast with the National Television Award for the Nation's Favourite Comedy Series at the ceremony in October 1999.*

CAFE

CHAPTER ONE

FISH & FUNERALS

The History of *Last of the Summer Wine* from 1972 to 2000

'Summer Wine *isn't so much a laughter show, as a smiling show.*'

BRIAN WILDE

Naturally, any successful comedy series begins with a very successful comedy writer. As it happened, Roy Clarke wasn't a successful comedy writer. He was, however, a successful writer for television drama. Having started his career penning two popular radio thriller serials under the production eye of playwright Alan Ayckbourn, Roy Clarke's first television credits came in the late 1960s. He wrote a notable episode of *The Troubleshooters* and later contributed to the fondly remembered Patrick Wymark industrial serial, *The Power Game*.

In 1970 he wrote and created the popular ATV comedy drama *The Misfit*, which resurrected a character from his work on *The Troubleshooters*. Basil Allenby-Johnson was played by that fine character actor Ronald Fraser in two series of *The Misfit* and won Clarke the Writers' Guild Award for Best Series. It was, ironically, these ITV shows derived from a BBC programme that brought the writing of Roy Clarke to the attention of the Comedy Department.

Clarke subsequently has gone on to script *Rosie*, *Open All Hours* and *Keeping Up Appearances*, but *Last of the Summer Wine* was the granddaddy of them all and has survived the longest.

The late Duncan Wood, a much-respected comedy producer who had worked on the television classic *Hancock's Half Hour*, invited Clarke to write comedy material for the BBC. However, their first meeting was as much about luck as anything else. Speaking in 1997, Wood recalled:

In 1971, I was Head of Comedy at the BBC. One evening I was watching a series called The Misfit *starring Ronald Fraser. Ronnie gave his usual excellent performance, but what interested me more than anything was the writing. It was supposed to be drama but had great comedy undertones.*

I wanted to meet the writer, so I invited Roy Clarke to come and stay with me and my wife. Down he came, drank most of our Scotch and we plied him with food and drink as we discussed some of his ideas. The one I was most interested in was the idea he had about three old men who had nothing to do and all day to do it in. A fortnight later in came the pilot script. I gave it to one of my esteemed colleagues, Jimmy Gilbert, to

The show's first producer, Jimmy Gilbert, toasts the present producer, Alan J.W. Bell, with tea rather than wine, on the café set in 1997.

Summer Wine's writer, Roy Clarke (second right), makes a rare visit to location filming with the familiar late-1980s' line-up – Peter Sallis, Michael Aldridge and Bill Owen.

produce and direct, and that's how it all started.

Roy Clarke remembers that fortnight as not the easiest time in his writing career:

I was trying to find some way to inject enthusiasm into this for me, let alone an audience, and I was on the point of turning it down and telling Duncan, 'Look, this particular idea is not for me. I can't make it work,' when it came to me. If the three men were free from all responsibilities and ties and were all, for one reason or another, living alone, and either unemployed, redundant or retired, then they had the same kind of freedom that juveniles at the other end of the age-scale have, and the moment I began to see them as carefree and, in effect, as young people, it clicked.

Indeed, everything did click in time for *Comedy Playhouse*. The series was a flagship presentation from BBC Comedy and served the very useful purpose of experimenting with ideas within a recognized format. The hope was for one of these self-contained episodes to hit the right mark so that a series would be commissioned. Probably the best-remembered *Comedy Playhouse* episode was *The Offer*, which led to the excellent *Steptoe and Son*.

The basic structure for the programme was fairly

Opposites attract – Bill Owen and Michael Bates enjoy a (non-political) chat during the filming of the Comedy Playhouse *episode.*

workmanlike. Clarke was told to pen a half-hour ramble concerning the lives of three old men. The result became a geriatric take on *The Goodies* – with Clegg the Tim Brooke-Taylor-like coward, Blamire the Graeme Garden-styled leader and Compo the Bill Oddie-esque scruff-bag.

However, this was not knockabout visual comedy and satirical bubble-pricking; this was a far more gentle, lyrical comedy style, mixing – as both Bill Owen and Peter Sallis have observed – *Just William* with *The Wind in the Willows*.

Roy Clarke remembers these early *Summer Wine* days very well:

I'd just turned 40 – which, OK, is way past acne and your first purchase of underwear not for comfort but for its lower drag coefficient – but it's still not the age when a writer's fancy likely turns to thoughts of varicose veins. The psyche was still more Marlboro country than at home on the geriatric range.

There was also the class factor. I was working for drama departments with people who do joined-up writing and discuss things called themes and dress as if they work in heavy industry and have absolutely no contact with inferior life forms in entertainment departments. It's called Light Entertainment to make sure nobody mistakes it for anything better.

So there I was. I didn't know sitcom. I didn't know old age, so naturally the BBC Comedy Department invited me to write a sitcom about three old men. And that was it. The full extent of the brief. We want something for three old men.

I never did learn why. Maybe they thought that age-

group as an audience wasn't being catered for, and I thought that it was never going to be catered for by me. Three old men? They must be joking. We'll never get it off the ground. And if we do fluke it somehow into being – it's never going to run, is it?

In Clarke's original script, these three old duffers are constructed as childlike, enthusiastic and lovable, happily treating their relative old age as a passport to carefree play. Wisely, Clarke wrote the trio as old school friends who are enjoying a second, even crazier childhood together without any ties of maturity. Thus, wives were either distant memories or non-existent, and there were no children to drag the ageing fun-seekers back to the real world. Only Compo and his long-standing obsession with Nora Batty could pull the lads back from the brink of excess adventure.

Although Roy Clarke was now comfortable with the premise, the show's producer/director, Jimmy Gilbert, was unhappy with the potential age of the characters:

I was a bit nervous of the three characters being in their seventies because I'd already had experience on a previous comedy where the audience was uneasy at laughing at old men and their problems. I asked Roy Clarke if we could make them younger so that they had ten or 15 years more of jolly good life inside them to enjoy themselves. And we really then treated them as children. Whenever we were stuck for a bit of business, I used to say to them, 'Well, how would kids do this?' and they used to kick a can or do something like three juvenile delinquents.

Brian Wilde, later to join the cast as Foggy, agrees:

Most wives will tell you that men never really get beyond the age of 12! The other reason the characters worked so well is that the men never gave up. We refused to be old and clapped out. We would not commit the ultimate sin – to despair.

Although still a relatively young man, Clarke, like Alan Bennett and Alan Plater, discovered a natural skill for creating believable northern dialogues. These three old men came alive with local mannerisms, references and comparisons. Their world was self-contained, where Huddersfield was the brightly lit Mecca, ferrets and fags could make up a perfect day, and philosophical conversation in a library could challenge the strongest preconceptions.

Clarke was told to pen a half-hour ramble concerning the lives of three old men. The result became a geriatric take on The Goodies.

Indeed, so involved were the trio in hushed bickering within the library walls that the favourite title, overall, for the opening programme was *The Library Mob*. This was later changed to Clarke's provisional title, *The Last of the Summer Wine*.

The only actor that was fully cast in stone was Peter Sallis:

I had done a couple of scripts for Roy Clarke before. One was with Sheila Hancock – a one-hour play; the other was an episode of something called The Spider, *which never took off as a series. So I knew Roy Clarke's work very well.*

Clarke wanted to create a situation comedy character especially for Peter, and the result was Clegg. The actor was charmed with the result.

When the script arrived from the BBC, it didn't entirely take me by surprise that I had been sent it. When I read it, I thought it was gold dust. It was funny and very witty in parts.

However, before filming started with a vengeance, the BBC needed the ideal northern location for the exterior work. Much of the studio-based material would naturally be recorded at BBC Television Centre, but Roy Clarke and Duncan Wood rightly felt a taste of local colour was required for the *Comedy Playhouse* episode.

Barry Took – one of comedy's most influential talents – played an important, often unheralded part in the success of *Last of the Summer Wine*. Having worked with Marty Feldman on scripts for television's *Bootsie and Snudge* in the early 1960s and radio's legendary *Round the Horne* later that decade, Took was appointed as a roving producer for BBC Comedy, finally bringing together the Cambridge faction of John Cleese and Graham Chapman with the Oxford boys of Michael Palin and Terry Jones for *Monty Python's Flying Circus* in 1969.

In early 1972 Took had been filming a half-hour programme as part of a BBC documentary series showing the British at leisure, entitled *Having a Lovely Time*. Six different well-known personalities contributed to the series. Took's effort, *At the Club*, looked at a run-down old venue, Burnlee Working Men's Club, which he himself had once unsuccessfully played in his struggling days as a stand-up comedian. A home for smutty gags, unsubtle striptease and crude drinking songs, the club was situated in a small town called Holmfirth in the West Riding of Yorkshire and, ironically, this very location – still looking slightly rundown but continually in use – is often utilized today as base camp for the actors and crew during production.

Although Took's *Having a Lovely Time* effort failed to impress many critics on its first broadcast on Thursday 31 August 1972 – the *Daily Mirror* commented on the 'lifeless, cheerless and dejected' feel of Holmfirth – the programme was the most popular of the series, making it to number 17 in the week's ratings.

More to the point, Took immediately saw the place's potential as a television location. Realizing that Duncan Wood was working on a *Comedy Playhouse* set in Yorkshire, Took suggested Holmfirth as the perfect place to film; both writer, Roy Clarke, and director, Jimmy Gilbert, agreed wholeheartedly.

Interestingly, Holmfirth was no stranger to pioneering British comedy. For many years it had been the home of Bamforth and Co., purveyors of the country's finest saucy seaside

Barry Took makes a belated return to Holmfirth for Summer Wine*'s 25th anniversary documentary.*

postcards. While Brighton became synonymous with the cheeky charm of naughty weekends, kiss-me-quick hats and oversized bathing belles, the actual factory where these titillating titbits were produced was based in Holmfirth, Yorkshire.

Today, Bamforth's has gone, but there is a postcard museum and pub, The Postcard, to serve as a permanent reminder of those long-gone halcyon days.

The factory itself had been owned by James Bamforth, a postcard printer since 1870, and it was he who utilized the surrounding countryside for primitive silent comedy films. As early as 1899 he delighted local audiences with his slapstick interpretations of Yorkshire folklore and comic stories. The locals of Holmfirth fully supported Bamforth and his film crews. The Holme Valley banks would gladly allow robbery scenes to be filmed outside their premises, the railway station helpfully provided mock trains for crash scenes and even Holmfirth Council allowed filming to take place in the park.

A century on, the population of Holmfirth continue to support filming in the area – welcoming *Summer Wine* producer Alan J. W. Bell and his crew.

Bamforth's success led to offices springing up in both London and New York, but a major order for a hundred films for the Russian market was quickly curtailed with the outbreak of the First World War in 1914. That was, fundamentally, an end to Bamforth's dream of international film-making, but his postcards continued to spread happiness. Moreover, the pretty local lasses who had brightened up his films were cleverly used for Bamforth's new war-conscious, sentimental line of product. Cards that had been popular during the Boer War were reworked and restructured for the new conflict, and a soldier far from home could be comforted with a pretty face and a loving collection of words.

After the war, the tide turned fully towards the risqué, by-the-sea postcards made famous by artists such as Donald McGill. A winking, ever-smiling, sun-drenched world of buxom blondes, henpecked husbands and shy newly-weds created the very essence of British comedy for generations – themes still very much in evidence in *Summer Wine* sub-plots. In post-war cinemas, the *Carry On* series basked in the warmth of saucy postcard innuendo and perhaps just a slice of that cheeky rebellion rubbed off on to Holmfirth's favourite son, Compo Simonite, as played by Bill Owen – himself a member of the early *Carry On* cast.

So it was that Barry Took pointed the fledgling *Summer Wine* production crew towards the beautiful locations of Holmfirth. In June 1972 a BBC camera crew made the journey to shoot location material for the *Comedy Playhouse* pilot. It was a match made in heaven: the local area has been used for all episodes in the 30 years since.

But back in 1972 the whole project was still a gamble on the part of the BBC. The plot was hardly the most earth-shattering, and the middle-aged cast (although mere babes in arms compared with, say, those in *Dad's Army* or *For the Love of Ada*) were not the stuff of radical, cutting-edge programming.

Fixed cast member Peter Sallis had been joined by the solid comedy actor Michael Bates, familiar from radio's *The Navy Lark*, and Bill Owen, the experienced film and stage performer. Roy Clarke, for one, was less than happy with the choice of Bill Owen. To the writer, Owen was completely wrong for the unkempt, ferret-loving, lusting Compo. For one thing, Bill Owen was a Londoner. He had played cockneys in a string of post-war British films, and for Clarke this characterization was totally wrong:

I couldn't see Bill Owen as Compo. Compo to me was

The first publicity photo – Peter Sallis, Michael Bates and Bill Owen pose for a mugshot to promote the Comedy Playhouse *pilot.*

the archetypal northern layabout, and Bill Owen for me was the archetypal cockney. I'd seen him in all the films he'd done, and he was always the very London Bill Owen. What I didn't know was that Jimmy Gilbert had seen Bill playing solid northern parts in the Royal Court Theatre. It wasn't until I went down to London for a read-through that I began to see Bill's potential. Of course, as soon as he was on screen, the rest of the world could see that Bill could play Compo.

While Clarke was concerning himself with the suitability of Gilbert's choice for Compo, he couldn't have known that Owen himself had already fallen in love with the part and was desperate to claim it as his own:

When I read the pilot script I knew there was something special about this. It was fresh, it was new and it had an elderly appeal. I think Roy Clarke foresaw the independence that would grow among elderly people over the next 25 years.

Hence, after a long, long haul, *The Last of the Summer Wine – Of Funerals and Fish* was finally aired on BBC1 on Thursday 4 January 1973 at 8 o'clock in the evening.

It was the first presentation in the 14th season of *Comedy Playhouse*. Other shows featured in the run included the Peter Jones-scripted tale of a wannabe suicide, *The Rescue*; Michael Robbins in the chauvinistic nightmare of *Home from Home*, and the John Le Mesurier domestic farce *Marry the Girls*. *The Birthday* cast Gordon Peters as a bemused loner wandering through life, and this pilot developed into the short-lived (only six episodes were made) *The Gordon Peters Show*. The season's highlight came with the Sherlock Holmes parody *Elementary, My Dear Watson*, starring John Cleese and Willie Rushton. Ironically, this was produced by Barry Took and failed to get a series commission. Twenty years on, when this excellent Holmes comedy had been long forgotten, John Cleese proved there were no sour grapes when he guest-starred in *Summer Wine*'s *Welcome to Earth* in 1993.

The *Comedy Playhouse* edition of *The Last of the Summer Wine* proved popular enough with the audience and, more important, with BBC bigwigs, successfully to secure a series.

The central trio of Michael Bates, Bill Owen and Peter Sallis were retained as the core of the series, as were northern battleaxes Kathy Staff and Jane Freeman.

Six episodes were written for the first series of what was now called simply *Last of the Summer Wine*, the first *The* being dropped, although still forever part of the show as Ronnie Hazlehurst's music testifies. Just sing the title to the music and you'll see what we mean! Jimmy Gilbert remained to produce and direct the first series.

The opening episode of Series One, *Short Back and Palais Glide*, was broadcast on 12 November 1973 and a television legend was here to stay.

Despite the fact that this opening series contains much of Roy Clarke's finest *Summer Wine* dialogue and a towering comic performance from Michael Bates, audiences were slow to respond to the programme.

Filming for the pilot episode was less than successful, as Peter Sallis recalls:

The audience at Television Centre, whose laughter we needed for the show's soundtrack, had never seen or heard anything like it before. After the first scene, Bill, Michael and I came off and we were sweating. We couldn't understand why the people weren't laughing. If you watch the pilot today, you'll notice that our voices are getting louder and louder as the episode goes on. By the end of the show, we were practically shouting our lines at each other to try and get the laughs. We had no idea how to handle a studio audience then – but the show survived, and it's gone on surviving.

The question of audience laughter tracks on his work has always concerned the writer, Roy Clarke:

Is it better to have your show with an audience so the viewer back home hears the laughter, or no audience and the viewer back home just gets the programme? I know we go to the cinema and there's no laughter on the soundtrack of comedy films, but there are hundreds of people laughing with you and that's the atmosphere. It's the same in a theatre. But when we get to television, we sit in our living-rooms, put that machine on, watch funny things, don't hear any laughter and somehow that's not right. I certainly wouldn't want canned laughter that wasn't genuine but I wouldn't want no laughter at all.

Surprisingly, the first episode of this simple-minded, endearing family entertainment was scheduled post-watershed – cropping up after the evening news on BBC1 at 9.25 p.m.

However, in a display of loyalty and trust rarely shown today, the BBC stuck with the show through its lean, fledgling years. Although in no mad rush to produce further editions, the BBC wasn't ready to pension off *Summer Wine* quite yet. Owing to a BBC strike that saw many projects curtailed, no programmes were actually screened during 1974. However, a second series, produced by Bernard Thompson, and starring Bates, Owen and Sallis, had already been commissioned before the strike action, and Roy Clarke had scripted seven half-hour episodes. Delayed in production, these programmes

were eventually made, and broadcast over March and April 1975.

The gamble clearly paid off, for two episodes from this second series made it into the top ten programmes of the week. The opening show, *Forked Lightning*, was watched by over 18 million people. However, it wasn't all plain sailing for this series. Michael Bates, who had starred in all the episodes, was forced to leave the programme owing to ill health. While he continued to appear in *It Ain't Half Hot, Mum*, Bates had to abandon the more physically demanding role of Blamire in *Last of the Summer Wine*. The actor subsequently died in 1978.

His replacement came in the guise of a confused military sign-writer by the name of Foggy Dewhurst. The character brought his skill for overambitious, military-styled plans that always ended in disaster, usually leaving Compo stranded in mud, water or a tin bath! In Foggy's debut episode, *The Man from Oswestry*, Peter Sallis brilliantly bridged the departure of Blamire and the introduction of Dewhurst. In the opening scene, Sallis reads a lengthy letter from the former leader, Cyril Blamire. In it, he discusses his love for a seductive temptress and heralds Foggy's appearance by mentioning the military man's desire to return home following dismissal from the army.

Brian Wilde, still filming the Ronnie Barker prison situation comedy *Porridge* for the BBC, was ideally cast as the dictatorial Foggy, and the trio of this era is widely regarded as the show's definitive line-up. Brian Wilde was an obvious choice for the new character, as *Last of the Summer Wine* producer Sydney Lotterby had made his name in BBC situation comedy, especially with the hugely successful *Porridge*.

Wilde's first episode was broadcast on 27 October 1976. The programme was still given the 9.25 p.m. slot, and none of Series Three's seven episodes made it into the top ten – although the final show, *Isometrics and After*, attracted over 15 million viewers on its repeat screening in spring 1977.

Also of note for this first Brian Wilde series was Roy Clarke's inclusion of a two-part episode. The fondly remembered trip to Scarborough, which was covered in *The Great Boarding House Bathroom*

Get on me step! A pensive moment for Kathy Staff and Bill Owen during the late 1990s.
Right: The Dream Team – Peter Sallis, Brian Wilde, Bill Owen and that stunning Yorkshire countryside.

Caper and *Cheering Up Gordon*, featured the regulars enjoying a charming holiday by the coast. A hilarious discussion between Sid and Ivy (John Comer and Jane Freeman) concerning their less-than-romantic sex life was a gem.

The fresh blood of Wilde and Lotterby played a major part in revitalizing the show, and shortly after a healthy repeat season of Series Three, the fourth series was screened from 9 November 1977. The late transmission time remained, but the three-way conversations and childlike behaviour of Owen, Sallis and Wilde were clearly beginning to bond. Eight episodes were broadcast over November and December 1977. Amazingly, other than a Christmas Special, *Small Tune on a Penny Wassail*, broadcast on 26 December 1978 at 10.40 p.m., almost two years would pass before a further series of *Summer Wine* was made and broadcast.

Last of the Summer Wine *was becoming less a situation comedy and more a comedic soap opera.*

It was to be this series that signalled the turning-point for the show's longevity.

The reason for *Summer Wine*'s apparent sudden rise in popularity was due mainly to an ITV strike, which lasted 11 weeks from 10 August to 19 October 1979. This effectively left television viewers with a choice of just two channels, BBC1 and BBC2. Appreciating that it had at its disposal far larger audiences than it could previously have expected to receive, the Beeb cleverly rescheduled many of its most popular programmes to boost its viewing figures further, and in the case of *Last of the Summer Wine,* the corporation attempted to entice not just regular viewers but a whole new group of untapped interest.

Series Five, therefore, was broadcast for the first time at a pre-watershed slot, running for seven episodes between 18 September and 30 October 1979 on Tuesdays at 8.30 p.m. Along with repeats, *Summer Wine* spent 11 weeks in the top ten that year. Indeed, the episode *Earnshaw Strikes Back* on 16 October received 22.2 million viewers and ensured *Summer Wine* a place in the top ten most-watched programmes of the entire year. After that, the series never looked back.

Also of importance for this fifth series was Roy Clarke's continuing pioneering experiment to present themed double episodes. Despite the fact that *Full Steam Behind*, a self-contained, unique three-hander centring around a Will Hay/*Oh! Mr Porter*-style railway exploit, proved most popular – it is Peter Sallis's favourite episode – four of the remaining episodes were effectively a pair of two-parters. *The Flag and Its Snag* was followed immediately by *The Flag and Further Snags*, while the series was rounded off with *Here We Go into the Wild Blue Yonder* and *Here We Go Again into the Wild Blue Yonder*. This allowed Clarke time and space to develop situations beyond the usual half-hour boundaries and also proved useful for attracting the viewing public back to watch the follow-up episode. Clearly, *Last of the Summer Wine* was becoming less a situation comedy and more a comedic soap opera.

Following this viewing success for the BBC, *Summer Wine* was rewarded with a second Christmas Special. *And a Dewhurst up a Fir Tree* was broadcast on 27 December 1979 at 8.30 p.m. This, some two hours earlier than the 1978 Special, saw the three old men celebrating Christmas at a far more sensible

A new arrival – Bill Owen and Peter Sallis welcome Brian Wilde's Foggy, as John Comer looks on.

time for the family audience. It also meant a slight change in Roy Clarke's expressive writing for the series. The early scripts had included a smattering of mild bad language, as Jane Freeman recalls:

The programme used to go out after the Nine O'Clock News, *so we were allowed to swear a little. I used to say 'bloody' every other sentence early on. But then, of course, it became a favourite among children as well, so we realized we had to clean up the act a little bit. Nowadays, the worst thing you will hear Compo call someone is a hedgehog's jacksey!*

Again, following the 1979 Christmas Special, there was to be a two-year gap in production, although following on from the programme's huge ratings success during the 1979 ITV strike, the BBC wisely repeated Series Four during the winter of 1980 with one episode – the Christmas Special, *Small Tune on a Penny Wassail* – reaching the week's number one slot for the first time in the show's history. Indeed, the other eight repeats all made it into the top ten.

Both the show and its audience received the finest Christmas present the BBC could offer when, off the back of this repeat season, as opposed to a new series, a Yuletide Special was commissioned for broadcast on Christmas Day 1981. The show, *Whoops!*, went out at 7.15 p.m., gained 17 million viewers and was only beaten to the number one slot by the ever-popular *Coronation Street*.

Even more impressively, the BBC's flagship premiere presentation of the 1939 MGM film classic *Gone with the Wind* was beaten by *Last of the Summer Wine*. Kathy Staff is very proud of this achievement:

We were on Christmas Day and Gone with the Wind *was on Boxing Day at around about the same time.* Last of the Summer Wine *got almost three million viewers more than the film. Of course, all the newspapers were then ringing me up and asking me what it felt like to be more attractive than Scarlett O'Hara! That was absolutely wonderful. We had really hit the top at that time, and we realized we were in something really rather special. We had always felt it was special, but you don't always get the public to think that.*

Ironically, Series Six of *Summer Wine*, which started just ten days later on 4 January 1982, was slotted back into its old post-watershed position of 9.25 p.m. It was this ground-breaking series that saw the entrance of Alan J. W. Bell as producer and director. Employed for his filmic eye – Alan was previously a film editor and therefore well used to location shooting – these seven episodes fully utilized the glorious Holmfirth locations.

Alan J. W. Bell recalls joining the series:

I hadn't long since finished making the science fiction epic (in BBC terms) The Hitch-Hiker's Guide to the Galaxy, *when, in 1981, I was given* Last of the Summer Wine *to produce and direct.*

It may seem a strange progression, but it wasn't really. Summer Wine *was a series that I had avidly followed since its first episode in 1973, so it was a bit like winning the lottery to actually be assigned such an original and superbly witty show. The BBC had, it seems, recognized my filmic bent and astutely realized that the high proportion of location filming in each episode would not be a problem in my hands. And so it was that without ever having produced a situation comedy, I found myself in charge of the jewel in the crown of the Comedy Department.*

Despite being given the later time-slot once again, the show was rewarded with high viewing figures for all its episodes and, at its height, Bill Owen's favourite episode, *From Wellies to Wet Suit*, was seen by over 15 million viewers. It is interesting to note that following the death of Bill Owen in July 1999, it was that episode that was chosen to be broadcast as a tribute to Bill. Some 17 years after it was first broadcast, *From Wellies to Wet Suit* was seen by almost 7 million viewers and earned itself a slot in the week's top five entertainment programmes.

Once again, 1982 saw the team present a *Summer Wine* Christmas Special. *All Mod Conned* was broadcast on Christmas Day. Two days later, Bill Owen, Peter Sallis and Brian Wilde reappeared in a special short version of the show as part of *The Funny Side of Christmas* entitled *How to Ignore Christmas*. The popularity of Compo's and Nora's ongoing love–hate battle led to a near-miss pop record and appearances by Bill Owen and Kathy Staff on the BBC's *Val Doonican Show* and *Children in Need*.

By now *Summer Wine* was a firm favourite in the ratings, and it wasn't just the grown-ups who loved it. Universally popular with children thanks to its childlike premise and visual buffoonery, the Noel Edmonds-fronted Saturday morning show *Multi-Coloured Swap Shop* even voted it Television's Top

A typical location day in Yorkshire – flimsy chairs, stone steps and cloth caps.

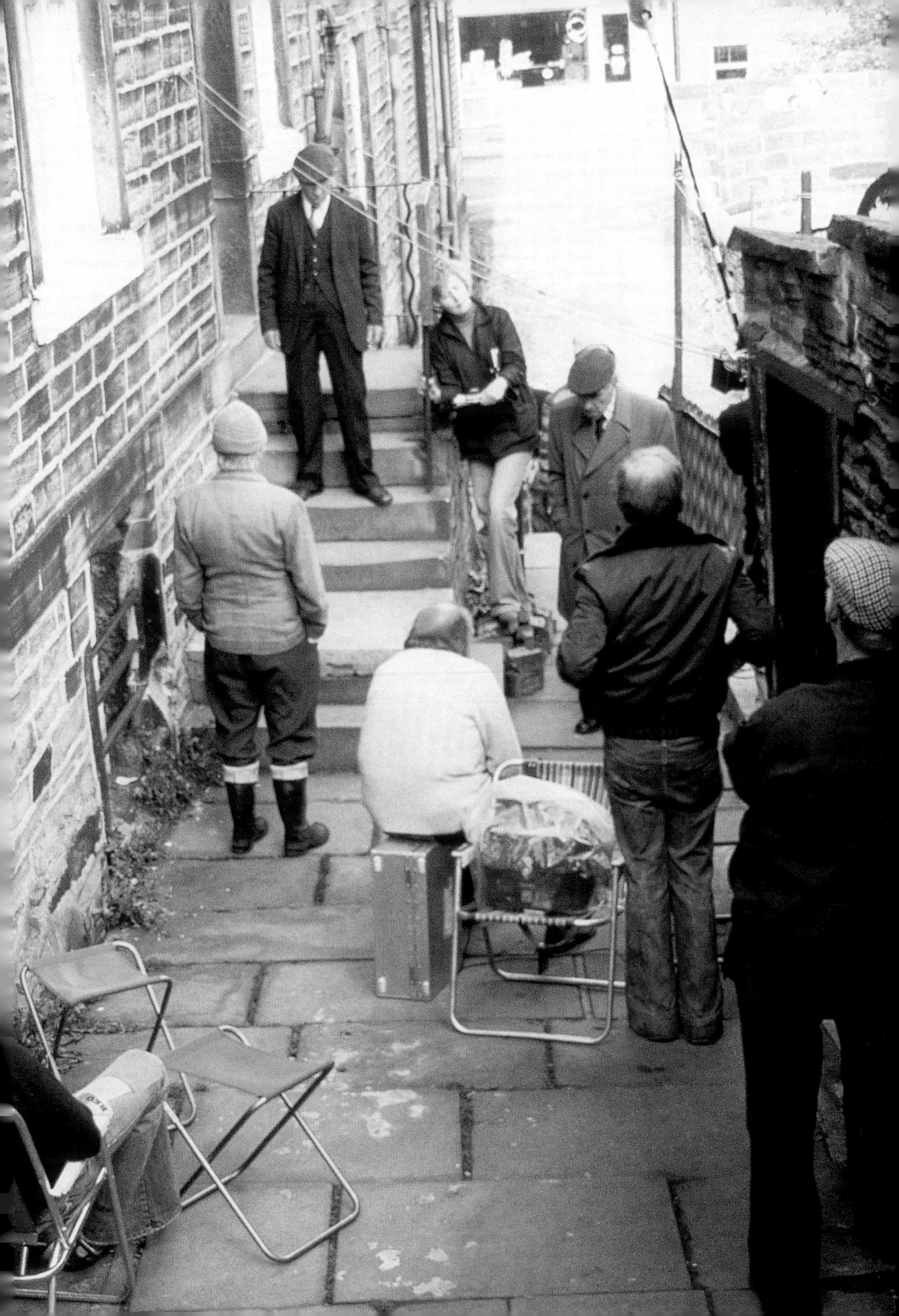

Programme. Moreover, the seventh series, broadcast from 30 January 1983, saw the show gain a peak-time Sunday evening slot of 7.15 p.m.

Unbeknown to the programme's loyal television audience, internal wrangling at the BBC and Brian Wilde's insistence led to the temporary return of producer Sydney Lotterby for this seventh series. Wilde had not been a keen fan of Alan J. W. Bell's style of producing and directing. Wilde preferred close-up shots of the men speaking their lines, whereas Bell opted for wider shots to allow the beauty of the countryside to be taken in at the same time as the humorous scripts. The matter more or less resolved itself with no loss of face on all sides when Bell was assigned to produce Spike Milligan in the sketch series *There's a Lot of It About*. Milligan – an admirer of Bell's work on *Hitchhiker's Guide* and *Ripping Yarns* – insisted on Bell working on his show. This allowed Lotterby to produce *Summer Wine*. As both series were being filmed at the same time and therefore needed two different producers at the helm, the BBC had found a way of appeasing both actors and producers alike.

Alan J. W. Bell returned to *Summer Wine* to produce the landmark feature-length television film *Getting Sam Home*. Bell gives the credit for the film to Bill Owen:

Bill had loved the Last of the Summer Wine *novel Roy Clarke had written several years earlier. Being a great film actor, Bill longed to make a feature-length episode based on the book. Sydney Lotterby hadn't been very keen, so Bill was delighted when I, a film person, came on to the show. Almost immediately, he came up to me and suggested the book as a source for a film. I went to John Howard Davies, who rather dismissively muttered, 'The BBC don't make films!' I reasoned with the simple request, 'Why?' and he couldn't really answer me. Anyway, the film was made – as* Getting Sam Home *– and it began a trend for situation comedy films, which* Summer Wine *was proud to have started.*

Roy Clarke's brilliant adaptation of his own novel proved to be the perfect springboard for *Summer Wine*'s next 15 years. The 90-minute film *Getting Sam Home* – a first for a situation comedy on television – was broadcast on 27 December 1983 and delighted in delicious black humour, with the three old men desperately trying to help their pal Sam enjoy one last night of lustful pleasure with a local glam girl, played by Lynda Baron – better known as Nurse Gladys Emmanuel from Roy Clarke's other great 1980s' hit, *Open All Hours*.

Although feature films had been produced from small-screen hits for years – *I Only Arsked!* had emerged from *The Army Game* in 1958 and, during the 1970s, everything from *Steptoe and Son* and *Up Pompeii* to *Dad's Army* and *Man About the House* made it to the cinema – *Getting Sam Home* was the first full-length situation comedy film made for television. *Only Fools and Horses* – among many others – has since followed its lead.

The return of Alan J. W. Bell came with the 1983 Christmas Special. At this time in the show's history, the slow rate of production saw just one series and a smattering of Specials every two years. Roy Clarke's commitment to *Open All Hours* was the main reason for this.

However, things were about to change. Not only was there to be a series every year from 1987, but the number of episodes increased from six or seven per series to ten, and even to 12 for Series Nine. Alan J. W. Bell also increased the use of location filming, stripping away completely the need for scenes filmed at BBC Television Centre.

A sell-out summer season presentation of *Last of the Summer Wine* played to packed houses in Bournemouth during 1984, though personal

The special *Big Day at Dream Acres* heralded the tenth series for October and November 1988, but Clarke felt that character-based loose ends needed tidying up. The deaths of Joe Gladwin and, earlier, John Comer had not been mentioned within the shows themselves. The excuse given was that continual repeat screenings included the actors, and the public would get confused. However, thankfully, this was rectified with the popular double-length Christmas Eve 1988 Special, *Crums*. The programme featured an emotionally charged farewell tribute to 'Wally' and 'Sid' from Kathy Staff's Nora and Jane Freeman's Ivy. Roy Clarke, blessed with the time and space to develop his characters, utilized the obvious spectre of death over his aged cast and welcomed real humanity into his comedy universe.

A further eight Michael Aldridge episodes were broadcast in 1989, with Series 11 screened from October and another Christmas Special, *What's Santa Brought for Nora Then?*, on 23 December. The season delighted in the usual anarchic, localized titles with, notably, *Oh, Shut Up and Eat Your Choc Ice* allowing Aldridge to lead his merry, gullible companions through yet another madcap adventure. The final show of the series, *Three Men and a Mangle*, was clearly an example of Clarke attempting to tap into modern, filmic puns – the Tom Selleck comedy film *Three Men and a Baby* was currently hot in cinemas across the country.

However, despite continued success, a major sea change was about to occur within the cast. Michael Aldridge, nursing his sick wife in London during time away from the Holmfirth locations, and himself sporting a serious hip problem, was forced to relinquish his role in the series. Heartbroken, the actor had no choice but to leave and, with late-1980s' sitcom projects having failed to gel, Brian Wilde eagerly returned to the fold as Foggy. In the first episode of Series 12, *Return of the Warrior*, Aldridge leaves on one bus just as Wilde reappears on another. The two 'third man' leaders never actually meet but pass like ships in the night at the start of Foggy's second coming.

Ten episodes and a Christmas Special was Wilde's reward, and the nation seemed to settle back into the classic line-up like a comfortable beanbag. With the introduction of *On the Buses* legend Stephen Lewis as Smiler, the full supporting cast were firmly in place. Alan J. W. Bell was in charge of the production, and the BBC merrily kept signing the cheques for the continuation of its flagship gentle family comedy product. A further six episodes and a Christmas Special appeared in 1991, with another ten programmes being broadcast in 1992.

Summer Wine yielded ten more shows in 1993, including the celebrated science

Former prime minister Harold Wilson returns to his home town of Huddersfield to visit loyal Labour Party member, Bill Owen.

fiction Christmas Special *Welcome to Earth*, featuring a guest appearance from John Cleese and an unforgettable ET-inspired bike fly-past.

A full year passed before the show's return – with an hour-long New Year's Day Special in 1995. Heralding the start of Series 16, which kicked in the following Sunday, *The Man Who Nearly Knew Pavarotti* headlined a guest appearance by British comedy great Norman Wisdom.

Despite continual press speculation and, indeed, internal memos at the BBC itself concerning the end of Last of the Summer Wine, *viewing figures still regularly peaked at over ten million.*

Roy Clarke appreciated Alan J. W. Bell's use of well-known comedy character actors for guest appearances in the show:

The one-off appearances by stars have been very satisfying personally because they've enabled me to have some connection, for a while at least, with people I was very much fond of before I got into the industry. For example,
I wasn't in the business when I saw Oliver! *for the first time with Ron Moody's wonderful performance as Fagin, and it's almost a completion of a little dream when you see someone like Ron appearing in a major part, even when it's only in one episode of the series you're doing.*

Amazingly, after a fairly lean period, 1995 saw the broadcast of 20 – yes, count them – 20 episodes of *Last of the Summer Wine*. Two complete seasons and a couple of Specials made the year a bumper harvest for *Summer Wine* fans.

Suitably exhausted after all that mucking about on the Yorkshire Dales, the cast took a year off – returning with the classic 1996 Christmas Special, *Extra! Extra!* Starring Oscar-winner George Chakiris, all the fun of the fair was injected into the programme. It also welcomed back Norman Wisdom, reprising his role as Billy Ingleton. Originally, plans were set in motion to include Norman as a regular player in the series. However, other work commitments and cast disquiet sadly prevented this from happening.

Despite continual press speculation and, indeed, internal memos at the BBC itself concerning the end of *Last of the Summer Wine*, viewing figures still regularly peaked at over ten million. While each and every new season was mooted with the thought that it would definitely be the last, Roy Clarke, Alan J. W. Bell and their loyal band of players kept on returning for more.

Veteran of *Summer Wine* Kathy Staff says the cast are equally surprised:

It's just been amazing over the years how the show has gone on. None of us could have envisaged that it could have lasted so long. When we were right at the top, we thought perhaps they would pull it then. And they didn't. Then when we had done 21 years, the BBC gave us a framed certificate, so we thought, that's it now. But no. At 25 years they gave us a dinner, and still we are going on.

The major achievement of having lasted 25 years on television was marked with an affectionate look back at the show's history, *25 Years of Last of the Summer Wine*. The documentary, produced and directed by *Summer Wine*'s Alan J. W. Bell, featured revealing interviews with the majority of cast members, as well as hilarious out-takes, a look behind the scenes at production and even an

Wind power! The trio enjoy themselves on location for the 1978 Christmas Special, Small Tune on a Penny Wassail.

interview with Barry Took – back in Holmfirth a quarter of a century after his *Having a Lovely Time* show had sparked off the connection.

The silver jubilee celebrations were continued with a further ten episodes in Series 18. Perhaps it was only fitting that with the seemingly divine mantle the programme now appeared to have achieved, this series was broadcast even earlier on a Sunday in what had previously been known within the business as the 'God slot' – a change of scene but not a change of time for one of the main characters, Thora Hird, who had presented *Praise Be!* for 17 years on Sundays for the BBC.

Following many years of speculation, it would have been feasible for the BBC to pull the plug on the series at this milestone. With the announcement that Brian Wilde was to leave for the second and final time due to ill health, it seemed this decision was inevitable. But no.

A Christmas Special for 1997 was already in the planning stages and the search was on for the next 'third man'. Once again Alan J. W. Bell's shrewd sense of the country's love for comedy nostalgia drew him towards casting a treasured favourite from among the portals of sitcom land. His inspiration was further fuelled by the highly successful repeat showings at Saturday teatimes of the ever-popular 1970s' department store camp romp *Are You Being Served?*

As Captain Peacock, Frank Thornton's sophisticated authority figure kept his band of merrie shop assistants together, and this characterization seemed perfect for *Last of the Summer Wine*. Ironically, *Are You Being Served?* was also originally conceived as a *Comedy Playhouse* and broadcast just as filming on the *Summer Wine* pilot had finished in 1972.

What made Frank Thornton's job harder on entering a series after 25 years was that his character's dialogue had originally been written with Brian Wilde in mind. As Truly of the Yard, Frank was given little time to work on character development, as he himself explains:

It was very much a last-minute casting for me. Brian had suddenly dropped out, so the scripts had to be adapted from Foggy Dewhurst to a new character. Obviously, the characters had to be similar.

Ironically, I had always cherished a dream. I used to watch the show and noticed that Foggy Dewhurst wore a Royal Air Force Services Club tie. I was delighted because Captain Peacock in Are You Being Served? *had also worn an RAFSC tie. I had a lovely idea that Peacock could go on holiday to the Yorkshire Dales and meet Foggy Dewhurst. Of course, it was a total fantasy because no writer would take a character from one series and put it into another series. But getting this part has been the nearest best thing.*

Instead of the usual practice of expecting to film a series before undertaking an annual Special, Frank was thrown in at the deep end, having to develop his character within the constraints of a Special before his debut series was broadcast.

The scripts for all ten episodes of Series 19 had been written with the Foggy character in place. Alan J. W. Bell was already facing a problematic season owing to Brian Wilde's desire to appear in fewer and fewer episodes. In the end, it was agreed that Foggy would appear in only occasional episodes. Six shows were built around the trio, with the remaining four featuring the Foggy character in very brief intro and outro moments. An old, discarded device of Foggy 'mind fogs' was reintroduced to leave the character stranded in a trance on the Yorkshire Dales while the plot revolved away from him. Brian Wilde ultimately pushed for just four actual appearances before his health condition reached a head and the character was abandoned

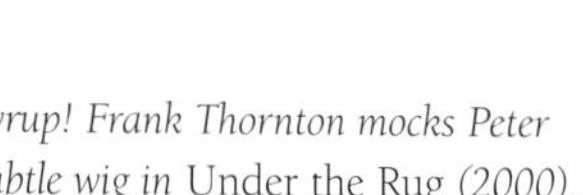

Smashing syrup! Frank Thornton mocks Peter Sallis's unsubtle wig in Under the Rug *(2000).*

completely. Thus, the authority figure – almost written out of several episodes – was reintroduced and reworked to fit Frank Thornton. Roy Clarke set about rewriting these ten shows to include Thornton's new character, Truly.

Importantly, Clarke, having been a policeman himself, found it easy to adapt this character at very short notice. Frank remembers his baptism of fire:

I only met Roy Clarke briefly when we had a meeting in London with Bill Owen and Peter Sallis and our director, Alan J. W. Bell. We read a few scripts, and over lunch I asked Roy about the accent. I was a little concerned about it. He said: 'I don't want too much of an accent. Compo has the fairly thick Yorkshire and Clegg has a much lighter accent. That would suit you.' I had been told that as a boy Truly had been taken to London by his mother. He had joined the Metropolitan Police, where he had served for 25 years. This would be my excuse if my accent shifted back to my native London!

The main problem facing Frank Thornton was that he had recorded half the new series before he filmed the Special that introduced his character for the first time. This was in order to give Roy Clarke the opportunity to write a brand-new episode that explained the disappearance of Foggy and the appearance of Truly.

Frank Thornton made his debut in the Christmas 1997 Special, *There Goes the Groom*. This double episode had to serve several purposes. Naturally, it was a seasonal celebration but, more intriguingly, Foggy needed to be written out and Truly written in. Although obviously not involved in filming, Brian Wilde saw his beloved character disappear into the back of a truck. Slightly the worse for drink after a stag-night celebration, only his legs were visible as he was driven away – kidnapped by an overzealous and oversexed post-lady who takes a shine to him. Foggy is whisked away to Blackpool, and the last we hear from him is via a telephone call to Clegg. A Clarke plot device akin to Blamire's letter in *The Man from Oswestry*, Foggy departed stage left without even appearing on screen.

Enter Truly of the Yard as another old school chum of Compo and Clegg, to solve the crime of the Yorkshire Dales and join in the wedding-based antics. Hence, a new authority figure was in place to control the unruly Compo and the philosophical Clegg.

Frank Thornton, the latest in a long line of characters set up to have his pomposity pricked, fitted into the ensemble cast like a tailor-made suit from Grace Brothers. Like the proverbial suit, his character has ridden with wear.

To the watching millions, the transition between Foggy and Truly appeared smoother than the production would indicate. Indeed, the season was very well received, and Alan J. W. Bell's continuing embrace of burgeoning television technology saw the introduction of digital wide-screen filming, giving an even clearer, enhanced quality of picture. Long takes and sweeping camera movements breathed new life into the old series and showed off even further the beauty of *Summer Wine* country.

Writer Roy Clarke had little trouble in adapting his work to these improvements:

There's no question that over the span of its time the show has changed. It began as a very talky, chatty thing with little action. A lot of film for its time, but still quite a small amount of film to what has been built in. It's now entirely on film in wide-screen, in digital, with very high production values, and as a consequence it looks beautiful and it has become, I think, more polished and, I hope, it has become funnier.

There seems to be no stopping the show. Since the early 1990s, when the programme became almost entirely location-based with interiors filmed within a closed studio set, it has become financially wiser to take the cast and crew to Yorkshire to film ten episodes rather than the standard six. Indeed, by not relying on a live studio audience, material can be shot quickly and, if necessary, out of sequence should the typical Yorkshire weather delay production of a particular scene.

In that respect, and with the experience of Alan J. W. Bell as film editor, the series has become more and more like cinema film production. Needless to say, this has aided the older members of the cast, allowing them short bursts of dialogue rather than the original long scenes of heavy conversation. *Summer Wine* was also the first comedy series to be recorded in stereo sound.

Thus, *Summer Wine* was and continues to be a successful and cost-effective programme to produce. And, what's more, the show continues to score heavily in the ratings.

Therefore the BBC had no problem with commissioning another series – the 20th. A further ten programmes were put into production. Many of the cast, now in their late 70s and 80s, were definitely moving more slowly, but their love for the show continued unabated. Bill Owen publicly announced that it was *Summer Wine* that was keeping him going.

The filming of the 20th series culminated in a special tribute held at the home of British film comedy, Pinewood Studios. Apart from the studio's glorious legacy of *Carry On* and *Doctor* films, plus classics such as *Genevieve* and Norman Wisdom comedies, it was also where the interior filming for this series of *Summer Wine* was undertaken.

The Pinewood event, held on Sunday 11 October 1998 and organized by the British Comedy Society, attracted most of the series regulars – including Bill Owen, Peter Sallis and Frank Thornton – as well as Roy Clarke, Alan J. W. Bell, the head of BBC Comedy, Geoffrey Perkins, and many other devoted fans of this longest-running of comedy television shows. A plaque was unveiled in the British Comedy Society's Hall of Fame, and a gala luncheon was enjoyed by all those who attended. Jeffrey Archer conducted a charity auction, and one item – a chance to appear in the 21st series, for broadcast in the year 2000 – was bagged by a super-fan, who paid an amazing £14,000 for the privilege. As Peter Sallis quipped at the time: 'That's more than we get for making the programme!'

The highlight of the day was the appearance of Michael Aspel and his famous red book, taking a moment to pop in, wish all at *Summer Wine* well and to say to one particular cast member: 'Tonight, Frank Thornton…this is your life!'

The series that had been in production up to October 1998 was to be broadcast from spring 1999. Impressively, the series included some of the funniest episodes in *Summer Wine* history. The common denominator was brilliantly embraced with Stephen Lewis and Mike Grady donning drag for the truly uproarious *Who's Thrown Her Tom Cruise Photographs Away?*, while Keith Clifford's unforgettable supporting role as the Yorkshire Robin Hood in *How Errol Flynn Discovered the Secret Scar of Nora Batty* proved hugely popular.

Not only that, but we, the authors of this very book, Morris Bright and Robert Ross, found ourselves swept up with the charm of Holmfirth and *Summer Wine* production.

Working on the Pinewood event, thoughts of a celebration book were discussed and Bright 'n' Ross were given the extremely taxing roles of Men at Bar in the episode *Howard Throws a Wobbler.* For us, it was a true honour to be working – however briefly – with comedy greats of the calibre of Bill Owen, Peter Sallis and Frank Thornton.

Series 21 – the millennium season – was already being written before Series 20 had been broadcast. The three old men of the Yorkshire Dales were finally coming of age.

As well as ten episodes, the BBC had agreed to commission a special millennium edition of *Last of the Summer Wine*. A 60-minute presentation, this emotive programme featured the touching and thought-provoking plot of the trio making a pilgrimage to war graves in France. Owing to the innovative way of filming this television comedy, the millennium Special was slotted in within the time-schedule for the ten standard episodes.

We again made the journey to Holmfirth, now in our honoured capacity of official historians for the series, and again we were invited to take part. It was clearly the millennium Special that was being treated as the season's focal point.

Fun and games on set and off were unabated. We were greeted at breakfast with Stephen Lewis repeating Nostradamus's prediction that the end of the world was due within 24 hours. We commented that this was a feeble excuse for not learning the lines for the day's filming. 'Well, there hardly seems much point, really,' came Stephen's reply.

Drunk with the success of our Men at Bar parts, we were both given two more (unpaid) roles to fulfil – Men Onlookers at Church during the millennium Special's pageant sequence and Boys Behaving Madly in a pub garden, Morris Bright attempting not to be run over by Thora Hird's car and Robert Ross chatting up the local talent.

With location filming in France as well as the usual Holmfirth, and guest appearances from Dora Bryan, Ray Cooney and a much welcome return from Keith Clifford, this Special was to prove very important.

However, the production was to be tinged with great sadness. During filming in France, Bill Owen was taken ill and on return to location in Holmfirth during June his condition worsened. It was with emotional respect that we watched Bill filming on his very last days of production. It was obvious to all who were on set that Bill was very sick indeed. Here, then, was a man of 85 who was so in love with the programme, so in love with his fans, and so in love with Yorkshire, that quietly and without complaint he continued working long hours around a hastily altered schedule in order that he could complete the essential scenes for the millennium Special.

The most touching moment came as Bill stood proudly in character, with Frank Thornton as Truly on one side and Peter Sallis as Clegg on the other. They were

Millennium madness – Summer Wine *salutes 2000 years of history in* Last Post and Pigeon *(2000).*

bedecked in medals from the war and standing to attention. Compo lifted a bugle to his lips to play, of all things, the Last Post. It was true to say that there were tears in the eyes of many who were on the set that day.

Bill died on Monday 12 July 1999. He had finished the millennium Special and three episodes of the 21st series. He was a true pro to the end.

Naturally, Bill's death was a tremendous blow to Kathy Staff:

I had been out for dinner in Blackpool with my two daughters. We knew Bill had been very sick, but it was still a shock when we heard the news that evening. We went home, looked at the television and saw the news that Bill had died. It was my birthday. So he died on my birthday. I think it is so sad that on my birthday, on Nora's birthday, Compo died.

The cast, though in mourning, got on with the job of filming, and Bill, according to a wish he had made some 20 years earlier, was laid to rest in Holmfirth following a private ceremony on 19 July 1999. Peter Sallis was the sole representative of the cast. Roy Clarke said he wanted to see the programme continue as a tribute to Bill and hastily set about rewriting the remaining episodes of the series. There was no talk of the character simply leaving the series – Compo had to die along with the actor who created him. The public would expect nothing less. The nation needed a chance to grieve.

It was perhaps rather ironic and just a trifle sad, in the light of *Summer Wine*'s tendency to be dismissed by the media, that Bill's death made national news headlines both on television and in the newspapers.

The filming of the funeral sequences following the television passing of Compo were filmed at Helme Church on Bank Holiday Monday, 30 August 1999. Friends and colleagues of Bill Owen, as well as townspeople, made up the congregation of 'mourners'.

The cast themselves got their own private opportunity to say their final goodbyes to Bill on the following evening when they gathered at St John's Church in Netherthong, for a special memorial service. Bill's son, Tom Owen, joined the cast and crew for the service at the church where Bill was buried. At the end of the proceedings, the congregation filed out to the accompaniment of a brass band playing the theme to *Last of the Summer Wine* and visited the graveside of their dear and much-missed friend. The view over the Yorkshire hills from his burial site is spectacular, and everyone understood why a typical cockney had chosen this very special resting place.

The very next day, Tom Owen started work on the series, coming in to play Compo's long-lost son. As an outsider looking in, Brian Wilde believes Bill would approve:

I think to have a son come in may be a surprise to the audience, but it is a perfectly natural progression. Families do it all the time. When the old man passes away, the son carries on and his son after that. It's a natural reflection of our lives.

The essence of *Summer Wine* is three old men who refuse to succumb to old age. Bill Owen was the first of the principal stars to die during production. If the remaining cast and crew, along with Roy Clarke, have their way, he won't be the last! Peter Sallis – with Bill since the very first episode – sums up their feelings:

I've reached the stage now where I don't want it to end. I'm hoping that as one by one we drop dead that, provided Roy is still alive, it will just keep going.

The prodigal son – Tom Owen dishes out calling cards to his father's old pals, Peter Sallis and Frank Thornton, in Some Vans Can Make You Deaf *(2000).*

CHAPTER TWO

THE WINOS

A Celebration of *Last of the Summer Wine*'s 'Three Wise Men' over the Years

'My love of Yorkshire and, in particular, the town of Holmfirth began the first day we arrived.'

BILL OWEN

Bill Owen MBE

BILL 'COMPO' SIMONITE: 1973 TO 2000

If anybody can sum up the spirit of *Last of the Summer Wine*, it has to be Bill Owen. The fun-loving gentleman of advancing age who refused to go quietly into the night, Bill set foot into the world of the Yorkshire Dales after a prolific career. While character actor legends such as Bernard Bresslaw and Peter Butterworth both passed away at the age of 59, Bill embarked on a whole new acting success story, which quickly overshadowed anything else he had done. As Compo, the slightly more twisted brother of Just William with a dash of Dennis the Menace for good measure, Owen became a headlining star for the last 30 years of his life. Although Roy Clarke's scripts were structured to create a three-way, mini-community between the men behaving badly in deepest Yorkshire, the nation soon took Compo to its heart. His carefree, shabby appearance, green bobble hat and equal passions for his beloved ferrets and Nora Batty's notoriously wrinkled stockings are part of the national identity. Compo is a television classic with an image totally alien from the real Bill Owen.

Roy Clarke believes:

The joy of Bill Owen's Compo is not what he does with the words but where he takes the character beyond what's in the script. He did this in a physical manner. It was only when I saw Bill on screen that I realized what a wonderful physical clown he was. When he did those silly dances and his odd walks, the quality was Chaplinesque – there's no question about it. Bill brought wonderful strength to the part with his instinctive movements.

Bill was born William Rowbotham on 14 March 1914. This most famous of television Yorkshiremen was in reality a true blue cockney, his father a London cab driver. The young Bill made his first mark in show business when he was appointed manager for Warners Holiday Camps, enjoying his first professional stage appearance with the Cambridge Repertory Company in 1934. Even as a young man of 19, his passion for left-wing politics shaped his choice of work. One of his earliest successes was with the Unity Theatre alongside the likes of H. G. Wells, Sean O'Casey and Paul Robeson. Although Bill began his association with the group as just a lowly understudy in the celebrated Clifford Odets play *Waiting for Lefty*, he soon graduated to leading comedy parts in politically geared revues and pantomimes.

Still acting under his own name of Bill Rowbotham, he made his first few film appearances in 1945, cropping up in the morale-boosting short film *Song of the People* and, most notably, his feature-film debut in the classic wartime RAF adventure *The Way to the Stars* with Michael Redgrave and Douglass Montgomery. Bill featured in the Robert Donat and Deborah Kerr romantic comedy *Perfect Strangers* for director Alexander Korda, and was cast by producer/director Peter Ustinov in the confused espionage yarn *School for Secrets* in 1946.

Bill married in 1946 and had one son, Tom. A valuable part of the Betty Box repertory company of screen players, Bill first encountered the clan – via writers Muriel and Sydney Box – in the gloomy dockside melodrama *Daybreak*. Released in 1948, it had been suppressed by the censors for two years while its tale of suicide, part-time hangman duties, Swedish sailors and hairdressing was cleaned up for the cinema-going audience. Ann Todd and Eric Portman starred, but Bill's eye-catching performance was enough to secure him regular film character-

Simply Compo. Bill Owen referred to his character as 'Just William in wellies'!

acting duties for over a decade. Featured roles came in the Jack Warner/Kathleen Harrison soap opera *Holiday Camp* and the classic Dennis Price/Edward Rigby football pools compendium piece *Easy Money* (both 1947), while the 1948 racing-car yarn *Once a Jolly Swagman,* with Dirk Bogarde, Bonar Colleano and Sid James, elevated him to the pole position of 'star' character player. The following year Bill co-starred with Jean Kent in the lovelorn, backstage Technicolor musical *Trottie True*, indulging his love for natty dressing and showbiz glitz. Into the 1950s Bill continued to notch up impressive supporting turns, notable among them *Hotel Sahara* with Peter Ustinov in 1952, and the Walt Disney adventure *The Story of Robin Hood and His Merrie Men* alongside a Lincoln green-clad Richard Todd. And occasionally pictures such as *The Square Ring* allowed Bill to develop his chirpy cockney mannerisms with added charm and clout to deliver a stunning dramatic performance – here as a cheerful boxer who desperately clings to his fame, fortune and female fans as his career begins to falter.

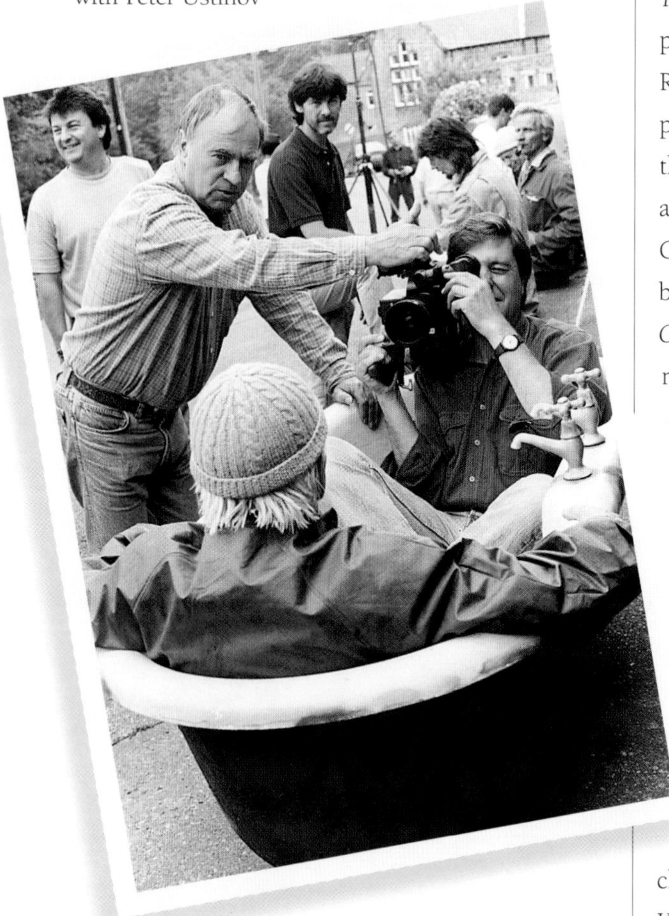

Alan J. W. Bell sets up the ultimate Summer Wine *cliché – the runaway tin bath!*

More average 1950s' fare included the horse-racing drama *The Rainbow Jacket*, the treasurable Brits-on-the-razzle-abroad fun of *A Day to Remember* with Harry Fowler, and the 1955 war film *The Ship That Died of Shame*. It was a shame the old ship died, particularly with folk such as George Baker and Richard Attenborough aboard. Bill had the dubious pleasure of appearing in *Davy* (1957), the very last of the celebrated Ealing comedies. A rather lacklustre and pathos-driven vehicle headlining the singing Goon himself, Harry Secombe, the film was written by the American William Rose, who had just penned *Genevieve* and would later script the 1963 comedy masterpiece *It's a Mad, Mad, Mad, Mad World*, and directed by Basil Dearden. At the very least, *Davy* had a strong supporting cast, including Susan Shaw, George Relph and future *Carry On* team members Kenneth Connor and Joan Sims.

Importantly, Bill himself was a regular member of the cast of the early Peter Rogers and Gerald Thomas *Carry On* comedy classics, starring opposite William Hartnell in the first, *Carry On Sergeant*, in 1958. Cast as the solid Corporal Bill Copping, the actor was called on to do little but look skywards in amazement at the clumsiness and barefaced cheek of Charles Hawtrey, Kenneth Connor and Kenneth Williams. However, his performance was a joy and Bill returned for the second film, *Carry On Nurse*. As the troubled patient

Percy Hickson, Bill was memorably saddled with a broken leg and an emotional wife, played with overflowing helplessness by Irene Handl. In 1961, the fifth film, *Carry On Regardless*, cast him as helping hand Mike Weston, featuring a classic sketch opposite Scottish Molly Weir and her collection of birds. Finally, in 1963, he completed his time with the team as grumpy taxi driver Smiley, in *Carry On Cabby* – ironically, years before Stephen Lewis played the equally miserable Smiler in *Last of the Summer Wine* and just at the same time as Bill was reunited with Sid James for the popular television series *Taxi*. Scripted by *Dixon of Dock Green* creator Ted Willis, *Taxi* was a ground-breaking mixture of earthy drama and laddish comedy screened by the BBC and, sadly, in the majority, wiped from the archives.

Although Peter Rogers had wanted to make Bill a regular member of the cast, the actor's reluctance to stay completely in comedy acting resulted in other, more diverse credits. These included such classics as the 1958 Virginia McKenna film *Carve Her Name with Pride*, the John Lemont-directed blackmailing drama *The Shakedown* (1959) with Terence Morgan, Donald Pleasence and Harry H. Corbett, and the 18th-century Keith Michell/Peter Cushing robbery romp *The Hellfire Club* (1961).

Bill had also kept busy on stage with West End appearances in Brecht's *Threepenny Opera* at the Royal Court and as Ko-Ko in *The Mikado* at Sadler's Wells. He starred as Hans Luther in John Osborne's *Luther* at the Phoenix, and battled opposite Spike Milligan in the Lyric Hammersmith staging of *Oblomov*, while still taking on less demanding roles in British films – including the blood and thunder Hammer hogwash of *The Secret of Blood Island* (1964) and Disney's men-in-tights romp of the same year, *The Fighting Prince of Donegal*.

Bill fully embraced cool Swinging Sixties England with a role in *Georgy Girl* opposite Lynn Redgrave and James Mason. Thanks to a freer attitude towards sex on screen, a spirit of fresh modernity and the Oscar-nominated title song written by Tom Springfield and Jim Dale, the film became a milestone in British cinema. Ironically, Bill's acting career seemed to hit a bad patch at this time, although he enjoyed success in other fields. He wrote the lyrics for many popular songs recorded by the likes of Cliff Richard and Guy Mitchell, as well as writing the West End musical *The Match Girls* in 1966 which, to this day, remains one of amateur theatre's most performed works. Bill felt that he owed a debt of gratitude to the distinguished director Lindsay Anderson, who cast him in two David Storey plays – *Celebration* and *The Contractor* – at the Royal Court in 1969. Bill believed that they salvaged his acting career. Speaking in the 1980s, he recalled:

At the time I was virtually finished in the biz and Lindsay picked me up.

A film version of *The Contractor*, *O Lucky Man!*, also directed by Anderson, appeared in 1973, while Bill had fully launched his major television career with the 1971 ATV situation comedy *Coppers End*. A sort of cross between Dixon and Bilko with a touch of Will Hay tossed in for good measure, this unfairly forgotten starring vehicle was created for Bill by Ted Willis. Cast as the lazy, cunning and corrupt police sergeant Sam Short, Bill ran his quiet, out-of-the-way police station with a lacklustre, semi-legal style. Richard Wattis played his ally and Josephine Tewson the bane of his life in 13 episodes broadcast in 1971.

Another small-screen favourite for Bill was *Coronation Street*. In the perennially popular soap opera he was memorably cast as a bolshie trade union official, while BBC situation comedy called on his services to play the equally bolshie father figure of George Chambers in *Whatever Happened to the Likely Lads?* As the flustered, rant-machine father-in-law of Rodney Bewes, Bill sparred to wonderful comic effect with on-screen wives Joan Hickson in the first series and Noel Dyson in the second. This classic resurrection of the 1960s' series starring James Bolam and Rodney Bewes saw the Dick Clement and Ian La Frenais scripts at fever pitch, and Bill's semi-regular appearances were beautifully delivered.

However, even by this stage, a pilot episode of a little Roy Clarke tale of three old chaps wandering the Yorkshire Dales had been commissioned and filmed. *Last of the Summer Wine* would take up the rest of Bill's life – even though, ironically, he wasn't believed suitable by many to play the part. Producer Jimmy Gilbert thought otherwise:

Bill Owen was right for the part because I had seen him play a very Compo-like character in a play with Spike Milligan called Oblomov. *I had also seen him in David Storey's play* The Contractor, *where he was a real tough northerner. Putting the two together, having seen him in comedy and having worked with him in musicals, he seemed to be the perfect casting. Even though a cockney at heart, Bill is very much an honorary Yorkshireman.*

From the first recording in 1972 through to when Bill's final four episodes were filmed in 1999, the familiar, beloved figure of Compo became a cherished national hero. Scruffy, lazy and ill-mannered, this carefree chap spent an idyllic lifestyle, chatting and bickering with contemporaries, betting on the horses, pampering his ferrets and shooting down hillsides in a tin bath. Happy with his lot in life and really rather fond of the ritual humiliation and ordering about dished out by authority figures from Bates to Thornton, Bill's regret at the departure of the Bates character Blamire was tangible on screen. In the first Brian Wilde episode, *The Man from Oswestry*, there's time for some charming, subtle and poignant pangs of loneliness from Bill – moodily stomping through life and disgruntledly supping his cocoa in Sid's Café. As he introspectively mopes about the lack of authority and argument in his existence since the departure of the trio's first, self-voted leader, the viewer sees inside the simpleton's mind. He needs that reassuring voice of authority to feel safe, and few actors had the ability and technique to convey that sense of need like Bill Owen.

The *Summer Wine* ethos conjured up an almost mythical, ultra-safe haven. It was a timeless, ageless and leisurely pace of life, which appealed to all. Bringing with him so much experience and performance success from a lifetime of acting, Bill could effortlessly inject moments of touching emotion into Compo's fragile, underdog persona. Overflowing with ripe, fruity comments, a childlike addiction to fun and, literally, the joys of living, Compo remains a masterly comic creation.

In Bill's own favourite episode, *From Wellies to Wet Suit* – screened in tribute to the actor the day after his death – all the physical comedy of a true pro is brought out of the locker room. Clad in a figure-hugging wet suit and, for much of the episode, mucking about in the water, Bill's brilliant, wordless vignette in the local newsagent's shop is a masterly comic moment. As the assistant and customer look on with amazement while not breaking their conversational flow, Bill gamely staggers and stumbles through his attempts at selecting a magazine. A perfect bit of mime, the ever-mounting task – as great swathes of journals and papers cascade to the floor – is one of Bill's finest moments of high comedy.

In the memorable episode *Going to Gordon's Wedding*, the endearing naive charm of Compo is

Bridge over untroubled water. Bill Owen, Michael Aldridge and Peter Sallis in the rolling Yorkshire hills.

allowed to inform and enhance the usual bumbling, work-shy, tatty comic observation. His pride in finding the perfect gift – a loud alarm clock, which provides the show's comic climax, pride in appearance – a suit worn with an oversized floral buttonhole for added splendour, and, more importantly, bubbling pride in acting as the big event's best man, all illustrate hidden depths to the basic standard character. Bill's acting was paramount to these subtle sea changes and emotional roller-coaster moments.

Bill rejoiced in playing the part on stage both in the *Summer Wine* summer season and later in various pantomime appearances when the Compo mannerisms guaranteed full houses. Appointed an MBE in 1976, Bill married his second wife, the actress Kate O'Donoghue, in 1977. Throughout, the glories of *Summer Wine* kept his spirit young, and in 1981 he was delighted to indulge in political activities when he was appointed Labour's Chairman of Arts. Stage and film assignments frequently filled Bill's time between *Summer Wine* work, and his distinctive vocal talent was heard in the charming children's film *The Smurfs and the Magic Flute*.

His final cinematic appearance was in the Channel 4-funded, Ealing comedy-style tale of geese-farmers, *Laughterhouse* – broadcast on television as *Singleton's Pluck* – while a long-standing ambition to film a second feature-length episode of *Last of the Summer Wine* was realized the following year when

Uncle of the Bride ushered in new team members Michael Aldridge, Thora Hird, Sarah Thomas and Mike Grady. Taking on the mantle of Roger Livesey from the celebrated Laurence Olivier film, Bill starred as beloved, aged music-hall favourite Billy Rice, opposite Michael Gambon, in the 1993 BBC2 presentation of *The Entertainer*. In 1994 Bill published his fascinating autobiography, *Summer Wine and Vintage Years – A Cluttered Life*.

A seemingly never-ending fantasy world, *Last of the Summer Wine* continued to get BBC re-commissions, and in 1997 it celebrated its 25th anniversary with a special documentary. Ever optimistic, Bill did ponder on the dreadful possibility of what on earth he would do when the show actually ended. As it happened, Bill happily saw out his days working on the series. Delighted that a millennium Special had been agreed on, Bill made the emotional trip to the war graves in France with Peter Sallis and Frank Thornton. Physically weakened by the cancer of the pancreas that would kill him, Bill made the strenuous trip and returned to his beloved Holmfirth for the final scenes. Bravely going through the touching and poignant Last Post climax with his two co-stars, Bill's professionalism and stamina seemed to push him through the pain barrier and on to his ultimate aim: simply to finish the programme. The actor knew this was the end. On his penultimate day of filming, he gave actress Kathy Staff the wink and slowly walked over to director/producer Alan J. W. Bell. Kathy remembers:

Just before we filmed it, Bill quietly told me that he was going to ask the producer to make a little change to the script. He just winked and walked off. I had no idea what it was all about until Bill came back and told me that after all these years Nora was finally going to kiss Compo. I knew Bill had been ill, but it was only after his death that I realized the significance of that kiss.

It is clear that Bill wanted to round off his time with the show in style. The Holmfirth exhibition was given his one, final lookover to make sure everything was perfect. The shocked Compo, having spent nearly 30 years in hot pursuit, goes out with a kiss of affection from the love of his life, and the actor Bill Owen can rest in peace knowing full well that the show he loved so much will continue to be enjoyed by countless generations.

Though no longer in the show, long-time acting partner Brian Wilde was deeply affected by Bill's death. As with so many friends, memories came flooding back:

He was a wonderful actor to work with, and I treasure the memory of us sitting in the churchyard where Bill is now buried. It was a nice sunny day, and Compo was looking around at the tombstones and their inscriptions. He asked, 'I wonder what they'll put on my grave when I'm dead?' and Foggy replied, 'Something very heavy I hope!' We all laughed then and it helps ease the sadness now.

In accordance with Bill's wishes, he was buried in his beloved Holmfirth, the place that had become his second home. As Bill remembered shortly before his death:

When I first came here, Yorkshire for me was just another excellent county with some good theatre dates if you were on tour. When we came to make the pilot, I really found out what Yorkshire was all about.
I remember coming into this little town quite early in the morning. I looked down the high street and it looked a bit tired and sorry for itself. There was a lot of unemployment. The recession had been on a long time, but I felt a sudden warmth for it. I was sitting in the pub, the Elephant and Castle, when an old Yorkshireman, sitting alone at a table next to mine, suddenly looked at me and said, 'Are you all rit?' and I said, 'Aye!' I had never actually spoken

the Yorkshire dialect before in my life, and that was when I felt something for this town that I've never felt for any other city I have been in. I knew I wanted to belong to it.

Peter Sallis

NORMAN CLEGG: 1973 TO DATE

Of the three principals first to venture through the Yorkshire Dales, it was Peter Sallis who was firmly fixed in the mind of series writer Roy Clarke. *Summer Wine* was primarily created as a situation comedy vehicle for Peter, and the intricate dialogues, languid comments on life's absurdities and rolling observations on the less-than-gentle stagger into old age, were perfectly suited to him. Peter has played the bewildered, witty and cowardly retired lino salesman in every single episode of *Last of the Summer Wine* – a record that makes his contribution to the series a unique and mind-blowingly long one. Whereas the length of the series and the expansion of the central cast might have blurred the edges and removed a lot of the magical, spiralling conversations that single out the first five years as masterpieces of scriptwriting, Peter can always be relied on for a delicious throwaway line that nobody wants to throw away. Dubbed 'Cleggisms', these pearls of wisdom are what give the series its warmth and comic heart. Interestingly enough, Peter Sallis the actor and Norman Clegg the character are remarkably similar, a point that Peter himself is happy to elaborate on. While on location filming, it is Peter who injects off-the-cuff comments and witty opinions on the world around him. Like Clegg, Peter can get the biggest laugh with a short, pithy aside, which instantly hits the funny bone:

I am Clegg. I'm a physical coward. I used to be afraid of women. And, of course, I don't like to get into any trouble. I just like to be safe! In fact, I've written the odd line for Clegg. The show is like manna from heaven for me as an actor because I don't have to act. Only on a few occasions do I have to think or do something which isn't entirely natural to me.

Born in 1921, Peter's first employment was as a frustrated bank clerk before a refreshing brush with amateur dramatics in the late 1930s fired his imagination and pointed the way forward for a career on the stage. During his war service with the Royal Air Force, Peter indulged his passion with regular appearances in camp entertainments, and on leaving the RAF he secured a place at the Royal Academy of Dramatic Art in London. Having graduated with flying colours – he was awarded the Laurence Olivier Prize for Most Promising Actor – Peter performed on stage and in film, making his feature debut in the 1952 production of *Child's Play*. In a cast headlined by the distinguished actress Mona Washbourne, the film's plot – concerning a bunch of youngsters harbouring nuclear power to aid their flourishing popcorn business – has a charm and quaintness all of its own. And with the very, very young Christopher Beeny – later to star in television's *Upstairs, Downstairs* and *In Loving Memory* with Thora Hird – there is plenty of opportunity for early star-spotting. Other notable films of the 1950s, such as *Anastasia* in 1956, featuring Ingrid Bergman's triumphant Oscar-winning return to Hollywood, the murderous Doris Day suspense thriller *Julie* (1956), and the aristocratic, criminally sophisticated production *The Scapegoat*, which reunited star Alec Guinness and director Robert Hamer a decade after *Kind Hearts and Coronets*, all cast Peter in effective, minor supporting roles of bemused authority. *The Doctor's Dilemma* again allowed for more of the same, this time opposite Dirk Bogarde and Alastair Sim, while 1960's *Saturday Night and Sunday Morning*

contrasted this with stark, realist imagery and a towering, on-the-brink performance from Albert Finney.

During the 1960s Peter found himself profitably involved in some of the finest and most endearingly successful film series. In 1960 he enjoyed a minor role of twittering devotion opposite Virginia Maskell in *Doctor in Love* for producer Betty E. Box and director Ralph Thomas. Moreover, the great Hammer horrors cast Peter in several standout productions. He suffered some unforgettable Oliver Reed snarling in Terence Fisher's garish classic *Curse of the Werewolf* in 1961, and fell victim to Christopher Lee's fiendish count in the 1969 chiller *Taste the Blood of Dracula*. He played alongside Peter Finch and Susan Hayward in the Robert Stevens-directed melodrama *I Thank a Fool*, cruised through a small role in the Orson Welles/Margaret Rutherford airport epic *The VIPs* and gamely took on the decade's obsession with the taming of outer space in the wayward Ron Moody satire *The Mouse on the Moon* (1963).

Peter also found himself a part of Charles Crichton's undervalued psychological and philosophical compendium *The Third Secret* (1964), John Guillermin's 1965 tale of mental anxiety, *Rapture*, and Albert Finney's sparkling champagne comedy adventure *Charlie Bubbles* in 1967. Peter grabbed a substantial supporting role opposite Nicol Williamson and Eleanor Fazan in a thought-provoking filming of John Osborne's play *Inadmissible Evidence,* and returned to all-out, Gothic horror for the treasurable 1969 terror-fest *Scream and Scream Again*. Despite its many faults, the last has passed into cinematic history for teaming Peter Cushing, Christopher Lee and Vincent Price for the first time, while detective Alfred Marks skilfully tried to make sense of all the murderous goings-on.

The first sip of Summer Wine. *Peter Sallis as Clegg in an early publicity shot.*

Film work during the 1970s was less and less frequent, while Peter's choice of material was often less than careful. He starred opposite Patricia Neal in a confused variation on *Night Must Fall, The Night Digger*, in 1971, and appeared in the mammoth James Mason horror spectacular *Frankenstein: The True Story,* which played in its full version on American television and crept out in an abridged format in British cinemas.

'Last of the Summer Wine *has transformed my life – good gracious, I could have been an actor!'*

Television had provided Peter with some interesting work throughout the 1960s and early 1970s, including a bit of earnest, snowbound angst in *Doctor Who: The Ice Warriors* with Patrick Troughton and *Carry On* favourite Bernard Bresslaw. Peter also supported that raffish charmer Leslie Phillips in a short-lived BBC situation comedy *The Culture Vultures*, co-scripted by fledgling Goodie Tim Brooke-Taylor. Playing Professor George Hobbs in this short-lived series (only five episodes were made and broadcast in 1970), Peter excelled with troubled befuddlement in this University of Hampshire-based dose of comedy.

His next major encounter with BBC comedy was far more successful. Writer Roy Clarke, having worked with Peter on a television staging of one of his plays, immediately set about penning a series especially for the actor. Injecting mannerisms, opinions and the vocal delivery of Peter, Clarke came up with an idea for three retired old chaps, unattached to wives and employment, who stagger through mad scrapes and reflective conversations in the Yorkshire Dales. The pilot formed part of the 1973 season of *Comedy Playhouse*, and the series, *Last of the Summer Wine*, is still with us some 30 years later. Peter's introspective, quiet and non-confrontational delivery became a mainstay of the comedy, and his way with Clarke's intricate dialogue has created some of the show's funniest moments. The relationship between actor and writer was strong from the beginning, as Roy Clarke remembers:

I'd recently finished a play – a drama – with Peter Sallis, and I knew from that moment that I wanted Peter for Clegg. In fact, I wrote Clegg with Peter very much in mind. Clegg tends to get the more reflective lines. I suppose he would have to be nearest to me because I don't wear wellies all the time on the one hand, and I'm not quite as authoritarian as Foggy on the other.

Peter himself was unaware of this for many years:

I didn't know Roy Clarke had written the part of Norman Clegg with me in mind. It was probably ten years or more before I found out. Roy would never have said it to me. But once I knew, we talked about it and shared a close personal moment. At the time I had no idea. I just thought I was well cast!

Norman Clegg proved the perfect sounding-board for Compo's bedevilled glee and for the various third man authority figures. He was also perfect for pinpointing the absurdity and hidden pitfalls concealed within the manic schemes of Blamire, Foggy, Seymour and Truly. In the Series Two classic, *Ballad for Wind Instrument and Canoe*, his reaction to the spirited enquiry,'Have you seen a canoe, fellows?' is greeted by the brilliantly uninterested 'What colour?' It may originally have been attributed to Harry Secombe when, during war action, Spike Milligan enquired about his missing cannon, but Sallis milks the ironic clout perfectly. It's definitive Clegg, and it's this programme that provides Peter with his most vivid memory of working on *Summer Wine*:

I remember we were shooting on the River Wharf – a shallow and slow-moving stretch of water, full of pot-holes. Michael, Bill and I had to paddle a canoe underneath a bridge and through the other side. That's all we had to do. It was a bank holiday, so a whole crowd had turned up to watch. I explained to the director, Bernard Thompson, that I couldn't swim and that if anything happened I must be looked after quickly. Michael, on the other hand, had made it clear that he knew how to swim and all about canoes. Just like his character, he wanted to lead and took the stern end. Bill didn't care either way and got stuck up the front – so I was in the middle.

We set off – it was a lovely bright sunny day. We did get past the bridge, and then I felt it going. I shouted out: 'We are going to go over!' Michael barked: 'No, we won't. Leave it to me!' And we promptly turned over! I managed to snatch a breath before I went down. I struck out with both legs to try to find somewhere to steady myself. I pushed against this object, and it just got me up high enough to claw my way up the bank and out of the water. I then made my way through the crowds, sopping wet, to the pub where we kept our things. One of the onlookers came up to me and asked: 'Excuse me, weren't you Samuel Pepys?'

I found out afterwards that the object I had got my foothold on was, in fact, Bill Owen's head!

Importantly, Peter escaped typecasting during the early *Summer Wine* days and happily accepted roles in other television comedies. He was extremely popular and successful as the devious and hiss-worthy Mr Gudgin in the children's classic *The Ghosts of Motley Hall*. Broadcast from 1976 through until 1978, this early evening ITV treat featured spectre turns from such priceless eccentrics as Freddie Jones, Arthur English and Sheila Steafal. In 1977 he appeared as Randall Todd in the second series of the wartime comedy drama *Yanks Go Home* for director Roger Cheveley, and a further ITV comedy favourite followed when Peter was cast as Arthur Simister, the mournful and pessimistic boss of David Roper in *Leave It to Charlie*. Four series were broadcast between 1978 and 1980.

On the big screen, the 1970s had provided Peter with a handful of notable roles, working with Mia Farrow on the 1976 haunted house chiller *Full Circle* and hamming it up in the Glenda Jackson biopic on the early life of actress Sarah Bernhardt, *The Incredible Sarah* (1976). He appeared in the gastronomic black comedy *Who Is Killing the Great Chefs of Europe?* (1978) with George Segal and a scene-stealing Robert Morley, while in the following year he sparred with the all-teeth-and-cloak madness of Frank Langella in the 1979 treatment of *Dracula*.

But it was the seemingly aimless wanderings of Clegg that the nation took straight to its heart. The three-way conversations, particularly of the very early shows with Michael Bates, allowed Peter to mutter and yawn his way through life's little problems and annoyances. The stunning letter-reading monologue that explains Blamire's leaving and introduces the off-screen spectre of Foggy in *The Man from Oswestry* was peerlessly performed, with every comic aside, bizarre situation and jaded comment in place. As a writer's device to lose one character and welcome another, it was hackneyed, to say the least – but Peter's beautiful delivery made it one of the season's high points. *Summer Wine* scripting was at its best in its rawest form and, indeed, Peter's own personal favourite episode, *Full Steam Behind*, is a perfect example of this:

I really loved doing Full Steam Behind. *There were only the three of us, Brian, Bill and myself, and we went to Haworth and rode on their steam trains. The episode had a charm about it. It has a marvellous opening with me*

The wild ones. Brian Wilde, Peter Sallis and Bill Owen pose for the 1993 Christmas Special, Welcome to Earth.

ironing as usual and Bill just chatting. Brian comes in wearing this awful railway porter's cap and carrying a green flag and whistle to rally us to go and see a steam train. We were really going train-spotting but literally ended up stealing the train. It was delightful!

On-screen chemistry with Bill Owen was firmly in place for 27 years, while battling banter opposite former RADA contemporary Brian Wilde resulted in the show's classic years. Fans and historians alike point to the Owen/Sallis/Wilde episodes as definitive *Summer Wine*. Throughout, Peter's nervousness over women, going into battle and even travelling at high speed down a hillside in a tin bath created an overflowing, endearing and comically inspired sense of growing tension. Deep in thought about the distance of sky from land or painfully concerned about the plight of flowers severed from their roots, Peter's mini-universe within the *Summer Wine* fantasy added further freshness and comic class with each new series.

Peter's comic experience and gentle irony were also welcomed by the 'alternative' crop of performers who invaded British television during the 1980s. Towards the end of the decade Peter was recruited to play a semi-regular character opposite the cunning, corrupt and less-than-conservative Conservative MP Alan B'Stard, as played by Rik Mayall in ITV's *The New Statesman*. His voice dripping with mild-mannered sincerity and patriotic duty, Peter cameoed as the frustrated pub landlord who revelled in cherished memories of being Britain's most prolific hangman. Despite the briefness and infrequency of the scenes, Peter's good-natured, ghoulish and traditional comic edge within the new small-screen environment created a treasured role. Familiar terrain was trodden with Peter's lead role in Mike Stephens's ingenious but short-lived attempt to turn the clock back on the *Summer Wine* gang. *First of the Summer Wine* related the wartime antics of Compo, Clegg, Foggy and the like as youngsters, with a wonderfully laid-back Peter playing the part of Clegg's eternally bemused father. It further adds to Peter's longstanding devotion to the series, as he appears in all *First* and *Last of the Summer Wine* episodes – to date a total of 205 programmes – a devotion matched only by the continuing adoration of the show by its millions of fans:

I think the viewers love it because they can live in this community for 30 minutes and they know all those people. They feel that if, say, Pearl and Howard came round the corner, they might bump into them. You feel you are there with them. You could say the same applies to soap operas – you could identify with the regulars in the Rover's Return – but that's different. That's trying to be real life. This is not. This is Wind in the Willows. *It's enjoyed by children as well as adults. Children, middle-aged people and the elderly absolutely love it. I think if I wasn't in it…I would still watch it!*

Peter's appeal to children was further reinforced when his delicious, languid voice was employed for the international success story of Nick Park's Wallace and Gromit short films, the animated Plasticine adventures of a meek and mild Yorkshire chap and his quick-witted dog. Oscar-winning classics sponsored by the BBC and showcasing an unlikely, totally lovable British double act of self-conscious action heroes, the films – *A Grand Day Out*, *The Wrong Trousers* and *A Close Shave* – remain timelessly enjoyable. With a passion for cheese, buttered toast and the wireless, Peter's lugubrious delivery of Wallace's dialogue has made him a hero to children of all ages.

In September 1999, Peter played part-time thespian Quince in *A Midsummer Night's Dream* – part of the BBC's landmark millennium Shakespeare season.

A national treasure, Peter remains one of the

country's finest and best-loved actors. Wisely, he has never allowed the fame to go to his head:

I was in Chichester doing a play and I rented a little house in a cul-de-sac. I would walk down it every evening to get to the theatre. I was going past one of the houses and a man was trimming his hedge. He came out and grabbed me by the shoulder and said: ''Ere, I know you. You were in the next cell to me in Wormwood Scrubs!' I said: 'I don't think so!' But he was insistent. I said: 'No, really, I wasn't!' And he said: 'Oh, I under–I understand! But I'll tell you what, my wife has seen you going past and said I should invite you in for a cup of tea one evening. Now wasn't that nice of her?' So I said, 'Yes' and I left. A few moments later he came running after me and said: 'Oh, Gawd, no. I'm terribly sorry…it was Doctor Zhivago*!' I wasn't in that either!*

Michael Bates

CYRIL BLAMIRE: 1973 TO 1975

Completing the original troublesome trio for Roy Clarke's initial batch of *Last of the Summer Wine* was another distinguished British character actor well known for comedy. According to Jane Freeman:

Michael Bates was a tremendous comedy technician. He was a very well-known theatre comedian, which suited the early shows. He spent a great deal of time showing me how to hit someone over the head with a tin tray. He would say: 'Wait, Jane – pause!' He was wonderful and very helpful, regaling us all with tales of film-making.'

Michael Bates was born in Janshi, India, on 4 December 1920 and could speak Hindustani before he could speak English. His military upbringing, style and demeanour shaped his most celebrated small-screen roles. As with Bill Owen, Michael found himself popular as a useful, jobbing actor for post war British cinema. He had a supporting role in the 1954 David Niven and Margaret Leighton courtroom drama *Carrington VC*, directed by Anthony Asquith for producer Teddy Baird. Other notable 1950s' appearances included the classic Boulting brothers' union satire *I'm All Right Jack* (1959) with Peter Sellers.

But it was on radio that Bates first fully made his mark in comedy. Joining the leading cast members of Jon Pertwee, Leslie Phillips and Stephen Murray in the Light Programme's *The Navy Lark*, Michael excelled as a vast array of comic stereotypes. Foreign and regional accents were a speciality, his vocal mannerisms perfect for ranting officious types, and, alongside the young Ronnie Barker, Bates helped colour in the background for this landmark series. As with the rest of the established cast, Michael continued to find time for the radio broadcasts right through the 1960s and into the 1970s. The series finally came to an end in 1977 after an amazing 19 years at the top.

On television, Michael found himself much in demand for similar character roles. They were all bumbling policemen, toffee-nosed eccentrics and befuddled gentlemen, although as early as 1957 he enjoyed a rare Shakespearean role as Bardolph in the BBC presentation of *The Life of Henry V*. He featured in the eight classic episodes of *Mr John Jorrocks* in 1966, which starred Jimmy Edwards as R. S. Surtees's celebrated sporting cockney who becomes squire of the village of Handley Cross. Michael staggered in for some eye-catching work as the Duke of Donkeyton. Written by Michael Voysey, the series was directed by Peter Dews for the BBC. Two years later, Michael starred as Antrobus, the First Secretary, in a one-off *Comedy Playhouse* production, *Stiff Upper Lip*. Richard Vernon, and Bernard Bresslaw as the thick-skulled embassy footman Percy, also appeared in this long-forgotten Barry Took adaptation of Lawrence Durrell's stories. Michael Mills produced.

Very much part of the late 1960s' swinging cinema of British film-makers, Michael seemed ideal to play the solid, unswinging figure of authority opposite the comic hero. He made a vital contribution to the surreal and totally fascinating world of Peter Cook and Dudley Moore's *Bedazzled* in 1967. This was an ultra-bizarre excuse to rework the Faust story within and around choice sketches from the duo's BBC series *Not Only…But Also*, and Michael was stunningly reserved as the dogged and super-suspicious detective on Dud's trail. In 1968 Michael appeared in the ground-breaking British comedy *Here We Go Round the Mulberry Bush* with Barry Evans and Trevor Howard. Directed by Clive Donner, its free attitude towards sex and swinging Britain made it an important and commercially successful piece of work. Michael enjoyed a leading role opposite Sammy Davis Jr and Peter Lawford in the hip murder mystery *Salt and Pepper* (1968).

Later that year Michael cropped up in the Jerry Lewis and Terry-Thomas comedy *Don't Raise the Bridge, Lower the River* and in the unsubtle James Bond clone *Hammerhead* with Vince Edwards and Diana Dors. However, Michael's finest film appearance by far came with the 1970 Oscar-winner *Patton*. George C. Scott portrayed the bombastic American general with tangible passion in this engrossing and thought-provoking epic, alongside Michael stealing some of the limelight with a peerless presentation of Field Marshal Montgomery.

Michael then drifted into more lightweight fare – notably mugging like a good 'un in Peter Cook's multi-media satire *The Rise and Rise of Michael Rimmer* (1970), and the all-out breakneck farce of *No Sex Please, We're British* (1973) with Ronnie Corbett and Arthur Lowe. Intriguingly, Stanley Kubrick cast Michael as Chief Guard Barnes in his harrowing, beautiful and emotive piece of work *A Clockwork Orange* in 1971. The following year Alfred Hitchcock teamed him with Alec McCowen as the bumbling London police officer Sergeant Spearman in that lovely thriller *Frenzy*.

Blamire! Michael Bates radiates Summer Wine *pride on location in Holmfirth.*

But by this stage in Michael's career, television had well and truly captured most of his time. On the box in the corner, Michael would be a very welcome face for most of the 1970s. He joined the cast of the Peter Jones and Sheila Hancock situation comedy *Mr Digby, Darling* for the third series in 1970. The shows revolved around Peter Jones, his wife, his sanctuary-providing office, Rid-o-Rat and his secretary. Michael played Norman Stanhope in this popular series scripted by Ken Hoare and Mike Sharland. In 1971 Michael enjoyed an impressive appearance in one of the *Six Dates with Barker*. The star was Ronnie of that ilk, and the episode *Come in and Lie Down* was written by *Monty Python*'s John Cleese. The show cast Michael as a paranoid fellow who pretends to be the gasman in order to chat to Ron's bemused psychiatrist. With a performance of nervous tics, hidden secrets and uneasy creepiness, Michael helped to create a uniquely dark slice of British comedy.

After a lifetime of supporting roles on television and radio, Michael was finally presented with his own series in 1972. Directed by Bill Hitchcock, *Turnbull's Finest Half-Hour* was written by *Mr Digby, Darling* creators Ken Hoare and Mike Sharland for Yorkshire Television. The series concerned the exploits and shortcomings of the very minor broadcasting power Pentagon Television, and featured *Carry On* favourite Liz Fraser and future *Yes, Minister* writer Jonathan Lynn in the supporting cast. Despite the fact that

An accident waiting to happen. The original trio – Michael Bates, Peter Sallis and Bill Owen – in Ballad for Wind Instrument and Canoe *(1975).*

only six episodes were made, Michael's sterling lead performance as a retired, authoritative, militant type desperately trying to keep a collection of misfits in order clearly pointed the way towards *Last of the Summer Wine* early the following year. Although other television assignments came along – Michael starred as Reg Forrester in a single ATV *Comedy Premiere* of *Honey* in 1975 alongside an annoying American (Sandra Dickinson) who comes to dinner, and his wife (Kathleen Byron) – it was in a couple of legendary, long-running series that he became a comedy star. Closely associated with two very different roles in two very different BBC situation comedies, Michael Bates ended his long career with his best-loved and best-remembered performances.

The first role was as the upright, polished, militant and dictatorial Cyril Blamire in *Last of the Summer Wine*. Starring in a total of just 14 episodes with appearances in the pilot, Series One and Series Two, Michael created the blueprint for the slightly aggressive, slightly pompous and slightly eccentric Yorkshire Dales authority figure – some of the characteristics of which spilled over into real life.

Bill Owen recalled that not all ran smoothly filming the pilot:

We all stayed at the Coach and Horses in June 1972. It wasn't much to look at then. There was a notice up which ran 'Sunday morning breakfast with strippers'. When I told Jimmy Gilbert he said: 'Are you sure it's not kippers?' I remember our first evening together when a heavy political argument developed between Michael Bates and myself. It got very heavy. Suddenly Michael ended it, got up and walked out, which infuriated me even more. After that we decided there would be no more politics, and there never has been since. We all got on famously after that.

Brian Wilde, Michael Aldridge and Frank Thornton have all had to follow in the footsteps of Michael Bates and inject traces of his persona into their characterizations. Michael's performance was a masterpiece of controlled anguish, bubbling temper and proud self-importance. Fired up by reckless displays of youthful enthusiasm, energetic gusto or any sign of the spirit of British adventure, Michael was the ultimate slightly tarnished *Boy's Own* hero living out his final days in clouded circumstances. He proved the perfect contrast to Bill Owen's work-shy Compo and Peter Sallis's cowardly Clegg. Blessed with Roy Clarke's first and freshest scripts, Michael delighted in the tightly constructed, well-written, three-way conversations between the retired gentlemen at the show's heart. Chatting in the pub, the library, Sid's Café or on the side of a hill about life, the universe and everything, the childlike trio captured the essence of growing old disgracefully.

Peter Sallis had met Michael 20 years before *Summer Wine*:

I had known Michael since he became engaged in 1953. We'd done some plays together, one with Orson Welles and another one with Laurence Olivier. Michael was meticulous – he was basically a theatre actor. He played television as though it was theatre. Of course, Summer Wine *in those days was like theatre being played out in front of a live audience. Everything had to be exactly right for Michael. If he bought a round of drinks, he liked to have the right money on him.*

Although many of the early shows were centred around long-winded and intricate conversational pieces, Michael's penultimate episode clearly pointed the way towards the future. The future was Brian Wilde and even more hare-brained schemes, but in *Ballad for Wind Instrument and Canoe*, Michael Bates proved he could be as hot-headed, ridiculous and foolhardy as anybody else. There's the classic café-based competition with Bates,

A stunning publicity shot of Michael Bates as his other classic BBC comedy character Rangi Ram in It Ain't Half Hot, Mum.

Owen and John Comer struggling to ascertain who has the biggest mouth before Jane Freeman bellows her way into pole position. Only Michael, donning swimsuit and military gait, betters this priceless vignette for his well-orchestrated, disastrous launch of the trio's canoeing antics, visual comedy and panicked dialogue coming together for a raucous comic close.

Michael's other landmark comic creation for the BBC was for Jimmy Perry and David Croft. The *Dad's Army* writers had come up with another wartime-based situation comedy, this time set within the confines of an Army Entertainment Unit in deepest Burma at the tail end of the conflict. *It Ain't Half Hot, Mum* was first broadcast on 3 January 1974 – one day short of a year after *Summer Wine*'s debut – and starred Michael as the Indian guru Rangi Ram. Browned-up, donning his own school snakebelt around his turban and injecting deliciously Indian mannerisms remembered from his youth, Michael was in his element as the fount of all knowledge. Like Frankie Howerd with his *Up Pompeii* prologues, Michael was permitted to act outside and away from the ensemble playing of the supporting cast and actually address the watching millions at home. Although the powerful military ranting of Windsor Davies ultimately became the show's leading comic turn, Michael's endearing and understanding performance was at the very core of the series. His own invention – the action of clearing his throat but pulling back before spitting out – became a much-loved recurring gag. He starred in 36 episodes.

Sadly, just as Michael Bates was carving out a dual-edged star career with BBC Comedy, in late 1975 the actor was diagnosed as having cancer of the groin. It was terminal. Faced with a bleak future, Michael was forced to choose between continuing with *Last of the Summer Wine* or *It Ain't Half Hot, Mum*; reluctantly, he selected the latter. Both shows meant the world to him, but the hectic Yorkshire Dale working scenes were proving too much for the actor. Besides, *It Ain't Half Hot, Mum* was his career favourite. Series co-star Christopher Mitchell, who played that 'lovely boy' Gunner Parkins, remembers the actor's bravery:

Michael was in great pain towards the end, but he didn't show it. In rehearsals David Croft wouldn't let him stand, even though Michael would stand for the scene in the studio. He was a sad loss, and he really enjoyed doing the show. It was like reliving his childhood.

Michael's final episode was screened on 29 November 1977, by which time Brian Wilde had already joined the *Summer Wine* cast. Michael Bates died on 11 January 1978 at the tragically early age of 57, a wonderful career in comedy cut short at its zenith. Amazingly, both Michael's greatest shows continued in the wake of his death. Naturally, *Summer Wine* marches on for ever, while *It Ain't Half Hot, Mum* survived for a further three series until 1981. However, the early loss of Michael's subtle and always likeable acting contributions saw both shows stripped of an irreplaceable touch of magic.

Brian Wilde

FOGGY DEWHURST: 1976 TO 1985 AND 1990 TO 1997

Michael Bates might have started the tradition, and Frank Thornton proudly takes it into the new millennium, but Brian Wilde's Foggy is undoubtedly the nation's best-known and best-loved *Summer Wine* 'third man'. Injecting befuddled military tactics and pompous self-assurance into the programmes, Wilde's bombastic, eccentric and nervous mutterings proved the perfect butt to Compo's jokes and Clegg's wry asides.

Roy Clarke is grateful to Brian for rescuing the show at an early crisis point:

Casting has been a major contribution to the programme's long run. When Michael Bates left, we thought we were at the end of the road. It was Jimmy Gilbert who suggested Brian Wilde to be written in to a slightly modified Blamire – a character now to be called Foggy Dewhurst. Brian pulled us out of the fire, put us back on track and we've been running ever since.

Born in 1921, Brian Wilde studied acting at the Royal Academy of Dramatic Art alongside long-term co-star Peter Sallis. The usual experience of repertory theatre and radio led to Brian's first major break on television – the medium where the actor would present his finest work.

Brian's first small-screen success came with the ITV situation comedy *The Love of Mike* in 1960. The series starred Michael Medwin as carefree dance-band trumpeter Mike Lane, Medwin's reward for huge national popularity in *The Army Game*. Brian Wilde was cast as the hero's flatmate and friend, who advised on and joined in the comic adventures. Leaving the show after just seven episodes, Brian's role was subsequently taken on by Bernard Fox.

A 1966 *Comedy Playhouse* pilot, *Room at the Bottom*, led to a single series in 1967. Notable as the very first television comedy scripted by John Esmonde and Bob Larbey (later to create the fondly remembered classic *The Good Life*), this series starred *Carry On* team member Kenneth Connor as the cunning maintenance man Gus Fogg. Brian played the much put-upon Mr Salisbury in this short-lived comic inspection of life and laughter in the Saracens Manufacturing Company. A similar position of inadequate power and disrespectful treatment came with the gritty and realistic Jack Rosenthal series *The Dustbinmen*. Brian, replacing Frank Windsor and John Woodvine in the role of big boss man Bloody Delilah – the flustered inspector at the Corporation Cleansing Department – brought a familiar edge of ineffectual bluster to the second and third series of this important television comedy. The programmes were broadcast in 1970 and clearly pointed the way towards Brian's two greatest television successes.

'My character's a good-natured, willing sort of bloke and pretty incompetent, but I don't think there's any harm in him. God knows there's enough of us about!'

In the meantime he had briefly flirted with film work. In 1967 he fleetingly joined the legendary *Carry On* team for a memorable sequence opposite a bedridden Frankie Howerd. Despite being only an innocent supplier of rubber sheets, Howerd's sense of impending doom and the helpful musical accompaniment of the theme tune from *Alfred Hitchcock Presents, The Funeral of a Marionette*, suggest the sinister thought of coffin-fitting. Brian proved useful as a comic stooge and was invited back for the 1970 romp *Carry On Henry*. Sadly, he proved dispensable here, for his cameo role opposite Joan Sims as Queen Marie ended up on the cutting-room floor.

It was the experienced producer Sydney Lotterby who catapulted Brian Wilde into sitcom super-stardom when he cast him as the overly friendly prison warden Mr Barrowclough in *Porridge*. Scripted by those multi-talented likely lads Dick Clement and Ian La Frenais, the series may have had a fairly limited run – only 21 episodes were made between

1974 and 1977 – but *Porridge* remains one of the BBC's flagship situation comedies. Ronnie Barker's perfectly detailed comic performance as Norman Stanley Fletcher almost made the idea of a life behind bars seem inviting. Richard Beckinsale embraced small-time corruption and endearing innocence as Barker's youthful cell-mate Godber, and Fulton Mackay stormed through the proceedings as the sarcastic Scots tyrant Mr Mackay. A peerless supporting cast included Peter Vaughan as Grouty, the incarcerated supremo of Slade Prison, and a young David Jason as the very old Blanco.

The basic comic premise was lifted entirely from the 1960 Peter Sellers film classic *Two Way Stretch*. For Bernard Cribbins read Richard Beckinsale, for Lionel Jeffries read Fulton Mackay and for George Woodbridge read Brian Wilde, but the by-play between the characters and deliciously structured scripts created a timeless piece of British comedy which easily stands on its own two feet as one of television's finest. Brian Wilde's quiet restraint, gullible and almost tangible willingness to believe his prisoners in the hope of reforming their characters, comes across as the warm, upright and hard-working face of prison life. Although the wool is continually pulled over his eyes, there is a touchingly understanding relationship between inmate and officer. As Fletcher observed in one episode, both men are, in effect, prisoners together. A feature film of the series was released in 1979. Directed by co-writer Dick Clement, the original cast recaptured the essence of the television series, and the film proved a fitting memorial for Richard Beckinsale, who died soon after its release.

That man! Brian Wilde's Foggy in definitive terms.

Brian remembers his disquiet during the making of the series:

I'd become disappointed in what I had to do in Porridge. *I thought it was pretty small stuff compared with the pilot, which was primarily Ronnie Barker and myself. I remember saying to Fulton Mackay during the second series that I thought I was being written out. He told me not to be paranoid. When we got to the third series, Fulton had less to do and he came to me and said, 'Brian, you're not paranoid!'*

Anyway, I went to see Jimmy Gilbert after the first series and asked if I could have more to do. But the situation didn't change until after Series Two, when Jimmy called me up and explained that Michael Bates had been taken poorly and would I like to take over in Summer Wine. *I didn't know much about it. I'd been too busy making television to watch it. The scripts arrived, they were very funny and I said yes.*

Between the *Porridge* and *Summer Wine* years Brian had cropped up alongside Les Dawson in one of Alan Plater's *The Loner* episodes – *Dawson's Complaint*, directed by James Ormerod for broadcast in 1975 – but Foggy was the future and the established *Summer Wine* team needed to be told. Peter Sallis recalls:

Jimmy Gilbert came to my house for tea one day when poor old Michael Bates was ill. It was generally accepted that Roy had to write him out. Jimmy told me the new character was ex-army and his name would be Foggy Dewhurst. He asked if I had any thoughts on who could play him. I said straight away, 'Brian Wilde!' Jimmy said, 'That's a bit of luck, we've just cast him!' I was delighted. I'd known Brian for many years. We had been at RADA at the same time and appeared in several plays together.

Starring as Foggy from the start of the third series, Brian fitted the tight-knit cast perfectly, donning iconic green jacket and cap and proudly clasping his stick with military precision. The two old favourites are instructed to welcome home their old, old school friend – Foggy – and the golden years of *Summer Wine* are uncorked. Initially, Foggy was very foggy indeed – lapsing into moments of silent, trance-like meditations, which amused Clegg and simply confused Compo. Because the audience didn't fully get the joke, these interludes lasted just a few episodes, but the name remained.

Wilde bursts into life immediately, hitting the floor running with military clout, suffering hassle from unfriendly bus employees and indulging a loving obsession for his collection of hand-painted signs. The feverish, angst-ridden, getting-to-know-you walk through the dales captures the three-way diatribes in an instant, and there's even a perilous downhill physical comedy interlude for the *Summer Wine* cliché collection. Brian's initial ten years with the series are, as often as not, considered the real vintage èra for *Last of the Summer Wine*. They provide his happiest memories too:

I enjoyed the one we did with the little railway engine – Full Steam Behind. *I liked it when the engine moved away and we thought Compo was on it and we looked round and he was standing next to us. The engine was going by itself and we all started running after it – that was a funny scene.*

Of course, we did have to do some of our own stunts and that could prove to be a nightmare. I remember filming Who Made a Bit of a Splash in Wales Then? *I had to have my leg in plaster and they put me in a wheelchair at the top of a hill, which I had to roll down. There was no offer of a double for the stunt, so I did it. I fell out several times on the way down. I was supposed to be asleep, so at least I could shut my eyes and not look. As long as you can't see it happening, it's not so bad!*

Interaction with John Comer's rotund café owner, an encounter with a giant carrot in *Greenfingers*, frequent step-based attacks from Kathy Staff's notorious Nora Batty, an obsession with brightening up the area with a Union Jack and uneducated, lyrical waxing on the Loxley Lozenge formed high points in Foggy's adventures.

It would be another five years until the character drifted back to life in the Yorkshire Dales. In the interim, Brian Wilde had flirted with the opening series of the ITV sitcom *The Kit Curran Radio Show* starring Denis Lawson. Brian played Roland Simpson – another bemused figure of officialdom – the ineffectual new boss for Lawson's cocky disc jockey. The show failed to ignite.

In 1988 the BBC unveiled a major new situation comedy that was headlining not just *Summer Wine*'s Brian Wilde but also *Are You Being Served?* favourite Trevor Bannister. Brian was cast as the authoritarian Major Wyatt in the lacklustre *Wyatt's Watchdog*. A timely tap into the late 1980s' obsession with neighbourhood watch schemes, the scripts from Miles Tredinnick failed to create interesting characters, interesting situations or interesting comedy – a slight drawback in character-driven situation comedy. However, Brian's central performance – a sort of Foggy with slightly more clout – was enjoyable enough. Ironically, the show was produced and directed by Alan J. W. Bell. It had been no secret that Brian was less than enamoured with Bell's directorial style, but with healthy rewrites and loving attention to detail, Bell pulled the pilot out of the fire and created something halfway decent.

Needless to say, however, the show didn't see a second series commissioned, although, importantly, it brought the *Summer Wine* ex-favourite and the *Summer Wine* current producer/director back together again! – so much so that Brian had even expressed an interest in returning to the series for the occasional guest appearance. Forever loyal to *Summer Wine* cast members, Brian attended the funeral of Joe Gladwin and again discussed the possibilities of making a return to the series. Indeed, a script was written which pitted Seymour against Foggy. The novel idea was to have the two leader figures bicker and banter throughout – akin to Patrick Troughton and Jon Pertwee in *Doctor Who: The Three Doctors*. Sadly, the script simply had Foggy repeating almost word for word every command that Seymour gave – less a competition and more a childish copycat battle. Brian declined the role, and the script was restructured.

However, the seed of a thought that Foggy could reappear was planted. When Michael Aldridge was forced to leave, Brian Wilde was very keen to resurrect his role on a regular basis. The apocalyptic episode *Return of the Warrior* began Series 12 on a high. Returning from painting eggs for a living, Brian's Foggy stepped back into *Summer Wine* action as if he had never been away and, what's more, Roy Clarke could inject moments of warm welcome – a free cuppa from Jane Freeman, a short greeting from Kathy Staff. There's real pathos and disappointment when Foggy believes his old chums have not missed him. Brian's performance – desperately trying to cover his sadness with forced delight over their militarily geared steady rejection of human emotion – is quite stunning.

Back in action with a self-propelled salad strainer, the suit that turned left and Captain Clutterbuck's treasure, a huge roster of episodes kept Foggy up to his neck in misadventure across two decades:

When I returned to the show in 1990, it was like starting again. There were so many new faces. I'm not sure that I enjoyed the second lot as much as the first lot. I was older and less happy about location work. All in all, doing Summer Wine *was 90 per cent happy, 10 per cent awful. All those years that we were together – and there was a lot of us – we all got on so well and fitted in with each other. We were a happy company. It's amazing there were not ructions and shows of temperament.*

His final episode, *A Sidecar Named Desire*, was broadcast at the close of Series 18. His 117 episodes include some of the programme's finest moments, and in terms of BBC video releases and national

A relaxed Brian Wilde during a break from filming and, far right, a rather more frantic moment from The Kink in Foggy's Niblick *(1976).*

popularity, Brian Wilde is the essential ingredient that makes Compo and Clegg the most bankable, respected and beloved old-age pensioners in the land.

Peter Sallis believes that:

The show has meant an enormous amount to Brian. One shouldn't make comparisons, but he was absolutely marvellous as Foggy Dewhurst. He held together every episode in which he appeared – often to the detriment of my character. I didn't mind; he was so good. After all, Clegg organizing something would not have been as funny as Foggy organizing something. Clegg is not an organizer. Foggy Dewhurst was, and Brian Wilde was brilliant as the character.

Always a man of humility, Brian plays down the compliment:

I'm a good, average actor – I suppose we all are. We were never going to set the world on fire. We were so lucky to find these wonderful scripts. We really landed on our feet, didn't we?

Michael Aldridge

SEYMOUR UTTERTHWAITE: 1986 TO 1990

When life in *Summer Wine* became just too much for Brian Wilde the first time round, the man who was Foggy left the series and was hastily replaced by a kinder, gentler, even more eccentric figure in the shape of Seymour Utterthwaite.

The actor who played him, Michael Aldridge, was born in Glastonbury, Somerset, on 9 September 1920. He was educated at Gresham's School in Holt and determined from an early age to take up acting as a career. Joining myriad dramatic societies with the sole aim of impressing one of his school governors – the Aldwych farce-writer Ben Travers – the young Michael joined the local repertory company immediately after leaving school. He made his professional stage debut in Terence Rattigan's *French without Tears* at the Palace Theatre, Watford.

Utterly Utterthwaite! A charming pose from Michael Aldridge.

Active war service as an air gunner, observer and navigator with the Royal Air Force interrupted his acting work, but on his demobilization in 1946 he jumped straight back into the character-building and invaluable experience of rep. In 1950 he cut his teeth playing in works by Shakespeare, Goldsmith and Molière for a season at the Old Vic in London. There followed work with the Bristol Old Vic and a 1951/2 season at Stratford and the Chichester Festival. During his time in Chichester, Michael joined the original cast of Alan Ayckbourn's celebrated play *Absurd Person Singular*. His prolific stage credits included everything from Brecht and Eliot to Greek tragedy and Chekhov.

A jobbing actor for most of his career, television was late to seize this fine character actor. He was a delight in the ITV adaptation of H. E. Bates's *Love for Lydia* in 1977, and an eye-catching support opposite Alec Guinness in *Tinker, Tailor, Soldier, Spy* followed. Other notable small-screen credits included *Mussolini – The Untold Story*, *The Man in Room 17* and Giles Cooper's *Love and Penguins*. He featured in *The Eleventh Hour*, memorably scripted by Tom Stoppard and Clive Exton.

However, despite a less impressive track record on television than the 'third man' pioneer Michael Bates, Michael Aldridge, too, left a lasting legacy of two hugely popular comic creations for the BBC. First, in an inspired piece of casting, Michael was offered the role of Caldicott in a major six-part comedy drama serial of *Charters and Caldicott* broadcast over January and February 1985. Deliciously and proudly English, obsessed with the fine art of cricket and rigorous in their split-second timing of tea at 11 o'clock in the morning, Charters and Caldicott had been created by writers and later influential film directors Sidney Gilliat and Frank Launder. Played by beloved eccentrics Basil Radford and Naunton Wayne in the classic 1938 Alfred Hitchcock thriller *The Lady Vanishes*, the duo played the roles – and several variations on the theme – for film and radio for over a decade. Arthur Lowe and Ian Carmichael re-created the British pluck for the really rather fine 1979 remake. Spiritedly pulled from retirement for these treasurable Keith Waterhouse-scripted episodes of the TV series, the late Robin Bailey brilliantly breathed fresh life into the bombastic, rather stuffy Charters, while Michael Aldridge brought an endearing, bumbling sense of playfulness to the well-meaning, brave and deceptively mild-mannered Caldicott. The series centred around a murdered young lady discovered in the club of Caldicott. Naturally, the two gentlemen give up their usual routine of tea and cinema to investigate, resulting in a delightful, eccentric and beautifully constructed slice of BBC entertainment. Granville Saxton and *Only Fools and Horses* player Tessa Peake-Jones were in support. Julian Aymes directed for producer Ron Craddock, and the central casting was deservedly highlighted by a glowing review in the *Daily Telegraph*:

Incredibly, Bailey and Aldridge, synonyms for sublime English pottiness, have never worked together before. Waterhouse must feel like the chap who introduced Gilbert to Sullivan.

Having played one beloved English eccentric, it was only natural that Alan J. W. Bell would consider him for another. Seymour in *Last of the Summer Wine* was quickly created to replace Brian Wilde's departing Foggy, and the character made his first appearance in the second feature-length episode, *Uncle of the Bride*. The uncle of Sarah Thomas's bride and brother of Thora Hird's Edie, Michael rejoiced in his role, quickly teaming up with the terrible twins – Compo and Clegg – and dragging his adopted 'schoolboys' through various madcap schemes and scientific exploits.

Peter Sallis recalls the introduction of Michael's character:

Over the garden wall. Michael Aldridge settles into Summer Wine *country.*

When Brian left the series, Michael Aldridge came on the scene. Michael didn't have much time to prepare for his role following Brian's hasty departure. I think that Roy might not have had as much time as he would have wanted to plan the new character. Seymour seemed to me to be the one character that presented the most problems. He was an engaging character in his own right. He just didn't quite fit in with us two – Seymour that is, not Michael Aldridge. His character was on a different planet half the time – always up in the air. He was an inventor and teacher, forever talking about Compo and Clegg as his 'lads'. Michael, though, was a fine actor and wonderful company. He was very gregarious and revelled in entertaining the entire cast and crew.

Perhaps Michael's series highlight came with his hilarious springing of Joe Gladwin's Wally from the clutches of Nora Batty in *Set the People Free* – note Ronnie Hazlehurst musically merging the familiar *Summer Wine* theme with *The Great Escape*. However, misconceived, nautical madness in *The Heavily Reinforced Bottom*, seasonal playfulness in *Merry Christmas, Father Christmas* and elongated manoeuvring of an awkward-to-park caravan in *Come Back, Jack Harry Teesdale* proved highlights. Notably, in the last programme Michael's huge debt to the legendary Will Hay was clear to see. Michael's detailed speculation and totally incompetent planning play like the classic pole-juggling sequence from the Will Hay film *Where's That Fire?* More idiotic and clumsy than his comic foils, Michael Aldridge milked the maximum comic juices from allowing his educated, self-important schoolteacher to tumble from the highest of the highs to the lowest of the lows. A delightful and charming comic character was the result.

Sadly, Michael was forced to leave the series in 1990. Nursing his sick wife and himself suffering from a very painful hip problem – as with Michael Bates, he could no longer walk comfortably across the Yorkshire countryside – sadly, he had to decline further appearances. He was, however, more than willing to leave at the start of a season – the 12th – and thus allow Brian Wilde to return to the fold with the smoothest of transition periods. Ironically, despite appearing for no more than five minutes in *The Return of the Warrior*, in the *Summer Wine* tradition of alphabetical credits Michael retained top billing. The actor considered Seymour to be the ultimate role of his career and, sadly, failed to find another to beat it in the public's affection. Michael Aldridge died suddenly at his London home on 10 January 1994. He was 73 years old.

Frank Thornton

HERBERT TRUELOVE, A.K.A. 'TRULY' OF THE YARD: 1997 TO DATE

Still new enough to *Last of the Summer Wine* to be called 'Baby Frank', in fact Frank Thornton has been one of the country's most prolific and welcome character actors during the post-war years. Creating at least one masterpiece of television comedy in the shape of Captain Peacock in *Are You Being Served?*, he has sparred with almost every great comedian of the last 40 years and settled into the twilight-age antics of *Summer Wine* with consummate ease and professionalism.

Frank is in the best position to compare these two highly popular and endearing programmes:

If you write something that is topical, it goes out of date very quickly. Are You Being Served? *was written about a shop which was, already then, totally out of date, so it had a historical quality. Therefore, it never goes out of date.* Dad's Army *is another example, written about a time which had long since past. Also, the more simple the idea, the more successful. A shop is a familiar*

environment – we all know them, we all use them. Add to that the simple, seaside humour we all love, and it became good, well-made, low British comedy. Summer Wine *is timeless too because it deals with the antics of elderly people and it is their behaviour we are focusing on – the time in which it takes place is purely incidental. Of course, one must not forget the writers. In the case of* Summer Wine, *no one could write it other than Roy Clarke.*

Born in 1921, Frank started his acting career in the classics – he was a distinguished Shakespearean performer in the 1950s – before discovering the secret of success was the banana skin, the slow-burn look of comic outrage and the well-timed prat-fall.

He first made his mark in serious roles within thriller and dramatic quota quickies. These included the 1954 mystery *Radio Car Murders* – his film debut – and *Portrait of Alison*. Directed by Guy Green, this latter film featured co-written work from Ken Hughes and, rather unconvincingly, allowed Robert Beatty, William Sylvester and the gorgeous Terry Moore to stagger through a hackneyed adventure involving murder and smuggling.

However, it was on television that Frank really found fame, sparring with the small screen's favourite comedy actor – Tony Hancock – in his best-remembered show, *The Blood Donor*. Having by now discovered the perfect figure of snooty authority, Frank could distastefully look down his nose at Hancock's desire for a do-gooder reward. His 'What do you want? Money?' could cut through stone. Frank also proved useful in several of Benny Hill's self-contained half-hour comedies for the BBC, but it was with Michael Bentine that he really excelled.

Frank Thornton in a publicity pose as Yorkshire's favourite ex-Scotland Yard policeman.

From 1960 until 1964, Frank was a regular stooge for the anarchic ex-Crazy Person in the ground-breaking, pre-Pythonesque sketch series *It's a Square World*. Produced by *Summer Wine* pioneer James Gilbert, Bentine's inspired flights of fancy also gave regular work to Dick Emery, Clive Dunn, John Bluthal and Deryck Guyler. It was primarily off the back of this historically important slice of BBC comedy that Frank Thornton found himself in demand for more off-the-wall, influential assignments. He played Ben Travers farce with Richard Briers and Arthur Lowe, appeared in work scripted by Marty Feldman, as well as several pilots from television's finest scriptwriters – Ray Galton and Alan Simpson – and during the late 1960s, he appeared opposite the granddaddy of them all, Spike Milligan, in *The World of Beachcomber*.

'It was daunting joining a series like Summer Wine, *which had been on the air for 25 years.'*

On the other channel, Frank jumped aboard the less-than-steady ship of the Rediffusion comedy *HMS Paradise*. This was written by Laurie Wyman and very much in the mould of his long-running radio series *The Navy Lark*. Richard Caldicott starred, with Frank cast as the frightfully sophisticated Commander Fairweather. It was a simple variation on the pompous figures of officialdom, which he has made his own over the years.

Very much as a result of this steady, important and familiar television work, Frank was quickly signed up for more of the same in British cinemas. He appeared in the 1962 Peter Sellers/Richard

TV comedy's finest moment as Tony Hancock's blood donor meets Frank Thornton and June Whitfield in 1961.

Attenborough legal comedy *The Dock Brief*, tackled Norman Wisdom mugging in *The Early Bird* and even ventured into the surreal world of *Gonks Go Beat* that same year. Delighting in a sterling comic cast – including Kenneth Connor, Terry Scott and Reginald Beckwith – Frank cropped up at the close as the hip and cool King of Music. Hardly earth-shattering at the time, the film now stands as a gloriously unkempt reflection of the decade's excesses and bizarre pleasures.

In 1966 Frank joined the ranks of the *Carry On* team with a single performance – as a disgruntled shop manager – in *Carry On Screaming*. Richard Lester cast him in the big-screen version of *A Funny Thing Happened on the Way to the Forum*, he strolled into Dudley Moore's enjoyable ego trip, *Thirty is a Dangerous Age, Cynthia*, and incongruously joined Telly Savalas and Edith Evans in Jim O'Connolly's madcap heist comedy *Crooks and Coronets*.

Frank was directed by the legendary Billy Wilder in the Robert Stephens and Colin Blakeley mystery *The Private Life of Sherlock Holmes* and became even more surreal with Spike Milligan's post-nuclear parable *The Bed-Sitting Room* and the Peter Sellers/Ringo Starr farce of greed *The Magic Christian*. He appeared in Peter Cook's media satire *The Rise and Rise of Michael Rimmer*, kept a straight face opposite Danny La Rue in *Our Miss Fred*, and had an early battle with Thora Hird in the inheritance comedy *Some Will, Some Won't*.

A regular part of television situation comedy spin-off feature films, Frank cropped up alongside Warren

Mitchell in *Till Death Us Do Part*, Frankie Howerd in *Up the Chastity Belt*, Sid James in *Bless This House*, Bill Fraser in *That's Your Funeral* and Harry H. Corbett in *Steptoe and Son Ride Again*. Other notable film roles at the time came in the screen version of the long-running West End farce *No Sex Please – We're British*, the Jim Dale children's fantasy *Digby, the Biggest Dog in the World*, and Richard Lester's cheerful swashbuckling romp *The Three Musketeers*.

However, despite interesting supporting roles in the David Niven cod horror *Vampira* and the Terry-Thomas/Leslie Phillips clash of the cads *Spanish Fly*, it was on the small screen that Frank reigned as a true comedy star.

This was, of course, in the classic situation comedy *Are You Being Served?* which ran from 1972 until 1985, notching up some 69 episodes – a suitable number for a show that relied so heavily on some of the sweetest innuendo around. Frank's stern, authoritative performance as Captain Peacock proved the perfect stooge figure for Mollie Sugden's endless line in 'pussy' jokes, Trevor Bannister's jack the lad and John Inman's scene-stealing mince machine. David Croft and Jeremy Lloyd created the series, and the characters, jokes, catchphrases and class system of Grace Brothers' department store became a vital part of the British way of life. A rather lacklustre, unsatisfactory and hastily filmed – in around ten days – feature film version limped into cinemas in 1977, and the majority of the old players (with the exception of Trevor Bannister) were resurrected for the enjoyable, albeit short-lived, BBC sequel, *Grace and Favour*. Twelve episodes were broadcast during 1992 and 1993 under the direction of *First of the Summer Wine*'s Mike Stephens, but the familiar characters just didn't seem at home without counters, florid clothes and displeased customers to interact with.

Towards the end of the original run of *Are You Being Served?* in 1984, Frank appeared with Mollie Sugden in a single Les Dawson playlet, *Holiday with Strings*, and gave more of the same official ranting when he featured opposite Glynis Barber in the wartime comic strip come to life, *Jane in the Desert*. But it was Captain Peacock that kept the actor in the comedy echelons. A huge cult success in America, Frank was in constant demand for conventions and television guest spots. Eventually, the BBC decided to repeat the programme and won huge ratings.

It was a natural progression for Frank to be enlisted into the tight-knit community of *Last of the Summer Wine* in 1997:

I couldn't be more pleased at how lucky I was. Any sensible man at my age has retired and has put his feet up and is collecting his pension. The cast all treated me so well. One thing I shall always remember is that after I had been filming for a couple of weeks and still thinking, 'Where am I?' Peter Sallis came over and quietly said, 'You know you've got it, don't you?' He meant that I'd got the character. It was very heartening to have my colleague say that.

Making his first appearance as Truly of the Yard in the Christmas Special *There Goes the Groom*, the 'former Mrs Truelove's husband' was a welcome addition to the cast. Ironically, Frank had in fact been a regular cast member in the only other *Comedy Playhouse* pilot from 1973 to make it to a series – *The Gordon Peters Show* – a unique double that makes his performances all the more historically important and treasurable. With true dignity, humility and professionalism, Frank Thornton has brought a fresh slant to the aged goings-on of *Summer Wine*. With emotive work in the millennium Special, pompous self-importance in all things criminal and a steady, unflappable edge of authority, Frank looks set for a lengthy run in the series.

THE
BATTLEAXES

CHAPTER THREE

THE STRONGER SEX

An Affectionate Tribute to the *Last of the Summer Wine* Women We Love to Loathe

*'I don't think Compo realized
Nora was fond of him,
but I believe deep down she was.'*

KATHY STAFF

Kathy Staff

NORA BATTY: 1973 TO DATE

Probably the most celebrated comic battleaxe on British television, Kathy Staff has created a lasting monument to strong, cold and unemotional northern women in her ongoing performance as Nora Batty – continually whacking her poor husband, Wally, over the head, shooing those childish men 'off me steps' with swift broom movements and looking with outraged horror at Compo's lustful advances.

Although appearing from the outset – Kathy is spotted hanging out her washing in the opening sequence of the *Comedy Playhouse* pilot – the figure of Nora Batty wasn't originally perceived as the focal point of Compo's comic business. Indeed, at the start her appearances were infrequent, and she was even billed simply as 'Mrs Batty'. Gradually and unexpectedly, the nation took this mournful, bellowing figure to its collective heart. Terry Wogan's Radio 2 mentions of Nora's wrinkled stockings created an indelible comic icon which has slipped into our cultural consciousness.

Born in 1927, Kathy gained invaluable theatrical experience with repertory companies before becoming every casting director's ideal miserable northern wife. Her film parts include an important supporting role in the 1962 gritty classic *A Kind of Loving* with Alan Bates, June Ritchie and future *Summer Wine* tea-drinking companion Thora Hird.

For Kathy, it was a dream come true:

Thora had always been my heroine. She's one of the best actresses we have ever had in this country. In the film, I was cast as Thora's

Kathy Staff is made up into comedy's favourite battleaxe, Nora Batty.

next-door neighbour, Mrs Oliphant. I had two young daughters who they wanted to use in the film, to play in the front garden. When we got to the location in Bolton, the garden wasn't big enough for two children, so only one was required. I was in a panic as to what to do with my youngest, Susan.

Now, the scene was Alan Bates coming back to the house of his mother-in-law to find that his pregnant wife had fallen down the stairs and had been rushed off to hospital. He hadn't been given a key by this dreadful mother-in-law, played by Thora, so I had to tell him that his wife was poorly.

My older daughter Katherine was riding round the garden on a bicycle while Susan, who was only two at the time, was being looked after inside the house by Thora. Today, Susan is a vicar. I often say to Thora, 'I wonder if it was thanks to your influence when you looked after her that day all those years ago.

Kathy's major break on television came with the pioneering twice-weekly serial *Castle Haven*, produced by Yorkshire Television. Kathy played Lorna Everett, with Roy Barraclough as her scruffy husband Harry. The 13 months' experience on that series proved immensely useful for Kathy:

My agent rang me to tell me that the producer, Jimmy Gilbert, wanted me to audition for this part of Nora Batty. I didn't fancy going because I'd just got back from holiday and, usually, auditions were held in London. This time, though, they were to be held in Manchester.

I went to see Jimmy and his first reaction was, 'Oh, I'm sorry. You're nothing like the character we want! But now that you're here you may as well say some lines. But you really are nothing like the character!'

The piece I had to read was from the very first scene, where the camera pans round from the beautiful countryside to show me hanging my knickers on the line. The first line was, 'They're taking his telly again!' and we saw two men were carrying out Compo's television set. Then Compo and I had a scene together. When I finished reading, Jimmy Gilbert said, 'That's amazing. That's just the character. But we were looking for a big fat woman.' He asked if I would pad up to look as fat as possible and as ugly as possible. And that's how Nora came to be... and I'm still wearing the padding to this day!

During the 1970s Kathy featured in ITV's greatest soap operas, enjoying a lengthy run as Doris Luke in *Crossroads* and a semi-regular part as corner shop assistant Vera Hopkins in *Coronation Street*:

I told the producers I was doing Summer Wine *for the BBC and they allowed me to go and film by writing me out for a few weeks at a time. This almost caused me terrible problems. In the early days of* Summer Wine, *there was one episode where I had to ride a bike with a basket full of groceries. Compo jumped out at me, and I had to fall off the bicycle and pelt him with vegetables. I did the fall and Sydney Lotterby came over and said, 'That was wonderful, but I need to film it from the other side, so can you fall in exactly the same position again?' I did that fall at least four times!*

My agent was very annoyed. She said that if I'd broken my arm I couldn't have done Coronation Street *for 12 months. I was badly bruised on my knees and elbows, but thankfully, wearing Nora's padding, my body was protected.*

Even as early as the Michael Bates era of *Summer Wine*, Kathy was spotted for other comic variations on the Nora Batty theme. Arguably the most important of these was for Roy Clarke's other major BBC success, *Open All Hours*. Kathy was reassuringly cast in the Nora-like role of miserable northern woman Mrs Blewitt, continually badgering Ronnie Barker's tight-fisted, stuttering shopkeeper.

On ITV, Les Dawson became a prolific and much-loved co-star during the 1970s, a working relationship that kicked off with a single appearance in his 1975 series of self-contained comedy playlets,

Dawson's Weekly. Ray Galton and Alan Simpson scripted a half-hour entitled *Where's There's a Will,* which cast Kathy as Minnie. The premise – Dawson must marry within seven days to inherit a fortune – may not have been the most original (a similar notion having been employed for Tony Hancock in 1961), but clearly Kathy suited the droll comic's style immediately.

She was invited to join the team for the 11th and final series of *Sez Les*. Broadcast towards the end of 1976, these seven sketch-based shows reunited Kathy with *Castle Haven* player Roy Barraclough and featured a string of hilarious comic grotesques for the actress. She was retained for Yorkshire Television's follow-up series *Dawson and Friends*, which ran for four hour-long programmes in 1977.

This fruitful association with Les Dawson led directly to notable work with ITV's greatest comedy star, Benny Hill. The Thames production *The Benny Hill Show* remains one of British television's biggest international successes, and Kathy brought her usual peerless touch of battleaxe business to Hill's raucous comic style. A notable sketch, *Me and My Shadow*, starred Kathy as Hill's non-stop talking wife, who is memorably murdered by her browbeaten husband.

Benny's producer Dennis Kirkland later recruited Kathy for the 1988 Eric Sykes black comedy *Mr H Is Late*, which co-starred Sykes regular Jimmy Edwards and a coffin that gets involved in a string of comic situations.

But it is Nora Batty in *Last of the Summer Wine* that has always proved to be Kathy's most popular role – a character which she feels is often misunderstood:

Underneath, Nora is a very warm-hearted woman, but she doesn't like to show her feelings. She's the type of woman who if she shows any feelings thinks it's a sign of weakness. But I don't think she would show her feelings to anybody – even her husband. He probably didn't even realize that she was so fond of him.

For that matter, I don't think Compo realized Nora was fond of him, but I believe deep down she was. She hasn't much sense of humour, which makes the situation even funnier. You could see what Compo was going to do, and you saw Nora and you knew there would be a clash and that she would show no signs of humour at all.

In 1988, the BBC presented Kathy with her first starring situation comedy vehicle, *No Frills*. Another northern characterization with a softer centre, Kathy played Molly Bickerstaff, a recently widowed lady who moves from Oldham to the London home of her recently divorced daughter. Despite the star attraction of Kathy, this standard generation-gap comedy settled more on the ongoing dispute

Baby, it's cold outside! Kathy Staff and Jane Freeman suffer for their art.

between the daughter, Kate (played by Belinda Sinclair), and the granddaughter, Suzy (Katherine Schlesinger). Janey Preger wrote the seven episodes, and Mandie Fletcher – fresh from *Blackadder II* – produced and directed.

Kathy's autobiography, *My Story – Wrinkles and All*, was published in 1997. Clearly, the title illustrates that Nora Batty still holds a unique and easily recognizable place in the nation's comedy affections. For Kathy, too, *Summer Wine* has not just been a job but a fun and happy part of her life:

My favourite memory came during the filming of the Christmas Special All Mod Conned, *where the three old men decide to spend the festive season in a caravan. Now, being Christmas, Nora was obviously going to have her hair done. The Costume Department got me one of these nets with little beads on it so that Nora could look a bit dressy for the special occasion. Compo had to bring his ferrets round for me to look after while the men were away. As Compo handed over the cage with the ferrets inside, he grabbed me to kiss me. Unfortunately, Bill got his buttons entangled in my hair net. We couldn't get separated! It was wonderful: if only they could have shown that!*

Happy days, indeed. I shall always treasure them.

Jane Freeman

IVY: 1973 TO DATE

The other major female to appear throughout the 30-year history of *Last of the Summer Wine*, Jane Freeman proved the perfect sounding-board for the trio's eccentric ramblings within their regular place of sanctuary – Sid's Café. As with Nora, there is hidden emotion in Jane's blood-and-stomach-pills performance as Ivy. Continually trying to drag her happy-go-lucky husband away from the bad influence of the old men, Ivy is a complex mixture of pride, anger, devotion and frustration. Hidden depths are revealed in her romantic fantasies and secret longings. Obsession with financial concerns and the business of tea and buns, and a real, tangible concern with her husband's fidelity all make for an interesting characterization. As a young actress, though, Jane was concerned at playing a stereotypical harridan:

Ivy is a cardboard cut-out character. I'm like one of those seaside postcard battleaxes. Probably less so now because the ladies have acquired their own characters. In the early days we were very much like ciphers – the men were warm and like little boys and we were the tough 'mothers' they needed. Each of the men were little warm souls with childlike qualities. Nora and I would shout at them when they climbed lampposts, and it was like Mum giving her child a clip round the ear.

Ivy is a complex mixture of pride, anger, devotion and frustration.

Since the death of her screen husband John Comer, Jane's contribution has been less vital to the comic proceedings, but her ample frame and bellowing instructions still provided useful starting points for yet another off-the-wall Yorkshire odyssey.

Jane Freeman started her professional acting career with the Birmingham Repertory Company. Her presence was keenly felt in several landmark BBC productions. Thanks to the corporation's commitment to good quality single drama, she made regular appearances in presentation slots such as *The Monday Play* and *Play for Today*. Jane's credits included *The Marriage* and the celebrated Brian Glover bitter-sweet comedy *The Fishing Party*.

While Kathy Staff enjoyed sparring with Les

Dawson and Benny Hill on ITV, *Summer Wine* popularity led to Jane Freeman's appearances opposite Max Boyce in the BBC sketch and stand-up series *It's Max Boyce*. The supporting cast included Richard Davies and Dorothea Phillips, with four half-hours being broadcast throughout December 1984. Gareth Rowlands produced and directed. It was a real turning-point in Jane's career.

In *Summer Wine* with John Comer gone, she had to build a new working relationship with the slow-witted Crusher, as played by Jonathan Linsey. The café sequences became even more based around physical comedy and moved almost totally away from the pathos-driven diatribes of the married couple. For Jane, it was never going to be the same. To this day her happiest memories of working on the show date back to her appearances with her late screen husband:

Perhaps my fondest recollection was from when we were filming Cheering up Gordon. *We were on location in Scarborough, and John Comer and I had to go out to film a sequence in a rowing boat. It was really early in the morning and I was standing there by the bank as the crew were setting up the shot. In front of us there was a husband and wife who were arguing and shouting, and finally the husband turned round and shouted, 'For God's sake, woman, bloody shut up...you're worse than bloody her!' And he pointed at me. The worst insult he could think of was to point at me.*

Men in those days used to give me a lot of aggravation because they would stand up for Sid. One man almost pushed me off a platform at a railway station once! Mind you, at least they recognized me. When we used to film at TV Centre I would often go down to get a cup of tea from the cafeteria. I didn't have time to change out of my costume, and irate people would come up to me demanding to know when the café was opening. They always thought that I was part of the staff!

Opposite: A rare moment of happiness as Jane Freeman poses for publicity.

Right: Typical Ivy antics as Jane Freeman force-feeds a scone to guest star Norman Wisdom in Extra! Extra! *(1996).*

Dame Thora Hird

EDIE PEGDEN: 1986 TO DATE

The prolific and justly celebrated career of Dame Thora Hird could fill – and indeed has filled – several books. Suffice to say that her acting talents have been fully utilized on film, stage, radio and television. Thanks to ground-breaking performances for Alan Bennett's *Talking Heads – A Cream Cracker under the Settee* and *Waiting for the Telegram*, Dame Thora has proved herself to be one of the most remarkable actresses of her generation. The staggering 1999 ITV drama *Lost for Words*, directed by *Summer Wine*'s Alan J. W. Bell, was no less impressive, while appearances in everything from *Memento Mori* to Victoria Wood's *Dinnerladies* and *Pat and Margaret* have endeared her to a nation. A vocal *Summer Wine* fan of long standing, Dame Thora has enriched the programme since the 1986 feature-length special, *Uncle of the Bride*.

Born in 1911, Thora's film career fully took off in the early 1940s. Her major break came when she played the sarcastic secretary to Will Hay in Ealing Studios' political romp *The Black Sheep of Whitehall*. Over the next decade Thora cropped up in enjoyable supporting roles, ranging from landladies and cleaners to barmaids and fretful mothers. She appeared in the milestone propaganda piece *Went the Day Well?*, the motor-racing adventure *Once a Jolly Swagman* with Bill Owen, the subdued Ealing comedy *The Magnet* with James Fox, and the Basil Radford vehicle *The Galloping Major*.

She featured in the Sid James rural satire *Time Gentlemen, Please!* and Val Guest's science-fiction classic, *The Quatermass Experiment* for Hammer Films. Flamboyant, comic battleaxes were blessed with the Thora Hird touch in *Sailor Beware!* and *Further up the Creek*. Thora's film parts continued to be supporting roles or contributions to ensemble pieces, spanning such gritty classics as the Laurence Olivier production *The Entertainer* (1960) to the lowbrow reworking of the Alastair Sim inheritance comedy *Laughter in Paradise – Some Will, Some Won't* with Leslie Phillips, Ronnie Corbett and Michael Hordern.

Where did you get that hat? Thora Hird as Edie Pegden.

By this stage, Thora was one of Britain's most respected stage performers, contrasting straight plays with rewarding variety work. At one time she was the highest-paid variety act in the country.

On television she had been much in demand for many years, enjoying her first major comedy success with the Freddie Frinton series *Meet the Wife*. Five series ran between 1964 and 1966, casting Thora as the eternally nagging and suspicious star of the show. Ronald Wolfe and Ronald Chesney scripted these hugely popular shows.

Dame Thora has proved herself to be one of the most remarkable actresses of her generation.

London Weekend Television presented two seasons of Harry Littlewood's *Ours Is a Nice House*, starring Thora as the befuddled owner of a Lancashire boarding establishment.

It was ten years later, however, that Thora landed her biggest situation comedy success. Despite starting life as a 1969 pilot – with Marjorie Rhodes – the first series of *In Loving Memory* didn't hit the small screen until 1979. Cast as undertaker Ivy

Unsworth, the cynical and farcical scripts were penned by Dick Sharples and ran for five seasons until 1986. Before the end finally came, Sharples had scripted another comedy hit, *Hallelujah!*, which continued the religious flavour, with Thora as Salvation Army captain Emily Ridley. A couple of seasons were broadcast during 1983 and 1984, with Patsy Rowlands providing valued support to the holier-than-thou comic business.

The BBC capitalized on Thora's religious leanings and invited her to host their traditional god slot programme, *Praise Be!*, a series that she relished introducing for 17 years.

Her all-time favourite television programme has always been *Last of the Summer Wine*, and in 1985 a dream came true when she was cast in the show, in what was originally planned as a one-off appearance. Over 15 years later she is still with the programme and still billed as giving a 'special guest appearance':

When the director Alan Bell first asked me to play a cameo role, I was delighted, but I honestly thought that would be it. I don't tend to have many lines in an episode, but I do enjoy having the chance to do a bit of business with the other talented professionals who make up the Summer Wine *team.*

As Edie Pegden, Thora has created a fresh variation on the standard northern nag monster that she has brilliantly brought to life throughout her comedy career. Mixing overtly refined mutterings with coarsened Yorkshire dialect, Thora has embraced this role of pompous self-importance, snobbish behaviour and marital embarrassment. Basking in the educated and professional glories of her brother – as played by Michael Aldridge – during her early association with the show, Thora as Edie can now moan for Britain about her car-mad husband, naive daughter and unambitious son-in-law:

People often come up and stop me in the street and say that all the women in Summer Wine *are horrid to our husbands. Of course, that's the author's fault! We like the fellas really. We're only pretending. We all get on really well, especially the women. We've known each other for years. Jane Freeman, Kathy Staff and I share a caravan on location. We have a chuck wagon with tea and coffee, and Kathy always goes and gets me a drink as I have arthritis in the morning.*

Make it a double! Thora Hird and her faithful stand-in, Amy Shaw.

We're known as Freeman, Hardy and Willis!

Thora's career was celebrated in September 1999 with a television retrospective at the National Film Theatre and a BBC tribute, *Dame Thora – A Tonic for the Nation*, which included behind-the-scenes *Summer Wine* film footage and contributions from Roy Clarke, Kathy Staff, Jane Freeman, Matthew Kelly and Dora Bryan.

Juliette Kaplan

PEARL: 1985 TO DATE

Juliette Kaplan grew up in South Africa. On her own admission she was an inveterate liar as a child, and, rather than be labelled as such, her mother suggested that instead of talking about her fantasies, she should write them down. During her formative years she moved to America, and then, in 1951, aged just 11, she came to live in England with an accent that was a mixture of 'Brooklyn, South African and nasal tone'. Her mother – understandably – sent her to elocution lessons. It was there, while learning to talk more fashionably, that she became interested in drama. She slipped easily into the life of a thespian, and the only stipulation her parents made before allowing her to go off and tread the boards as a career was to gain a teaching qualification as something to fall back on.

Juliette spent many years performing in rep., pantomime and corporate films. As with her screen husband, she first joined the cast during the second *Summer Wine* summer season, playing the dreaded Pearl on stage at Bournemouth.

I'd been going through quite a difficult time, and I really thought it was time to give up acting. I decided to put my picture in Spotlight *for one last year, and on my return from a holiday I was confronted with the offer of an audition – the next day. I said I couldn't possibly go – I had too much to do. But I finally relented. I dashed to London, performed the audition and to my surprise and frustration I had to go back again the next day. I was told the part required a feisty and aggressive actress, and by this time I was pretty feisty, demanding the script, ranting at the producer and generally thinking I had no chance of getting the part.*

I was offered Pearl the next day, which was a Thursday. We had to start on the Monday, which gave me just three days to find someone to look after my late husband's business.

Wait till I get you home! Juliette Kaplan gets rough with wayward husband, Robert Fyfe.

Juliette believed that after one summer season it would all be over, until one evening, near the end of the run, she was approached by a senior cast member:

Peter Sallis came over to me and asked if anyone had mentioned the possibility of doing an episode on the box. It was something I had never imagined and could hardly believe would happen. The next day the director, Alan J. W. Bell, telephoned and invited me to read some lines. If I was shocked to be asked, I was even more surprised when he offered me the role on television. And I'm proud to say I've been here ever since.

Pearl's thin-lipped, super-suspicious blank stares have become an ongoing comedy favourite with audiences, while Juliette injects well-measured droplets of acid into the celebrated coffee-morning sequences.

Of course, it's not always rich tea and sympathy on set, as Juliette painfully recalls:

I remember one day tripping on the steps of the make-up truck. My foot immediately swelled up and went black. It was very painful, and Alan, being the kind director that he is, dashed over, took a look at my foot and promptly said: 'You're going to hospital...just as soon as we've finished the day's shoot!'

More recently, Juliette's acting has reflected her past profession when, for an episode of *London's Burning*, she played a casino croupier. But it's as the hard-boiled, though ultimately soft-centred, Pearl that Juliette is happy to be recognized, although time is beginning to take its toll:

When I started Summer Wine, *it used to take an hour and a half to get me to look like Pearl and 20 minutes to put me back as myself. Fifteen years on, it's 20 minutes into Pearl and an hour and a half to put me back the way I used to be!*

Opposite: Juliette Kaplan as Pearl.
Right: Stephen Lewis is dragged into another one of Jean Alexander's money-making schemes.

Jean Alexander

AUNTIE WAINWRIGHT: 1988 TO DATE

One of television's best-loved actresses for an entire small-screen generation, Jean Alexander is still very much remembered as *Coronation Street*'s endearing gossip, Hilda Ogden. With her hair in curlers, henpecked husband Stan, iconic ducks in flight firmly in place on her wall and frequent trips to the Rover's Return, Jean reigned supreme on the street for over 25 years. Indeed, there was a sense of national loss when Hilda finally moved away and Jean departed the series in December 1987.

The actress soon started work on *Last of the Summer Wine*, having joined to play the Irish, money-pinching, bric-à-brac shopkeeper Auntie

BOUGHT &

Wainwright for the Christmas Special of 1988. Her flustered twittering, determined attitude and overbearing persuasiveness have been the bane of Peter Sallis's ever-fearful Clegg ever since. There is also much comic mileage gained from Stephen Lewis and the outlandish situations 'Auntie' gets him into for the sake of a few quid. Jean describes her character quite simply:

She's another nutter...they're all individual nutters. Anybody in their right minds wouldn't believe the things those characters do. It's a complete suspension of disbelief – though while it's happening you can believe it could happen. Auntie Wainwright is a grasping old lady who is determined to make a crust and sells anything that comes to hand. She doesn't care what it is and whether they want it. People don't buy things in Auntie's shop – they get sold them!

Away from the Yorkshire Dales but not from Yorkshire Television, Jean appeared in the David Nobbs-scripted comedy *Rich Tea and Sympathy* with Patricia Hodge, Denis Quilley and Lionel Jeffries in 1991. She guest-starred in the ITV children's adventure series *Adam's Family Tree* in 1997 and, over a decade since leaving, returned to re-create her *Corrie* favourite, Hilda Ogden, as host for an exclusive video looking back at *Coronation Street*'s women over the years.

Jean continues to rule out a return to the *Street* but has no intention of retiring quite yet:

Some things seem to go on for ever. I think Summer Wine *can continue for many years to come. I don't intend hanging up my costumes for some time – I don't mind playing this part until I'm 90...if I get that far!*

Jean Alexander as the determined shopkeeper, Auntie Wainwright.

Sarah Thomas

GLENDA WILKINSON (NÉE PEGDEN): 1986 TO DATE

Perfectly cast as the daughter of Thora Hird's Edie Pegden, the talented comedienne Sarah Thomas was a much-welcome addition to *Summer Wine* following her debut appearance in the 1986 Special, *Uncle of the Bride*. Whether it's shaking her head with marital dismay and crying 'Oh, Barry!' or simply following in her mother's footsteps and putting on the hard-nosed, northern wife attitude, Sarah's contributions have enlivened the past 15 years of the series.

'Anybody in their right minds wouldn't believe the things those characters do. It's a complete suspension of disbelief.'

Coming from the comic stand-up circuit rather than the acting tradition, Sarah first found fame with satirical sketch comedy on the radio series *Peter Dixon's Night Nurse*. In 1979 she was enlisted to join the fun of *Worzel Gummidge* with Jon Pertwee, playing the cheeky young waitress in the village tea-shop. With the casting of Joan Sims for Series Two, Sarah was recast as Enid Simmons, the flighty young maid of the country estate, remaining with the show until the end of Series Three – when Joan Sims decided to leave the programme.

Adept at playing serving maids, Sarah delighted in several similar roles on the stage, and she was appearing as a cheeky teenager in the Victorian

comedy *When We Are Married* when the opportunity arose for work in *Last of the Summer Wine*:

I was working at the Thorndyke Theatre, Leatherhead, and I wrote to about half a dozen BBC producers. Alan J.W. Bell happened to live nearby, and he came to see the show with his wife, Constance. He invited me to come and see him and said that if Thora Hird would play Edie, he would take me on as her daughter. By the time I got home, the phone was ringing – it was Alan offering me the part! I was so excited, and I remember getting dressed up specially for the first day's filming. I was wearing lovely, brand-new white leather shoes, and as I got out of the car on location I stepped into an ankle-deep puddle of mud. And that's how I was introduced to everybody – with dirty shoes!

Building a delightful comic relationship with Mike Grady and reacting with fine timing opposite Dame Thora Hird, Sarah's popularity in the series has led to many notable farces and pantomime credits, with *Summer Wine* stardom making her a familiar stage performer. But, of course, it's the television series that remains her most successful role, and it's developed considerably since her *Uncle of the Bride* debut:

Glenda has changed over the years. She's always been the baby of the company, and the women still tell her how she should behave with men. She's still rather innocent, but after 15 years of married life, she is getting stronger with Barry. I feel she is becoming a bit more like her mother as she learns all the tricks during the coffee mornings. Eventually, she'll be as tough as the other women, but not quite yet...I hope.

Sarah Thomas as the ever-patient Glenda.

Rosemary Martin

MRS PARTRIDGE: 1973

The 'Marina' figure to Blake Butler's 'Howard'-inspiring character, Rosemary Martin twittered and flushed her way through two seasons of *Last of the Summer Wine* as the prim, proper but sexually eager librarian's assistant. Very much part of the Michael Bates era, these characters failed to gain a foothold in the nation's affections and were dropped.

Rosemary subsequently went on to appear in the 1975 sitcom *How's Your Father?* with Michael Robbins and Arthur Mullard, landed the indomitable role of Vera Parkinson opposite Bill Maynard in *Oh No – It's Selwyn Froggitt* and appeared alongside Derek Nimmo in the Yorkshire Television success *Life Begins at Forty*.

Her latest major comedy work was in the second series of Richard Harris's *Outside Edge*, the celebrated cricketing sitcom full of middle-class banter.

Jean Fergusson

MARINA: 1984 TO DATE

Almost ten years after Rosemary Martin had departed *Summer Wine*, the slightest essence of her character was resurrected for the Eastbourne summer season of the series. A blonde, brassy, mini-skirted sex goddess to play opposite and tantalize 'Howard' was created by Roy Clarke, and actress Jean Fergusson landed the part. Little did anybody know that the character, Marina, would go on to be written into the television episodes and remain a constant blonde bombshell tease for some 15 years.

Jean, perhaps more than any other member of the cast, suffers for her art. While all the other stars are able to use their costumes to help keep warm on the often cold and damp Yorkshire hills, Marina's tarty outfits leave little to the imagination and even less to insulate her against the rigours of location filming:

My character doesn't get to wear an overcoat. There's no room for thermals! I never knew what teeth-chattering meant until I came to do this series. I remember we were filming Uncle of the Bride *and we had to do one big cast shot outside the church. I was wearing this thin chiffon number. The cast members in heavy coats were cold, so you can imagine just how I felt! Mind you, at least I get to choose my own costumes, even if most of them do come from a local charity shop! In the past it used to be Miss Selfridge and Top Shop but now Marina's gone a bit economical!*

Jean first got involved in acting during the mid-1960s when she appeared with Brian Way's Theatre Centre, a children's theatre that toured schools and performed plays such as Louis Maliesse's *Christopher Columbus,* as interactive pieces. She gained invaluable experience with both St Anne's and Southport repertory companies, performing *A Christmas Carol* for Duncan Weldon. Serious plays were offering Jean some of the most challenging roles of her career – Martha in *Who's Afraid of Virginia Woolf?*, Linda in *Death of a Salesman* – but it was popular television that would make her a star.

During the 1970s she enjoyed regular work on the hugely successful soap opera *Crossroads*. Other television work has included a notable comic cameo in Dennis Potter's celebrated *Lipstick on Your Collar* – but it has been as Marina that audiences have taken Jean to their hearts.

Regular summer seasons and pantomime work based on the character led to the role that dominated Jean's time for much of the 1990s:

In 1990 I was doing panto in Darlington. The manager, Michael Vine, said, 'Here, you don't half remind me of Hylda Baker!' I was in character as Marina the Fairy with the glittery mini-skirt and the glittery bike, trying to look glamorous, but he said, 'There's something about the way you work the audience.' I decided then and there to research her life.

The result of Jean's research was the definitive book on the legendary comedienne, *She Knows, You Know!*, and a one-woman play of the same name, directed and performed by Jean, which finally opened in the West End at the Vaudeville Theatre in October 1997.

Ironically and, perhaps, even more sadly, Jean recently missed the filming of the funeral scenes for Compo. She was, in fact, filming another funeral – for the world's longest-running soap opera, *Coronation Street* – where she was playing the mother of Gary Mallett, whose wife, Judy, had just died.

It was an odd experience. I was surrounded at the Granada Studios by people I knew and had worked with over the years, but somehow I felt I should have been on the other side of the hills.

As with her fellow *Summer Wine* actors, her funniest memory is from filming:

Roy Clarke writes his stage directions as beautifully as his dialogue. There was a scene where Howard and I were backpacking in the hills, and Roy had written that the weight pulls us over on to our backs and, with our legs flailing in the air, we looked like a couple of beached turtles!

The scene also required paint to be poured over us – all well and good, except immediately after we got into position, and with the paint covering us, Alan called a tea break. It was freezing cold, and for continuity I wasn't allowed to move. Dear Peter Sallis was outraged at the treatment of one of his fellow actors and went off to have stern words with the director. The ensuing discussions took so long that I was lying on the ground far longer than if everyone had just had a quick cuppa. It was a very kind thought. But then Peter is a very kind man.

Nice doggie! The short-sighted Danny O'Dea gives Jean Fergusson an unexpected treat.

CHAPTER FOUR

THE HENPECKED

A Sympathetic Look at *Last of the Summer Wine's* Much Put-upon Menfolk

'Sid and Ivy would shout at each other all the time, but there was never any doubt that they loved one another.'

JANE FREEMAN

John Comer

Sid: 1973 to 1983

If Jane Freeman embodied the strong married woman with a suspicious mind, then she found the perfect stooge figure in John Comer's Sid. A brilliantly etched character study, here was one of the boys quite clearly under the thumb. Not quite as cowardly and controlled as Joe Gladwin's Wally Batty, John Comer's character was allowed tantalizing glimpses into the carefree life of the three old men. Longing to be free of his cares, wife and work, John created a figure whose wings – although clipped – were almost ready to spirit him into the eternal childhood of Compo and company.

John Comer started in entertainment as a slightly near-the-knuckle stand-up comedian delighting in pub and working-men's club performances throughout the north of England. Fans of classic British comedy films will fondly remember him as part of the lacklustre workforce under the unionist control of Peter Sellers in *I'm All Right Jack*. A satirical masterwork from the Boulting Brothers, John's work-shy banter with Kenneth Griffith, Sam Kydd, Victor Maddern and his other 'brothers' created a realistic, comic-slanted look at the underbelly of British industry.

A prolific character actor, John's lifetime of comic experience on stage and film was fully utilized with Roy Clarke's *Last of the Summer Wine*. John was in at the very beginning and became a vital part of the fun for the first ten years of the series.

Roy Clarke has fond memories of the actor who brought his ultimate henpecked husband to life:

John was always believable, always spot-on with his lines. Funnily enough, John's relationship with Jane Freeman's character in the café was always battle, battle, battle, and he loved to let audiences believe his own very happy marriage was exactly the same. John and his real wife ran a little boarding house near Manchester Airport. His pet trick was to come down in the morning when there was a new guest at breakfast and go into the kitchen, bang a tray around and make out a huge argument was taking place. The guests suddenly thought they were in Summer Wine *country!*

Longing to be free of his cares, wife and work, John created a figure whose wings – although clipped – were almost ready to spirit him into the eternal childhood of Compo and company.

John's beaming banter with Ivy became one of the most popular elements of the programme. A small-screen star was born. Indeed, other television companies were not slow in coming forward when it came to John's unique mix of gruff bombast and roly-poly childishness. Yorkshire Television signed him up to play Wilf opposite Diana Dors in the comedy drama *All Our Saturdays*. A spin-off of sorts from Diana's hugely popular *Queenie's Castle*, this series – which ran to just six episodes – retained familiar supporting face Tony Caunter (now familiar as Roy Evans in *EastEnders*) as Ken Hicks. The show was produced and co-directed by Ian Davidson and was transmitted from Valentine's Day 1973. Dors starred as Di Dorkins, the owner of the textile company Garsley Garments and chief coach for the firm's rugger team, the Frilly Things.

John was a semi-regular as the cheery landlord of the Hare and Hounds in the Sid James ITV situation

A potentially smashing time – Jane Freeman and John Comer in the café.

comedy *Bless This House* during the early 1970s. In 1975 Granada Television cast John as George Pollitt in the seven episodes of *The Life of Riley.* A good idea – Bill Maynard starring in the double life of insurance bod by day and sex beast by night – failed to gel with audiences, although it set things up nicely for his comedy success, *Oh No, It's Selwyn Froggitt.*

From 1975 to the fourth and final series in 1979, John starred as the much put-upon northern chappie Les Brandon in the BBC's *I Didn't Know You Cared.* Written by Peter Tinniswood, it was produced by *Summer Wine* anchorman Bernard Thompson. Still at the Beeb, John appeared as Sidney Bogart in two seasons of *Potter's Picture Palace.* Transmitted in 1976 and 1978, these starred Eden Phillips as the charming, eccentric owner of a fleapit cinema, and the supporting cast, including Melvyn Hayes and, in the first series only, David Lodge, proved a useful background for plenty of cinematic magic.

But it was *Summer Wine*, by now having fully hit its stride with Brian Wilde's Foggy in residence, that really made John Comer a household favourite across the nation. A big man in every sense of the word,

John's larger-than-life comic performance was a real asset for the series. Sadly, during 1983 the actor was diagnosed with cancer of the throat. Although cast in the first feature-length episode, *Getting Sam Home*, John couldn't deliver his lines, and the dialogue was re-recorded. Familiar comedy actor Tony Melody – having found BritCom immortality as the postman in *Steptoe and Son*'s *Come Dancing* – dubbed John Comer's lines with near perfection.

This was to be John's last acting appearance. He died in 1984.

Jane Freeman has missed her co-star ever since:

Sid and Ivy would shout at each other all the time, but there was never any doubt that they loved one another. They would have been lost without each other.

John Comer was a lovely person to work with. He was a nice big chap and he would go round bashing his stomach and saying: 'Eh, my money belt!'

Joe Gladwin

WALLY BATTY: 1975 TO 1986

A comic pro to the tips of his toes, Joe Gladwin joined the cast of *Summer Wine* in 1975, by which time he was already one of the country's best-loved and most familiar supporting players. The easily swayed, henpecked, flat-cap-wearing innocence of Wally Batty elevated him to national stardom. Struggling to enjoy life under the same roof as Nora Batty, desperately trying to allow Compo to take his wife off his hands and gratefully accepting any small crumb of carefree fun as provided by the three principals, Gladwin's hard-done-by characterization proved to be one of the show's most popular ingredients.

Joe's career stretched back to before the Second World War, when he was the multi-talented stooge to variety and working-men's club comedian Dave Morris. Morris, a brilliant comic specializing in an attitude of work-shy, cocky and crafty arrogance, gleefully embraced the slow-witted, mournful mugging of Joe Gladwin as his second banana. The pair proved so popular north of the border that the BBC Home Service gave them their own radio show – *Club Night* – which ran from 7 November 1950. The basic format was simply lifted from the duo's stage work, with Morris holding court and taking control, while Gladwin filled in with comic business and misunderstandings. The shows were hugely successful and remained on the airwaves until 1956.

The format was reworked for television, albeit with less success. Written by Morris and Frank Roscoe, the producer was Ronnie Taylor. However, despite Gladwin's peerless performance as Cedric Butterworth, the series failed to gel. The team made a single return – live from the Palace Theatre, Blackpool, in June 1958 – but it was eventually decided to take the popular duo in a different direction for the small screen.

In 1959 the BBC unveiled its six-part series *The Artful Dodger*, which again recruited Joe as Cedric Butterworth and headlined Dave Morris as the eponymous wheeler-dealer. Again, these shows were penned by Morris and Roscoe, while the producer was future Morecambe and Wise guru John Ammonds. Sadly, any further collaboration between Morris and Gladwin was tragically cut short when Morris died in 1960.

Like any surviving half of a popular double act, Joe found work hard to come by in the early 1960s, although his late partner's writing colleague, Frank Roscoe, tried to come to the rescue in January 1964. The BBC screened the pilot episode of a comedy

Joe Gladwin as the much-loved Wally Batty.

Joe Gladwin and Kathy Staff in a rare moment of domestic harmony in the Batty household.

called *The Mascot,* starring Joe as Arnold Birtwistle – a lifetime supporter and lucky mascot of the northern footie team Northtown FC. Sadly, a series failed to materialize, although its critical success was enough to secure Joe some valuable stage work.

Film roles, including *Three Hats for Lisa* with Sid James in 1965, and further television work emerged in 1968. He played Sesame Ingram in the pioneering prison situation comedy *Her Majesty's Pleasure*, which ran for two series in 1968 and 1969. Ken Jones – five years before appearing as 'Orrible Ives in *Porridge* – was the star.

ITV also presented Joe with the priceless, gleeful and wide-eyed supporting turn of Stan the pickler in the classic Vince Powell and Harry Driver sitcom *Nearest and Dearest*. Powell, who had co-written *The Mascot*, was delighted to secure Joe for the role, brilliantly going over the top opposite flamboyant star turns from Hylda Baker and Jimmy Jewel. The series, produced by Peter Eckersley and Bill Podmore, was a smash situation comedy hit and ran from 1968 until 1973, leading to a Hammer film version and establishing the working relationship between Gladwin and his *Summer Wine* wife, Kathy Staff.

During this flush of small-screen success, Joe also cropped up in the *Comedy Playhouse* episode *Don't Ring Us…We'll Ring You,* scripted by Mike Craig and Lawrie Kinsley. Despite its interesting credentials – Norman Rossington and John Junkin starring as a couple of inept northern theatrical agents – the proposed series failed to get off the ground. But Joe didn't fret. His appearances in *Summer Wine* were justly celebrated, and his bank account was kept healthy with regular income from his Hovis commercial voice-overs. His 'He were a great baker were our dad' monologue made him a national institution. Indeed, even serious theatre work was frequently interrupted by some wag from the audience shouting out, 'Where's your loaf of bread, mate?' Vince Powell – in the immediate wake of the death of his writing partner Harry Driver – put together the ill-fated Liverpool-based comic soap opera *The Wackers*, which featured Joe as Joe Farrell. The show lasted for just six episodes, transmitted during 1975.

In 1978 Joe was cast as Dennis Breene in the situation comedy *The Wrestlers*. Seemingly a sure-fire hit, the series starred Leonard Rossiter as a manager of bumbling wrestlers but, again, the idea failed to attract audiences and only one series of six episodes was filmed.

By then, of course, Joe Gladwin's stardom was already assured. He delighted in mournful, depressed banter with Bill Owen's Compo and scored huge laughs with his hound-dog reaction shots to Kathy Staff's biting comments. A regular and most welcome part of the cast, his role was often reduced to the merest of cameo roles, but the actor never failed to leave his mark. He made his final appearance in the 1986 Christmas Special, *Merry Christmas, Father Christmas*, and died in March 1987 at the age of 82.

Gordon Wharmby

WESLEY PEGDEN: 1982 TO DATE

Of all the regular cast members of *Last of the Summer Wine*, Gordon Wharmby is the only one who was never a professional actor before joining the series. He wouldn't claim to be a professional actor now. Simply, Gordon enjoys himself hugely tinkering with his motor cars, quietly nodding in agreement to his wife's nagging and giving plenty of priceless reaction shots of complete bemusement to all and sundry.

A local of Holmfirth, Gordon had gained minor experience with the Oldham Repertory Company. In him, the director and producer of *Last of the Summer Wine*, Alan J. W. Bell, spotted a natural talent and cast him as the bumbling, overall-clad figure of Wesley Pegden.

Alan remembers his unforgettable first meeting with the actor:

Gordon came to audition for just one line in the episode In the Service of Humanity. *In the programme, Foggy is taking charge yet again and removes a ladder from the side of a house. He leaves a man on the roof who simply had to look annoyed and shout, 'Bring that ladder back!' I went to audition some actors in Manchester, and Gordon was one of those who turned up for the job. I asked him what he had previously done, and he mentioned some credits with the Oldham Playhouse and one or two other parts, but added, 'I'm a painter and decorator really.' I asked him, 'Do you consider yourself quite good?' and he replied in all seriousness, 'The best. I can decorate a house, give it two coats of paint and do all the windows in less than two days!'*

Of course, I meant how did he rate himself as an actor, but he seemed far prouder of his decorating skills than any theatrical ability. Anyway, he amused me a great deal and we tested him. He read the 'Bring that ladder back!' line and sounded great. I had already seen several actors for

the role of Wesley, but I was so impressed with Gordon that I also got him to read some of that character's lines as well. He was considerably better than the other character actors I'd auditioned in London. I really wanted to cast Gordon as Wesley but had the dilemma of giving a major guest part to an actor who had done very little.

I asked him again how he rated himself. 'The best,' he said again. 'Convince me,' I countered. 'Well, there's this big house with two floors. I can strip the wallpaper off in next to no time.' I cried: 'No, as an actor I mean!' Anyway, he said, 'Just give me the chance.'

I was worried that he had no track record, but I brought him to London anyway, worrying how he would cope with nerves in front of a live television audience. He was so good that Roy brought him back for another episode, and the character has been with us ever since. In fact, Gordon has been with the programme as long as I have.

Finding his finest hour in *The Loxley Lozenge*, Gordon's characterization has problems and commitments thrown at him from every angle. Initially, it was the three old men reluctantly dragging him into madcap antics and mechanical tomfoolery. Latterly, the bane of his life has been a continually nagging characterization from Thora Hird. Forever put upon to smarten himself up and present a sophisticated image, he and Thora have taken on the 1990s' mantle of Kathy Staff's Nora and her henpecked hubby, Joe Gladwin.

Opposite: Gordon Wharmby's Wesley Pegden tinkers under the bonnet. Below: He holds court with the trio in The Loxley Lozenge *(1984).*

Blake Butler

MR WAINWRIGHT: 1973 TO 1976

The only actor to inspire the character names for two favourites in *On the Buses*, the late Blake Butler was a familiar and very welcome face in stage and television drama from the 1950s onwards. Situation comedy, televised plays and courtroom dramas all benefited from his perfectly etched figures of authority and bumbling eccentrics.

He made his first major mark in television comedy with the role of Froggy in the 1963 Trevor Peacock-penned *Comedy Playhouse* episode, *Underworld Knights*. Future *Summer Wine* guest star Ron Moody also starred. A decade later Butler appeared opposite Michael Bates in the series *Turnbull's Finest Half-Hour* before reuniting with Bates for the first batch of *Last of the Summer Wine* in 1973.

Nervous, sexually active and under the thumb, Butler's timid but earnest librarian Lothario acted as the blueprint for the beloved Howard of Robert Fyfe. However, with the three old men still in fledgling form and Clarke's scripts keen to explore their multi-layered personalities, the Butler character was under-used and ultimately phased out. The actor died shortly afterwards.

Howard is a fairly traditional, henpecked husband but he has this wild escapist vision of himself. Not quite Don Juan perhaps, but certainly something of a Lothario.

Robert Fyfe

HOWARD: 1985 TO DATE

Robert Fyfe came up through the ranks of acting in repertory theatre and on radio to land his first major television assignment – as Bill Simpson's first patient in the opening episode of *Dr Finlay's Case-Book* in the 1960s. Many stage and television roles followed, including appearances on *Crossroads* and *Coronation Street*. A favourite of writer Jan Butlin, Robert appeared opposite Derek Nimmo and Nerys Hughes in the 1982 comedy series *Third Time Lucky*. Later, in 1989, he played the granddad in Butlin's suburbia-based tale of sex, lies and sellotape *No Strings*, with Edward Petherbridge and Jean Marsh.

By then Robert had been cast as the mild-mannered, passionate bundle of nervous energy, Howard, in the second presentation of the *Last of the Summer Wine* summer season, this time in Bournemouth:

The show was tremendous fun. It was a romp, not a serious play, and I had a marvellous time. Jane Freeman was the only person I actually knew, and she was a great help making me feel part of the troupe.

The character proved so popular that Roy Clarke wrote him into the television shows, where he has remained ever since. Making his debut in the television series alongside Juliette Kaplan and Jean Fergusson in the 1985 episode *Catching Digby's Donkey*, Robert was incorporated into the cast as a semi-regular:

Howard, Pearl and Marina were brought in as a package. Originally, we didn't do every episode but

Battered and bewildered – Robert Fyfe as the Yorkshire Lothario, Howard.

gradually, over time, this changed and suddenly one found oneself in all of them!

The characterization proved no problem for the actor. Although born in Scotland, he did his drama training in Bradford, from where he then toured the north of England for three years. Of Howard, Robert says:

Howard is a fairly traditional, henpecked husband but he has this wild escapist vision of himself. Not quite Don Juan perhaps, but certainly something of a Lothario. He doesn't think he's as old as he is, and he always sees Marina as a young lady, even though it's becoming increasingly obvious that she's not in the first flush of youth.

Robert is keen to emphasize that there is very little of Howard in him:

We are totally dissimilar, although I was looking at a photo of my son's wedding the other day and there I was, standing like Howard with hands clasped, and I thought, No, no, that will never do...I'll have to watch that!

Philip Jackson

GORDON SIMONITE: 1976

One-time *Summer Wine* regular Philip Jackson was recruited as the gormless Gordon – nephew to Compo – for several early Brian Wilde episodes, including the hilarious two-part Blackpool outing. A blueprint for the put-upon married figure of Mike Grady's Barry – *Going to Gordon's Wedding* plays like a dry run for *Uncle of the Bride* – Gordon has led to Philip becoming one of television's most in-demand actors.

He starred with Sharon Duce in the 1981 situation comedy *Coming Home*, appeared opposite Frances de la Tour in the 1994 series *Downwardly Mobile*, supported Dawn French in *Murder Most Horrid* and has recently enjoyed success in the AA versus RAC comedy of the roads *The Last Salute*.

On stage he sparred with three of the Young Ones – Rik Mayall, Ade Edmondson and Christopher Ryan – in Samuel Beckett's *Waiting for Godot*. However, Philip is perhaps best remembered as the dogged Inspector Japp in the classic ITV presentation of *Agatha Christie's Poirot* starring David Suchet.

Mike Grady

BARRY WILKINSON: 1986 TO 1990 AND 1996 TO DATE

One of Britain's busiest and most popular comedy actors, Mike Grady has found the perfect niche for himself in *Last of the Summer Wine*. Making his first appearance in the feature-length favourite *Uncle of the Bride*, Mike's beloved, bumbling, naive character Barry married the blushing bride of Sarah Thomas and embraced her family – particularly Thora Hird's mother-in-law from hell – as part of the bargain:

I was thrilled to get the part of Barry, although at the time it was a one-off appearance in the feature film. I had never seen the show before...and for that matter I still haven't – at least, not regularly!

Barry's youthful angst, attempts at improving business skills and a finger slightly on the pulse of modern life have brought an extra dimension to the comic goings-on. Indeed, Mike sees a great chunk of the character in himself:

I do identify with Barry's gullibility. When someone tells me the word 'gullibility' doesn't appear in the dictionary, it takes me a minute to get that! The fact is that Barry wants to be a success and to be driven and

Mike Grady in an informal publicity pose as Barry Wilkinson.

'I hate you, Barry!' Mike Grady is attacked by a power-mad Stephen Lewis in How to Create a Monster *(1997).*

more forceful. I'd also like to be like that. In fact, the more I think about it, I think Barry is me. Roy Clarke must have been observing me from a distance for quite some time!

Mike was born in 1950 and made an early mark on stage and television. He notched up a notable supporting role in the celebrated ITV situation comedy series *Doctor in the House*, injecting some uneasy theatrics into the 1969 episode *Keep It Clean*, scripted by Graeme Garden and Bill Oddie. The following year Mike was briefly involved in the perennial *Carry On* series – *Carry On Loving* cast him as Boy Lover, forever caught by Terry Scott, Richard O'Callaghan and Sid James in amorous clinches with Valerie Shute. Mike remembers the experience as 'the sweetest way ever of making a living'.

Back on television, Mike cropped up in the 1976 one-off, John Stevenson-scripted *Comedy Playhouse* episode *Just Like Mum*, opposite Peggy Mount. The following year he landed the prime part of Ken in the classic series *Citizen Smith*. The first major success for *Only Fools and Horses* scriptwriter John Sullivan, the programme made a star of Robert Lindsay. Mike's endearing, slightly confused character proved the perfect sounding-board for Lindsay's slightly militant anti-hero, Wolfie. Screaming 'Power to the People!' for the common cause of the Tooting Popular Front, the show ran until 1980. Produced by seasoned comic master Dennis Main Wilson, the show remains gleefully nostalgic rather than uncomfortably anarchic.

In 1983, Mike was cast as Dr Ballantine in the BBC situation comedy *Sweet Sixteen* – a series starring Penelope Keith as the boss of a building firm. Douglas Watkinson wrote the scripts, Gareth Gwenlan was in charge of production and an eye-catching supporting turn from Victor Spinetti stole the limelight.

Following Mike's enlistment into *Summer Wine* country, he joined the cast for the second series of the ITV religious comedy *Troubles and Strife* in 1986, when he played Christopher. However, his finest post-*Citizen Smith* sitcom opportunity came with the Mel Smith series *Colin's Sandwich*, something of a Hancock for the 1980s. With this, *Smith and Jones* writers Paul Smith and Terry Kyan fashioned a brilliant, tightly structured comment on the problems of getting a book published, working for British Rail and generally getting through life. Mike played Des, again the naive friend to the star, peerlessly staggering into situations, putting his foot in everything and staggering off again without any idea how irritating he had been. The on-screen chemistry between Smith and Grady was superb. Sadly, only 12 episodes over two seasons were made.

In 1990 Mike decided to leave *Summer Wine* in order to accept a major role in the ITV sitcom *Up the Garden Path*. The series lasted until 1993 and cast Mike as quiet, cosy, dependable Derbyshire schoolteacher Dick Barnes, forever trying to win over the show's heroine, Imelda Staunton, and failing miserably throughout. Sue Lamb wrote the scripts from her radio original; Humphrey Barclay produced. Meanwhile, in 1992, Mike had appeared as Honeywell in the ITV children's adventure *Tales from the Poop Deck* – a 17th-century romp with Helen Atkinson Wood and Charles Gray.

Barry's youthful angst, attempts at improving business skills and a finger slightly on the pulse of modern life have brought an extra dimension to the comic goings-on.

During his five-year sabbatical, Sarah Thomas's Glenda had made continued reference to her absent husband and, therefore, a return to *Summer Wine* in 1996 was made with a swift, smooth action. The relationship had hardly changed, even if several of the characters had:

When I arrived back after six years away, there were all these new characters who used to be in other series. There was Stephen Lewis from On the Buses *and Jean Alexander from* Coronation Street. *I hardly knew what series I was in. It was like an amalgam of every sitcom you had ever seen. I almost expected Tony Hancock to turn up at any minute!*

Jonathan Linsey

CRUSHER MILBURN: 1985 TO 1990

With the death of John Comer in 1984 it was felt that Sid's Café and, more to the point, Jane Freeman's Ivy needed a replacement stooge figure. That replacement was a rotund, youthful, thick-skulled chap by the name of Milburn, who first

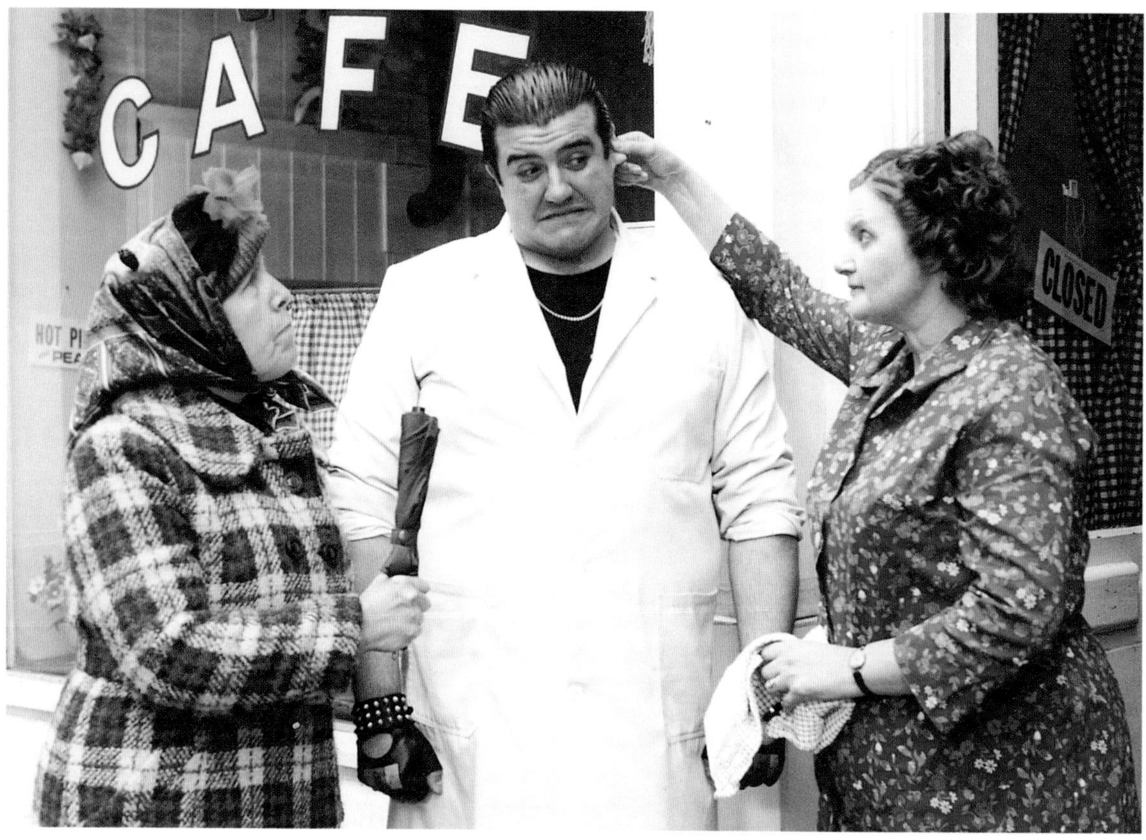

The café's punch-bag, Jonathan Linsey's Crusher, is pounded by Summer Wine*'s favourite harridans, Kathy Staff and Jane Freeman.*

appeared in the stage show. Dubbed 'Crusher' by the old men in response to his hulking form, Linsey's performance was an endearing mixture of childlike bumbling and 'doesn't know his own strength' power. The character was the show's gentle giant, often led astray by the madcap antics of the three lead men. Steeped in the tradition of quiffed 1950s' rock 'n' rollers, Linsey stayed with the programme from Series Eight in 1985 until the close of Series 12 in 1990, and in 1985 he played Chunky Livesey in *First of the Summer Wine – Ain't Love Dangerous*. Having suddenly decided to go on a crash diet, the actor who played Crusher was suddenly crushed and couldn't continue playing the role. However, in 1999 Jonathan was back, louder, prouder and as big as ever, in the successful Edinburgh Festival 25th anniversary revival of Steven Berkoff's controversial play *East*. The production transferred for a limited period to the West End's Vaudeville Theatre.

Danny O'Dea

ELI DUCKETT: 1986 TO DATE

Danny O'Dea's contribution to *Last of the Summer Wine* is a unique and hilarious one. As Eli, the Mr Magoo-styled bumbler of the Yorkshire Dales, O'Dea

Blind as a bat! Danny O'Dea as the accident-prone Eli Duckett.

has utilized almost every silent slapstick trick and visual gag known to man. Reheating ancient routines and bits of comic business for a whole new audience, his brief but potent appearances are justly awaited with eager anticipation by fans of the series.

One of the country's finest and most prolific pantomime dames, O'Dea's other stage credits have included the 1976 Scarborough summer season, *Carry On Laughing*, with Jack Douglas, Kenneth Connor, Peter Butterworth and *Summer Wine* guest star Liz Fraser.

Born in 1911, O'Dea was a veteran of variety in the music hall and on radio and television before *Summer Wine* brought him back into the public eye. From his first appearance – in the 1986 episode *Jaws* – O'Dea has proved a firm favourite. He appeared subsequently in the Victoria Wood playlet *The Library*, in 1989, but for the last decade it's been *Summer Wine* antics that have kept him busy.

Jean Alexander says of him:

Danny O'Dea kills me. He only ever does one line; sometimes he doesn't even speak. But it's what he does that makes you fall about. Like when he came out of a pub, walked across a few cars, thought he was getting on a bus and ended up on the rising platform of a dustcart. He shouted out, 'Right away, conductor!' and he was off. The best one, though, was when a hearse drew up. It was a hot day, and Eli banged on the window and said, 'Raspberry ripple please!' He's a wonderful man and I always enjoy watching him work.

Stephen Lewis

CLEM 'SMILER' HEMINGWAY: 1988 TO DATE

Thanks solely to just one outstanding, landmark and priceless comic creation, Stephen Lewis is still valued as one of the funniest men in the country. His towering, Hitleresque alter ego, Inspector Cyril 'Blakey' Blake of *On the Buses*, is a stereotypical comic grotesque, certainly, but a well-timed, 'Oh, my Gawd... Get that bus out!' can reduce the authors of this book to hysterics.

Stephen was welcomed with open arms into the tightly knit comic community of *Summer Wine*, gleefully playing a slight variation on his old, beloved, face-pulling misery from *On the Buses* in the shape of Smiler. Having appeared in a one-off, self-contained, guest-starring episode, *That Certain Smile*, in 1988, Stephen fully joined the squad in 1990:

Smiler's not that far removed from the Blakey character I used to play. He's quite a dour person, whose laughs derive from the miserable time he's having. My characters' mottoes have always seemed to be, If I can spread misery and gloom I'm happy!

'My characters' mottoes have always seemed to be, If I can spread misery and gloom I'm happy!'

Having first found fame acting with Joan Littlewood's workshop company, Stephen co-wrote the 1960s' cockney smash hit *Sparrows Can't Sing*. In 1969 he played Inspector Trimfittering in the London Weekend Television comedy playlet *Mrs Wilson's Diary*. *On the Buses* co-star Bob Grant also appeared, and the two joined forces almost immediately to write a *Comedy Playhouse*, *The Jugg Brothers*, for the BBC. Playing the central roles themselves, they failed to win a series, but instant comedy stardom had already come with the classic ITV situation comedy *On the Buses,* starring Reg Varney.

The show – a glorious, low-brow wallow in smut, lust and booze – quickly became the corporation's flagship comedy series, running for 74 episodes from 1969 to 1973. Many of the episodes were penned by Lewis and Grant themselves. Lewis had already stooged successfully for Max Bygraves on television and was cast in the short-lived *Buses* spin-off series *Don't Drink the Water*. This followed Blakey to his retreat in the Spanish sun with antics revolving around his sister, Pat Coombs, and a lazy porter, Derek Griffiths. Two series were made in 1974 and 1975. More importantly, *Buses* had spawned three hugely popular spin-off films for Hammer. The first, *On the Buses*, appeared in 1971 and remains the most financially successful Hammer film ever released for the home market. *Mutiny on the Buses* and *Holiday on the Buses* followed on in 1972 and 1973.

Stephen played a variation on the Blakey role – a moaning park-keeper – opposite Ronald Fraser and Arthur Howard in an instalment of Graham Stark's comedy compendium film *The Magnificent Seven Deadly Sins*, penned by Graham Chapman and Barry Cryer. But it was on television that Stephen found lasting fame. In 1982 he played Royston Flagg in the theatrical company comedy series *Rep* with Iain Cuthbertson.

Continually called on to re-create Blakey for pantomime, summer season and charity appearances, Stephen became a firm favourite on *Jim Davidson's Generation Game* and *The All New Alexei Sayle Show*. In 1996 he was cast as Harry Lambert in the David Croft railway comedy *Oh, Doctor Beeching* and continues to enchant comedy fans with *Summer Wine* tomfoolery. As he says:

I do like to work at entertaining people and making them laugh if I can. It can be a sad world, and if Last of the Summer Wine *can bring people a little happiness, then I'm very proud to be a part of it.*

'Oh, my Gawd!' Back on the buses, as Stephen Lewis recreates Blakey anguish for Summer Wine *publicity.*

CHAPTER FIVE

FROM SCRIPT TO SCREEN

Behind the Scenes of Television's Longest-running Comedy Series

'In order to keep the show fresh, we have to come up with new places to film.'

ALAN J. W. BELL
PRODUCER AND DIRECTOR

A wise television comedy director once wrote that, generally speaking, the funniest comedy arises from either unreal characters placed in a real situation or real characters placed in an unreal situation. Most people tend to agree that *Summer Wine* fits the latter description.

The task of actually creating that comedy is primarily the responsibility of just a couple of people – the writer and the director. The writer puts the characters and situations down on paper; the director sees that they get to our screens. Often that comedy is augmented by the work of the musical director, whose compositions can in themselves be pointers to laughter and comic signifiers in their own right.

The funniest comedy arises from either unreal characters placed in a real situation or real characters placed in an unreal situation. Most people tend to agree that Summer Wine *fits the latter description.*

In the case of *Last of the Summer Wine,* it is rather apt that this long-running series, dealing, as it does, with a trio of aged men, should itself be steered behind the camera by a most important trio (of slightly younger men!). Like the series, two of these have been with the programme since the very beginning and, suitably, the third man – as in the show itself – is the leader. He is also the director and, like the third man, has changed more than once over the years.

The Clegg of the operation is, of course, scriptwriter and creator of the series Roy Clarke. Ronnie Hazlehurst, the show's music man, injects the Compo-like cheeky charm that makes the programme even more of an audible feast, while the military precision of their third man leader is ably demonstrated by the show's producer and director, Alan J. W. Bell.

The problem with a show like *Last of the Summer Wine* – as with most productions – is that the characters are so indelibly printed in our minds that we often tend to forget the people and the work that goes into putting characters in front of us in the first place. And why should we think about them? We watch television to get away from the hustle and bustle of working-day life and, after all, television is such a glamorous job to be in. Isn't it? Well...

This chapter seeks to redress the balance slightly. Without underestimating the huge talents of all those who appear in front of the camera on *Summer Wine*, we want to take you on a trip through the several stages that take place before, during and after filming the world's longest-running television comedy series, and to make people realize that in order to present a programme that has a tranquil feel about it, actually making it can often be anything but tranquil.

In a constantly changing television world, most people are inclined to believe that *Summer Wine* has stayed exactly the same, but this is far from the truth. The programme has continued to evolve over the past 30 years to the extent where the only things that are the same as when the first series was

Summer Wine *creator, Roy Clarke, with his prized BAFTA.*

transmitted in the early 1970s are the writer, a few of the actors and the theme tune. And even the sweeping, melodious sounds that used to greet the beginning of each episode have now been moved, to allow a pre-credit sequence to entice the audience to watch more. As if Ronnie Hazlehurst's familiar theme were not enough!

The tune, which almost everyone in the country can whistle or hum, would not have become part of British television life if it hadn't been for Ronnie's insistence:

When I was asked to write the music for Last of the Summer Wine, *it was simply for a* Comedy Playhouse, *a one-off programme. I was given a script and a fair amount of licence, although there wasn't much money. I decided on a string quartet and three different instruments – one for each of the three principal characters. The BBC didn't like it. They said it didn't suit what they considered a comedy programme. They wanted it played faster or changed completely – anything to get us out of trouble.*

I stuck to my guns and, though I did agree to play it a little more quickly, that's as far as I was prepared to compromise. Anyway, there wasn't any time or money left to re-do it.

I always considered the programme to be less about belly laughs and more about gentle chuckles, and that's what I wanted the music to portray.

The man who has the task of continuing to keep the audience chuckling after almost 200 episodes is writer Roy Clarke. He has a set pattern and discipline to writing the show after all these years – a job that he says has actually become easier rather than more difficult:

It's changed over the years. It's got much easier because you can hear the voices, you can hear how the characters will respond to ideas and you've seen the actors doing the part. The changes have very often been audience-led. One of the advantages of having a live audience is that I've gradually woken up

Bom, bom, bom, bom, bom, bom, bom. Summer Wine *composer Ronnie Hazlehurst.*

Producer/director Alan J. W. Bell consults the latest Summer Wine *script on location.*

to the fact that three talking heads is not as funny as when you include some physical comedy in the programme.

Of course, there are live audiences and live audiences. Until the late 1980s, all the interiors for the series were filmed in front of a live studio audience at BBC Television Centre in London. But as the years went by, the actors got older and the amount of location work increased, while studio work became a drain on time and finances. The latter was eventually done away with by Alan J. W. Bell – the producer and director, who, with a history of comedy work recorded on film, took the ultimate step and turned *Summer Wine* into the first comedy series on television to be filmed completely away from a studio audience. *Summer Wine* does continue to have a laughter track but, at the insistence of its director, the laughter is real and not canned. This involves getting an audience to come to watch a show that has been completely pre-filmed – not always an easy job when most fans want to meet or at least see their favourite comedy actors in the flesh. Alan remembers the dilemma that faced him over making the change:

I was concerned about moving entirely to film. Would all the laughs still be there? I always insist on using real laughter, not the canned sort, and I had a difficult experience on one occasion in the late 1970s, during a showing of Ripping Yarns *to an audience. The show had also been completely shot on film, and the audience were less than responsive. They laughed for a few minutes, then nothing. I suppose there was a feeling that if they were watching a film, why bother to come and watch it at a studio when they might as well be at home watching it on TV?*

To this end, Alan shrewdly hit on a novel idea – to use *Summer Wine* cast members as the warm-up entertainment before a screening. This would include Bill Owen singing 'You Must Have Been a Beautiful Baby' to Kathy Staff, as well as comic turns from Stephen Lewis, Robert Fyfe, Jean Fergusson, Frank Thornton and Thora Hird. The stars then sit with the audience while the programme is played. The audience feel they have seen a show, met their favourite actors and watched the new programmes. Their laughter is genuine and is recorded on to the soundtrack.

Sometimes the laughter can be too much for a particular joke. When filming in front of a live audience, actors can judge the audience reaction and pause accordingly, but when the show is pre-filmed that luxury is not available. There are two ways in which this problem can be ironed out. One is to cut back the laughter on the soundtrack when it is recorded; the other and more preferred choice is to allow the filming 'to breathe' – to make the actors build in pauses when filming where a laugh is anticipated. This is a practice that works most of the time, but not always, and sometimes causes differences of opinion between the actors and the director, as Alan J. W. Bell recalls:

There was a line for Gordon Wharmby's Wesley in my first series, which prompted Compo to stick two fingers up. As he walks away, we pan to Clegg, who says, 'Probably a good driver, but not very good with hand signals.'

Peter Sallis came up to me after the rehearsal and said that the timing was bad. 'The time taken between Bill sticking his fingers up and me delivering my line is too long.' I pointed out that there would be a laugh and that we had to allow for it on the track. Peter insisted that the

Opposite: Alan J. W. Bell acts as stand-in for a beating as Kathy Staff warms up for the attack.
Right: A hard job but someone has to do it! Sound assistant John Crossland wires Jean Fergusson for sound.

laugh would be nowhere near as long and it would look wrong.

On the night of the recording, the audience were enjoying the episode immensely, and the joke got a huge laugh – the biggest in the show. If I had cut the film any shorter, it would have completely drowned out Peter's line. To his credit, he apologized. The actors love the programme as much as I do, and they like to have their say.

By the time an audience gets to see a show, most of the work has already been done. An episode of *Summer Wine* starts its long route to transmission many months before. Roy Clarke is commissioned by the BBC to write a series of episodes, and he likes to spend around a fortnight preparing each one. As the scripts become available, he passes them on to Alan J. W. Bell at the *Summer Wine* production office:

From the word go I've had a very easy working relationship with Alan. He leaves me to do my bit, and I leave him to do his. Mostly we communicate over the phone. I trust him. It's made life much easier having Alan in the saddle.

Alan J. W. Bell came to *Summer Wine* in the early 1980s not just as a long-standing fan but as a director with a mission:

I'd always felt there was something missing on Summer Wine. *I couldn't work out what it was. Roy's writing was brilliant, and the surroundings were beautiful. So just before I started working on the show I watched a few episodes and it clicked with me what the problem was – there were too many close-ups on the actors. One episode I watched might as well have been filmed on Ealing Common because you saw so little of the beauty of Yorkshire.*

It's that beauty that draws him back not just for filming but for the all-important pre-filming recce required to establish locations for shooting. Most viewers are inclined to imagine that the crew, after 27 years at Holmfirth, would know every inch of the surrounding countryside and that little would still be available as virgin shooting territory. Alan says:

That's partly the problem. In order to keep the show fresh we have to come up with new places to film. The last thing we want is for the audience to say, 'We've

When is a bridge not a bridge? When it's in Holmfirth! Chief designer Stephan Paczai and his assistant Eugene Zelim survey their handiwork.

Typical location weather. Juliette Kaplan, Sarah Thomas, Thora Hird, Jane Freeman and Kathy Staff take cover!

seen that before.' They will think the show is a repeat and possibly turn off. And remember: we don't shoot just in Holmfirth. The Yorkshire hills are rich with beautiful countryside locations. We could be here another ten years and still not run out of places to film.

It may be Roy Clarke's words and Ronnie Hazlehurst's music that provide his inspiration, but it's Alan's vision that provides the show with its unique look:

The programmes are made according to how I see them in my mind. If I read the scripts and I cannot see the pictures, I have to have the script worked on because it means it's unclear. I'm sure directors who've previously been film editors are all similar – I don't think I'm unique in doing this.

When I read the script, I see the men walking across the countryside and I also hear the music. This means that when we go filming, I tell the actors to walk for a while before they speak so that Ronnie can establish his works. It's all exactly as I see it. It's never shot and then thought about afterwards.

Roy doesn't come on location and doesn't express an opinion about how anything should be done. I do refer to him – often about the look of the programme and the way that the characters should be dressed. A number of authors would come down and get in the way. Roy doesn't do that. He never interferes. He's complained once or twice that perhaps we're going over the top with Marina, making her a bit too bizarre and overly tarty, but on the whole we seem to see eye to eye on Summer Wine.

The crew set up another one of Brian Wilde's madcap schemes as Bill Owen prepares himself...

Following the technical recce, the cast and crew assemble on location for the first tranche of filming. A shoot for a series of ten episodes usually comprises four weeks on location, ten days in a studio – Elstree, Shepperton or Pinewood – for interior scenes, then a break, before going back on location for a further four weeks, followed by a final fortnight in studios to finish off.

Filming on location usually starts at 8 a.m. and finishes at 6 p.m., six days a week. It's hardly surprising, therefore, that being away from home for long periods and almost living in each other's pockets mean that emotions can on occasions get a touch strained and actors can become a little difficult. It's been the job of Alan J. W. Bell to keep cast and crew happy, though he's not averse to resorting to dirty tricks when pushed:

Actors do grumble a lot, and older actors even more so. But I can be mischievous, too, and in my early days on the programme I was rather bolshie.

I remember we were filming the last scene of From Wellies to Wet Suit *in 1981. The final shot was of the men walking down a track. The piece was needed for the end credits and had to last about 40 seconds. So I told*

Brian, Peter and Bill to keep walking and not turn round until they heard me shout 'Cut'.

They started walking, the stopwatch was running and they delivered their lines. After 40 seconds, the crew and I sneaked off and hid in the bushes. The sound was still running and the men had their mikes on, so we could hear what they were saying: 'They must have done it by now.' 'Did you hear "Cut"?' 'I didn't hear "Cut".' 'We'd better not stop because we'll have to do it again.' And so on.

Eventually, Bill said, 'I'll walk backwards. My character has done that before, so it won't look odd.' He turned round and the next thing we heard was, 'Those bastards! They've gone!' It was very funny.

Bill Owen, of course, could see the funny side. He was, after all, a seasoned veteran of location filming. His cinematic career had lasted 30 years before he even donned the famous wellington boots. And he was a past master at the art of clowning around. However, as *Summer Wine* progressed through the years, he became concerned that the emphasis of the show's humour was depending more on the physical slapstick and less on the gentle three-headers that had made the show famous in the first place. His thoughts appeared to be echoed by writer Roy Clarke:

There was a period when we became too reliant on the physical business, and I regretted that. Thankfully, the programme has returned more to its grass roots – partially because the actors are getting too old to be chasing around the hills. There's a lot more chat between the characters, and that's like it used to be, but now it's shared among a dozen cast members in various locations. So the pace always seems fast, even when there may not be much happening.

Cutting back on the physical humour has forced me back to dialogue-led laughs, and I've had to think far more carefully about the scripts. I'm very pleased with the show at the moment. It's going through a very sharp period, and hopefully we'll be able to continue with that.

Of course, both Roy Clarke's and Alan J. W. Bell's work has become more problematic during the filming of the millennium series, following the sad passing of Bill Owen at the beginning of July 1999, only a third of the way through production.

Roy Clarke explains how he has had to adapt to a very emotional situation:

There was no great foreknowledge that Bill was ill. All the scripts for the series had been written before I knew there was a problem. I had no time to think about anything, really. If we were going to rescue the series, I had to write seven new scripts and very quickly. They'd done three with Bill in, but the rest became redundant. So even though I usually like about a fortnight to write an episode, I didn't have that luxury on this series. I was writing all day and all evening to complete seven episodes in eight weeks.

...and poor old Compo takes another tumble.

Peter Sallis and Frank Thornton provide reaction shots as the stunt man delivers another comic fall.

The major problem I had to overcome was how to deal with the death of a fictitious character. Somewhere there was a real family who was grieving. It was OK for me to show Compo's funeral and even to get some laughs out of the sadness, but how funny were Bill Owen's family going to find it? The best thing that happened was bringing Bill's son, Tom, on board. He saw the scripts, and if anything would have hurt the family, he would have told me.

While Roy Clarke was under intense pressure to rewrite episodes at speed, Alan J.W. Bell was faced with the prospect of returning to Holmfirth for the second tranche of location shooting without all the scripts ready to be filmed – a worrying prospect for any director, though if he found the experience daunting he certainly didn't let on:

It's not been as bad as you might think. When Bill said he was ill, my immediate thoughts were, to hell with Summer Wine*; let's worry about him. We're all human beings, after all. But Bill wanted to work on. He was angry that life was running out, and he was desperate to finish the series. Roy saved the day by coming up with three tremendous scripts. They were very touching and cover the death of Compo in a poignant yet funny way. He's kept the show going when it might so easily have crumbled.*

It hasn't all been plain sailing. There's been some considerable effort needed to keep the continuity going

The other Summer Wine *trio – stand-ins Tony Simon, Robin Banks and Denis Mawn.*

The complex rigging for a standard scene in Wesley's van. Gordon Wharmby, Bill Owen and Peter Sallis wait patiently.

and to ensure that Bill's wish to appear in the millennium episode was fulfilled. In a few scenes, I had to take shots of Bill which were filmed in the spring and merge them into scenes which were shot after he died. They were done very skilfully. Technically, it's taken a bit of time, and we've used doubles when necessary.

Of course, stand-ins and doubles have been part of the *Summer Wine* team for many years – though it's only recently that anyone has actually admitted to their existence. In the early years of *Summer Wine*, many of the stunts were performed by the players themselves. Indeed, Bill Owen would hang from trees and fall off walls well into his 80s. But many of the more dangerous antics were given to stunt men to perform, and some of the basic setting-up shots that required much hanging around utilized the talents of three regular extras on the show – Tony Simon, Denis Mawn and Robin Banks.

It was in the mid-1980s that one of the leading players suggested the idea of using stand-ins for the more senior cast members. Alan explains:

It was Michael Aldridge's idea for us to have doubles for the leading actors. When the men have to appear as little dots on the countryside, you can't tell if it's them or not. So why use them?

Realistically, there's a certain lack of mobility – not incapacity – but the men are not as agile as they once were. Michael said that though it would cost money, the

Corpsing in a pigeon suit. Bill Owen loses it and sets Peter Sallis, Joe Gladwin and John Comer into fits of giggles.

doubles would actually save on filming time. A lot of people use it as an opportunity to be disparaging about the show, but I don't know any film that doesn't use doubles. Roger Moore sliding down a hillside on skis and shooting off an abyss and pulling a cord which releases a parachute...do people really think it's Roger Moore? They're loonies if they do. And he's a loony if he does it!

The only reason I don't like to publicize it is because I don't want people to watch a show trying to see if they can spot a double. It spoils the programme. Mind you, I recently watched an episode from a few years ago and I couldn't work out if we'd used doubles or not. You aren't watching the actors; you're watching the characters. That's the difference.

Remember, we have to get an episode in the can in five to six days – rain, sunshine or snow. That's a lot of filming, including stunts. Using doubles has certainly helped us to continue the heavy schedule.

Robin Banks, who's played Bill Owen's stand-in for over a decade, got an opportunity to pay his own on-screen respects when he and his fellow doubles were cast as mourners for the funeral sequence of Compo.

It was one of the hardest days filming that the cast and crew were ever likely to be involved in – with feelings having to be put to one side and professionalism brought to the fore to help bring to the screen the emotion of the funeral trilogy.

Last of the Summer Wine

MONDAY 30 AUGUST 1999

SHOOT DAY: 08

Here's a diary of the day's filming of Compo's funeral. If any day was worth recording as an example of the show's professional production, then this was it. Not exactly a typical day, certainly not a particularly happy one, but probably the most important in the show's history:

Breakfast	**0700**
Crew Call	**0800**
On Set	**0830**
Lunch	**1300**
Unit Base	Field near Helme Church, Slades Lane, Helme

Four scenes are to be filmed today – two that take place in a church, one outside the church and one up in the hills. There are 15 artistes appearing, plus 25 extras for the church sequences and four actors' doubles, as well as four pallbearers, a funeral director and a 13-piece brass band.

Vehicles required include a hearse, two funeral limousines, Barry's car, a tractor and several crew cars to help make up the funeral cortège at the end of the day.

07.30 Crew arrive. Most of the equipment has already been set up from the evening before, allowing a slightly later start. Breakfast is available.

07.55 Arrive at muddy field adjacent to church where today's filming is to take place. As befits a bank holiday Monday, the day is cool and breezy.

Alan J. W. Bell sets up the cast, the extras and the authors of this book for Compo's funeral service.

The authors of this book are already in mourners' costumes – Robert has brought his own dark suit and tie, and hastily conceals its Elvis Presley motif; Morris has been given a grey suit by the BBC Costume Department and is wearing a black tie borrowed from the policeman father of a Huddersfield hotel receptionist.

Meet Juliette Kaplan, who is already dressed as Pearl. She's wandering around the field eating a piece of toast.

08.15 Compo's coffin arrives via hearse and is taken into Helme Church. Extras start arriving, including the three men who usually act as doubles for the three lead actors – Tony Simon, Denis Mawn and Robin Banks.

08.30 All extras into church. Solemn atmosphere as crew continue to set up cameras and lighting.

Extras positioned by director Alan J. W. Bell. Morris ends up sitting next to the vicar of the church. Robert takes up the first of several different positions of the day.

08.45 Female cast members arrive on set, including Kathy Staff, Jane Freeman, Sarah Thomas, Thora Hird and Jean Alexander.

09.15 Assembled 'congregation' are filmed singing 'All Things Bright and Beautiful'. Roy Clarke has written a scene of a funeral 'rehearsal', which allows for a certain amount of comedy in the lead-up to the real funeral sequence – Auntie Wainwright's mobile phone going off to alert her that there's a customer in her shop, and so on.

09.36 Female cast members leave to get changed from funeral rehearsal costumes into 'real' funeral attire. Someone points out that perhaps we should all have brought a change of clothing for the sake of continuity.

09.54 Extras repositioned for 'real' funeral filming. Morris replaces Danny O'Dea, who is brought nearer the front. Robert takes up second position on other side of church.

10.15 Peter Sallis and Frank Thornton arrive and are placed in Clegg's and Truly's positions in front row of pews.

10.23 Liz Fraser arrives as the character Reggie, and filming of the funeral proper begins.

11.43 High-angle shot of church has to be re-shot following the discovery of a hair in the gate which has ruined the picture.

12.25 The main cast are released for lunch. Extras stay for close-up shots with Liz Fraser.

12.51 All break for lunch.

14.05 All re-convene at church. Cast have make-up and hair retouched, while crew reposition lighting for new shots. Robert chats up new make-up girl (and fails!).

14.50 Congregation and main artistes dismissed – except Peter Sallis, Frank Thornton and Liz Fraser, who are required for close-up shots.

15.13 Interior shots of church completed. The crew begin setting up cameras and lighting outside church.

15.30 Director Alan J. W. Bell meets up with the conductor to discuss the music the brass band will shortly be playing. The conductor is not sure of the key required, but it has to fit in with the music proposed by composer Ronnie Hazlehurst at the editing stage. A quick call is made on a mobile to Ronnie's home in Jersey.

15.50 The music problem ironed out, the band warm up. And they need to...it's now very cold indeed.

16.03 Local residents and fans watching the filming are used as extras and placed in position outside the church for the next scene.

16.18 Compo's coffin, replete with wellies on top, is brought out of the church to the hearse, accompanied by Clegg and Truly. The band play in the background. The coffin reaches the hearse, but the boots are too high and there is a problem getting it into the hearse. Wellies are turned down by Bill Owen's former dresser. The scene is re-shot.

17.14 Artistes board the cortège limousines for final shot of the day.

17.50 The camera has been set up on top of the hills. Crew are out of shot. A wide shot is filmed of the funeral cortège taking Compo across the hills one last time. Morris and Robert in blue hired Renault form part of cortège along with members of the crew.

17.57 Director calls a wrap and filming finishes.

As shows are recorded, the rushes are sent back to London to the editor, who starts to piece them together according to the wishes of the director. Alan J. W. Bell, having himself been a film editor, shoots only what he knows is required and therefore the job of the editor becomes slightly easier.

Ironically, the editor of *Last of the Summer Wine* is Andrew Wilde, son of former Foggy actor, Brian Wilde.

Summer Wine may seem old-fashioned but it has certainly embraced the burgeoning technology of the 21st century in its editing procedures. That also includes the use of special effects. Yes, *Summer Wine* does use special effects! The millennium Special, in particular, needed the longest computer-generated imaging sessions that *Summer Wine* has ever used. The opening sequence shows Keith Clifford dressed as New Age Man blessing the rising of the sun on a new dawn. In reality, by the time Keith had got up, the sun had already risen and disappeared again behind some clouds.

Four hours of work on special effects later, the sun appears to dawn on a new millennium, taking *Summer Wine* and its much-loved cast into a brand-new era.

Once a show has been edited and before it can be viewed by an audience, there is one final but essential ingredient that must be added to the brew before the fermentation process is complete. Ronnie Hazlehurst spends more time looking at the shows than even the most ardent fan:

It can take me as long as ten hours to get all the syncopation points down for an episode of Summer Wine. *It's a painstaking job. At that point I haven't yet made up my mind if the music needs to enhance the comedy of a scene or not. It's only at a later stage that I decide exactly what to use and what not to use. I love helping the comedy with the music, especially the bits like Nora chasing Compo down the steps with her broom, or composing a little tune to fit in with Howard's footsteps as he walks along the road, or something more militaristic for Foggy's marching.*

I often think that writing the music for Summer Wine *is like writing for the cartoon* Tom and Jerry. *It may not be obvious at the time, but the music enhances the action without you noticing it.*

Of course, sometimes Alan asks me to bend the theme up hill and down dale to fit different situations. We've had the Summer Wine *theme as a march, as a two-step, as a waltz – which, of course, it basically is – and one time he even asked me to bend it around to sound like the theme from* Dallas.

Sometimes we augment the orchestra – usually in the Christmas episodes. We like to go out with a bash and increase the orchestra by maybe three or four different musicians to give it a slightly richer sound for the festive season.

The programme is now complete to play in front of the expectant audience – first at the studio, then finally before the millions who watch the show at home.

One of those millions seeing the show for the first time is the writer of the series, Roy Clarke:

I only watch the programme when the nation sees it. It's the only time it's real for me. The moment I hear the laughter, I know if I've got it right or wrong. It's very necessary for me to know that I'm seeing it along with everyone else.

I have no idea about this medium technically. I know my script and the end product, but nothing in between. And that's enough for me.

CHAPTER SIX

IRREGULAR TIPPLERS

An A–Z of *Last of the Summer Wine* Guest Stars

‘Norman Wisdom’s performance proved so popular that his character, Billy Ingleton, was brought back for a cameo role in the Christmas Show, Extra! Extra!*’*

From the earliest *Summer Wine* days, the three old men of the Yorkshire Dales have been aided and abetted in their childlike antics by a succession of featured players, guest artistes and interesting bit players. As the thematics moved further away from dialogue-packed discussions in the pub and the library, big-name actors were wisely brought in to keep the comedy fresh and the audience interest at a peak.

A seasonal, extended-length Special was made even more special with an Oscar-winning Hollywood name or a British comedy institution drafted into the cast. Extras, walk-ons and surprise appearances have peppered the series, ranging from a pre-stardom role for star of *The Lost World: Jurassic Park*, Peter Postlethwaite, to a quiet homage to classic slapstick with an appearance from Stan Laurel's daughter, Lois. Here, then, is an A to Z celebration of those notable guests who have been enlisted into television comedy's longest-running success story.

Kriss Akabusi

The celebrated British athlete, Olympic medallist and long-term *Summer Wine* fan appeared as a disgruntled milkman opposite Bill Owen in the 1997 Christmas Special, *There Goes the Groom*.

Trevor Bannister

Having forged an impressive acting career in everything from the ITV bitter-sweet comedy *The Dustbinmen* to the West End revival of Neil Simon's *The Odd Couple*, Trevor is still best loved and remembered as the dithering Mr Lucas in the classic BBC comedy *Are You Being Served?* Although absent from the cast reunion for *Grace and Favour*, he ironically guest-starred in the 1992 *Summer Wine* episode *Who's Got Rhythm?* And what did this fine actor, well known for selling menswear in a department store, play in the programme? Why, a tailor of course!

Lynda Baron

A favourite actress in the comic world of Roy Clarke, Lynda had starred in the hit Ronnie Barker situation comedy *Open All Hours* since the first series in 1976. Twenty-five episodes were made until 1985, and many of Barker's stuttering, lustful comic vignettes were based around his lustful, black stocking-obsessed relationship with buxom Nurse Gladys Emmanuel. For the landmark, feature-length *Summer Wine* episode *Getting Sam Home,* Lynda was similarly cast as a sexy icon, albeit of easier virtue, in the shape of Lily Bless 'er. As the narrative pivot for the comedy – she is helped to one final night of passion with the ill-fated Sam by the trio of old men – Baron's performance suitably dripped with northern permissiveness. Her other credits have included the Bill Maynard situation comedy *Oh No – It's Selwyn Froggitt*, the Peter Davison science-fiction romp *Doctor Who: Enlightenment* and the 1992 cinematic innuendo-fest *Carry On Columbus*.

Geoffrey Bayldon

A celebrated small-screen eccentric thanks to his spellbinding title performance as the ancient wizard Catweazle, Geoffrey carved out an inspiring string of supporting grotesques in British film. The Dirk Bogarde thriller *Libel*, Michael Winner's *A Jolly Bad Fellow*, the tongue-in-cheek James Bond adventure *Casino Royale*, Hammer's blood-soaked *Dracula* and a glorious homage to Ernest Thesiger in the 1972 horror compendium *Asylum* all benefited from his expert touch. He was a much-welcome addition to the *Summer Wine* cast as Broadbent in the 1995 episode *Adopted by a Stray*.

Lynda Baron joins the trio as Lily Bless 'er for the 1983 feature-length episode Getting Sam Home.

John Bluthal

Popular today as Frank Pickle in *The Vicar of Dibley,* John has enjoyed a long career in comedy, with regular appearances in *In Sickness and in Health*, a supporting turn opposite Kenneth Williams in *Follow That Camel*, and sketch assignments with Spike Milligan, Michael Bentine and Dick Emery. He played a barber who has a close shave with Brian Wilde in the 1995 *Summer Wine* show *Brushes at Dawn.*

Jean Boht

As Ma Boswell in *Bread*, the popular situation comedy about Liverpudlian dole fraudsters, Jean became one of the country's foremost comic actresses. Representative of the 'greed is good' mentality of the 1980s, the series was a BBC ratings winner for inventive scriptwriter Carla Lane. Married to composer and conductor Carl Davis, Jean had previously made a single appearance in *Last of the Summer Wine* in the early Brian Wilde adventure *Who's Made a Bit of a Splash in Wales Then?* back in 1977. Playing the sister of Jane Freeman's Ivy, Jean's heart-to-heart conversational scene stands as the semi-blueprint for the celebrated Edie coffee mornings of the 1990s.

Jim Bowen

Smashing, great, super, northern club comedian Jim Bowen came fully to the nation's attention as the fast-talking, obvious quipping host of ITV's Sunday evening game show *Bullseye!* Embracing general knowledge, skill at darts and players with an ability to smile graciously when awarded a ceramic, T-shirt-adorned bull, the hugely enjoyable pub quiz-styled entertainment enjoyed a lengthy run. A former school-teacher, Bowen found fame with the series and continued to bask in dart-based in-jokes for self-parody appearances in such shows as *Noel's House Party* and various other schedule time-fillers. He has thrice been invited to wallow in the Yorkshire sunshine for high-profile cameo roles in *Summer Wine*. He was a passer-by in the 1988 Christmas Special *Crums* and, later, a flustered librarian in 1992's *Ordeal by Trousers*. He also made a gag appearance in the very next episode, *Happy Birthday, Howard*.

Paul Bown

Fresh-faced comedy actor adept at anguished, put-upon facial expressions. His starring role as Malcolm Stoneway in the 1987–1993 Granada situation comedy *Watching*, written by Jim Chatfield, made him a small-screen star. Paul played a mild-mannered bird-watcher caught within the observational lifestyle of sisters Liza Tarbuck and Emma Wray. At the end of 1993, Paul was recruited to be a different type of watcher – an alien-spotter – in the science-fiction *Summer Wine* favourite, *Welcome to Earth*.

Duggie Brown

Northern star comedian who found nationwide fame with early, regular, corny joke appearances on Ted Rogers's haven of quizzical kitsch, *3-2-1*. Having recently gone legit to play the Fool in *King Lear*, Duggie guest-starred as Verny in the 1997 *Summer Wine* episode *A Double for Howard*.

Dora Bryan

One of the great names in British show business. Dora's West End musical credits and film appearances have been numerous and prolific, including *Mame*, *Carry On Sergeant* and *A Taste of Honey*, for which she won a British Film Academy award. Through her film work in the 1940s Dora was typecast as a 'tart with a heart' – cockney waitresses and cheerful barmaids. Supporting roles came in such films as Carol Reed's *Odd Man Out* and *The Fallen Idol*, *The Blue Lamp*, the Arthur Lucan and Bela Lugosi horror romp *Mother Riley Meets the Vampire* and the wartime comedy *The Desert Mice* with Sid James. Dora guest-starred in the momentous *Summer Wine* millennium Special as Ros, the flirty

Opposite: Kathy Staff sees off Duggie Brown in A Double for Howard *(1997). Below: Paul Bown tries to convince the men that the aliens are coming in* Welcome to Earth *(1993).*

sister of Thora Hird's Edie. Within the narrative of the script the character has returned to the village for good…so further appearances cannot be ruled out.

Dora Bryan guest-starred in the momentous Summer Wine *millennium Special as Ros, the flirty sister of Thora Hird's Edie.*

Jim Casey

Popular northern working-men's club comedian who made a career out of resurrecting the celebrated music-hall routines of the masterly Jimmy James. Puffing a dog-end cigarette with the style of a spiv, sipping whisky and staggering around the stage in smart dinner clothes, James's major legacy was the cardboard box routine performed with Casey's subsequent colleague, Eli Woods, and Roy Castle. His 'I thought I heard a rustling!', as an entire exotic menagerie is hinted at within the box, brought the house down every time. Jim made three appearances in *Last of the Summer Wine* seasonal Specials, each time teaming with Eli Woods and resurrecting the drunken persona of James in *Crums*, *Welcome to Earth* and *A Leg up for Christmas*.

George Chakiris

For the 1996 *Summer Wine* Christmas special, *Extra! Extra!* director/producer Alan J.W. Bell felt the need for a high-profile, Hollywood, Oscar-winning star. That star was the American music man George Chakiris, who had worked his way out of the chorus and on to film stardom in *Brigadoon* and the Academy Award-winning *West Side Story*. Drama roles in *Flight from Ashiya*, *633 Squadron* and the British film *The High Bright Sun* followed in the mid-1960s. In his *Summer Wine* appearance he played famous Hollywood director Max Bernard, who employs the three old men for his latest epic.

Twang! Keith Clifford amuses pub landlord Ron Backhouse in
How Errol Flynn Discovered the Secret Scar of Nora Batty *(1999).*

John Cleese

The funniest man in Britain – probably – Cleese first found fame in the revue *Cambridge Circus*, radio's *I'm Sorry I'll Read That Again* and television's *The Frost Report*. He starred in the 1967 sketch series *At Last the 1948 Show* and created the world-beating *Monty Python's Flying Circus* with Graham Chapman, Eric Idle, Terry Jones, Michael Palin and Terry Gilliam in 1969. Situation comedy immortality came with two series of *Fawlty Towers* in the 1970s. Films have included *Time Bandits*, *Fierce Creatures*, *Clockwise* and the international blockbuster *A Fish Called Wanda*. Cleese agreed to a gag guest appearance in the 1993 *Summer Wine* Christmas Special, *Welcome to Earth*. Billed as Keith Bread, he played an almost unrecognizable alien-spotter. Cleese had previously been given a tiny walk-by part in Alan J. W. Bell's *Ripping Yarns – Golden Gordon* in 1979.

Keith Clifford

A brilliant character actor and comedian who has successfully trodden the boards as his music-hall hero, Frank Randle, Keith's one-man stage show has won him acclaim as a writer and performer. He has also played the great comedian for BBC radio. More recently, Keith has become a firm, semi-regular favourite as Les Battersby's turkey-providing pal Charlie West in *Coronation Street*. In the 1999 series of *Last of the Summer Wine* he left a major mark as the Yorkshire Robin Hood, Billy Hardcastle, in *How*

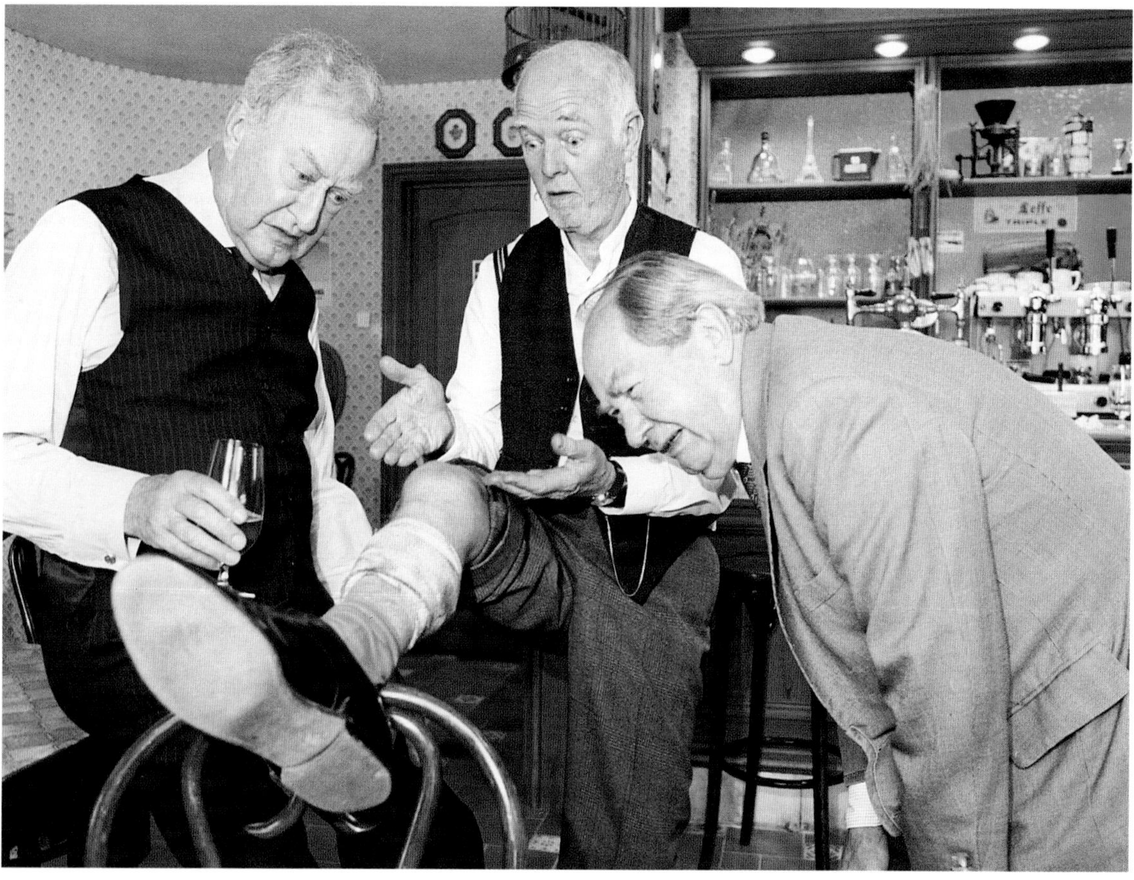

Frank Thornton, Ray Cooney and Peter Sallis in the millennium classic Last Post and Pigeon *(2000).*

Errol Flynn Discovered the Secret Scar of Nora Batty. The character proved so popular that he made a hasty return in the millennium Special and, following Compo's death, Keith crops up twice as Truly of the Yard's next-door neighbour. As for the future, the unique comic charms of Keith Clifford's Billy Hardcastle could make him an invaluable regular. We certainly hope so.

Ray Cooney

The greatest modern-day exponent of stage farce, Cooney has dropped his trousers, offered tea to vicars and slammed countless doors in theatres throughout the world. Frequently in film farces, such as the vastly underrated *Not Now, Comrade*, and notable début presentations, including *One Good Turn* with Geoffrey Davies, as a writer, director and actor, Cooney has made farce his own. His unique art for slapstick clowning was profitably employed for the *Summer Wine* millennium Special, where his wordless, energetic French peasant was a rare treat.

Kenneth Cope

A television legend, thanks to the 1960s' satirical success *That Was the Week That Was* and early soap opera fame in *Coronation Street*, Cope is undoubtedly best remembered for that ultimate cult classic *Randall and Hopkirk – Deceased*. As the sadly demised part of the detective duo, Cope's iconic white suit, continual cries of 'All right Jeff!' and hasty disappearing act were a major part of late-1960s' television viewing. Other television assignments have included *Doctor Who*, *Miss Marple* and *Truckers*. On film he has appeared in such comedies as *Rent-a-Dick*, *Carry On at Your Convenience* and *Carry On Matron*. He guest-starred as Lance in the *Summer Wine* episode *The Love Mobile* in 1997.

Alan Curtis

Our best-loved pantomime villain, Alan has appeared in two *Carry Ons*, *Doctor Who* with William Hartnell, *The Morecambe and Wise Show* and *Whoops Baghdad* with Frankie Howerd. He played Danny in the 1975 episode *A Quiet Drink*.

Anita Dobson

A familiar jobbing actress on stage, television and radio before instant superstardom came with her celebrated performance as Angie Watts in *EastEnders*. A cast member from the beginning of that series, her on-screen chemistry with Leslie Grantham's charmingly nasty 'Dirty Den' kept audiences glued to their screens, and the classic Christmas divorce episode is still considered by many to be the show's dramatic high point. Subsequent television roles have included Len Richmond's hairdressing sitcom *Split Ends*, and the Ray Galton and John Antrobus-penned TB sanatorium-based comedy *Get Well Soon*. Anita was invited to appear in the *Summer Wine* Christmas Special for 1995, *A Leg up for Christmas*, playing a bemused and surprised lady in the pub shocked at the familiar, unrevealed object kept in Compo's matchbox.

Elizabeth Estensen

Despite being a recent, short-lived addition to the cast of *Coronation Street* as former hairdresser Fiona Middleton's mother, Elizabeth is still fondly remembered as one of the *The Liver Birds* in Carla Lane's celebrated BBC situation comedy of the 1970s. Starring as Carol Boswell opposite Nerys Hughes from 1975 through to the close in 1979, her Scouse charm created the perfect working-class heroine. Ironically, just after the series had been revived – with original co-star Polly James – Elizabeth guest-starred as an educational adviser in the 1997 *Summer Wine* episode *How to Create a Monster*.

Yvette Fielding

Undoubtedly the most fanciable *Blue Peter* presenter of the late 1980s – she hosted the popular BBC young people's magazine programme from September 1987 to June 1992 – Yvette first found acting fame as feisty teenager Sandy Shelton in the boarding-house-based children's show *Seaview*. Two series were aired, the first in 1983 and the second in 1985. However, during Yvette's *Blue Peter* days, she made a welcome return to comedy acting, guest-starring as the delectable Fran in the 1988 *Summer Wine* Special, *Crums*.

Liz Fraser

Liz has worked with most of the top comedians of the post-war era, making appearances opposite Jimmy Edwards, Benny Hill and, most frequently, Tony Hancock, with featured roles in several episodes of *Hancock's Half Hour* and the 1961 feature film *The Rebel*. She played the blonde, buxom and sexy daughter of Peter Sellers's union leader Fred Kite in *I'm All Right Jack* and raised temperatures with a seductive striptease in the Ian Carmichael/Sid James boating comedy *Double Bunk*. In the 1970s she made scantily clad appearances in the *Confessions* films, and played the battleaxe wife of Windsor Davies in *Carry On Behind* – a belated return to the

Keith Marsh

Keith has proved a popular situation comedy actor since the 1960s, working with Sid James, Peggy Mount and John Le Mesurier in the ITV hit *George and the Dragon*. Bigger success came with Harry Driver and Vince Powell's racial tension series *Love Thy Neighbour*, in which his role as Jacko gave invaluable, mournful, pub-based support for Jack Smethurst's torrent of dismay and injustice. Marsh played a cheerful chimney sweep in the 1997 *Summer Wine* episode *A Clean Sweep*.

Joe Melia

Having made his big-screen début in the George Cole versus Terry-Thomas heist movie *Too Many Crooks* in 1959, Joe has etched out an impressive career as a useful character player. As part of the criminal gang comprising future *Carry On* legends Sid James and Bernard Bresslaw, Joe left a mark as the whispering thief. Years later, in 1982, he gave his finest film performance as the foul-mouthed Sergeant Len Bonny in *Privates on Parade* with John Cleese and Denis Quilley. He guest-starred in the Series Six *Summer Wine* episode *A Bicycle Made for Three*.

Tony Millan

Familiar from the situation comedy *Lame Ducks*, with Lorraine Chase and Brian Murphy, Tony first made his name as the disgruntled Tucker in *Citizen Smith*. He guest-starred as the pessimistic Gunnershaw in the 1997 *Summer Wine* episode *According to the Prophet Bickerdyke*.

Norman Mitchell

A regular on television, film, radio and the stage, Norman has chalked up appearances in most of the great comedy shows – *Yes, Minister*, *Dad's Army*, *Are You Being Served?*, *Porridge*, *Steptoe and Son*, *Whatever Happened to the Likely Lads?*, *Only When I Laugh* and *Ripping Yarns*, to name but a few. He has featured in five *Carry On* films, the *Pink Panther* series, *Doctor Who*, *Z Cars*, *Crossroads*, *William Tell* and Hammer's *Frankenstein and the Monster from Hell*. Familiar as a rotund, bumbling policeman in everything from classic whodunit *Why Didn't They Ask Evans?* to *Worzel Gummidge*, Norman added *Last of the Summer Wine* to his long list of credits in 1998 when he played the depressed and stony-faced contemporary of the three old men, Coggy Duckworth, in Frank Thornton's first regular episode, *Beware the Oglethorpe*. Brilliantly illustrating what could have been the fate of Compo, Clegg and the others if they had let go of their boyish attitude, Norman's character, sadly, wasn't developed for regular appearances.

Left: Joe Melia in A Bicycle Made for Three *(1982).*
Opposite: Jean Fergusson and Ron Moody in Captain Clutterbuck's Treasure *(1995).*

Ron Moody

Justly renowned for creating the unforgettable character of Fagin for Lionel Bart's *Oliver!* in the 1960s, Ron Moody played the role on the West End stage and in the classic Carol Reed film of *Oliver Twist*. He also resurrected his money-grabbing charms for *Comic Relief* in 1997. Moody's other film credits have included the last Ealing comedy, *Davy*, with Harry Secombe, the legal comedy *A Pair of Briefs* with Liz Fraser, and Michael Bentine's wordless masterpiece *The Sandwich Man*. Moody sparred with Norman Wisdom in *Follow a Star*, turned on the flamboyant theatricals for the Margaret Rutherford Miss Marple film *Murder Most Foul*, and found Hollywood stardom in the 1970 Mel Brooks production *The Twelve Chairs*. Other film appearances include the 1975 horror *The Legend of the Werewolf* and the 1979 Walt Disney fantasy *The Spaceman and King Arthur*, where his Merlin perfectly fitted in with the strong British cast, which included Jim Dale and Kenneth More. Perhaps his most power-ful performance has been as Grimaldi the Clown. Moody excelled as wittily charming con man Lieutenant-Commander Willoughby, retired, in the 1995 *Summer Wine* favourite, *Captain Clutterbuck's Treasure*.

Larry Noble

Celebrated stage comedian and actor, who leapt to fame with the Whitehall farces starring Brian Rix. Larry starred in the original production of *Reluctant Heroes* and created the role of the chirpy French jockey in *Dry Rot*. He played the miserly Mouse in *Summer Wine*'s *A Quiet Drink* (1975). Larry died in 1993 at the age of 78.

Tom Owen

The actor son of Compo himself, Bill Owen, Tom performed with the Royal Shakespeare Company in the 1960s and had a featured role in the Peter O'Toole remake of *Goodbye Mr Chips*. As a family tie-in joke, Tom cropped up briefly as Man at Cash Dispenser in the episode *Cash Flow Problems* in 1991. Following the death of his father, he was recruited to join the cast on a more regular basis. Appearing in the immediate post-funeral show, *From Here to Paternity*, Tom features as Tom Simonite in all the remaining episodes of the 2000 season.

Bert Parnaby

The late northern club comic played the eponymous hero of the 1989 *Summer Wine* show *Come Back, Jack Harry Teesdale*. He proved so popular that he was hastily invited back to re-create his role in *The Charity Balls* (1990).

Trevor Peacock

Popular comedy character actor Trevor Peacock is probably best loved as the ramshackle Jim Trott continually crying 'No, no, no, no, no…yes!' to Dawn French in the Richard Curtis-penned BBC situation comedy *The Vicar of Dibley*. Trevor has also featured in the ITV comedy *Born and Bred* with James Grout and the 1970s' series *Thick as Thieves* with John Thaw. He played Clutterbuck in the *Summer Wine* episode *That's Not Captain Zero* in 1990.

Bryan Pringle

Bryan first came to prominence as part of Joan Littlewood's ground-breaking theatre company, working on *Sparrows Can't Sing* with Barbara Windsor. He became a small-screen comedy star as the discontented Cheese and Egg in the 1969–70

Tom Owen with his ventriloquist's dummy, Waldo.

cast as the flustered, ineffectual wife of the vicar (John Horsley) in the Special episode *Jubilee*.

Norman Wisdom

How can you encapsulate the career of one of British comedy's finest actors in a few lines? Suffice to say that Norman Wisdom is a legend of stage and screen, whose beloved gump figure in the ill-fitting suit can have an audience in the palm of his hand with the merest cry of 'Mr Grimsdale'. Winning a British Academy Award for his first feature film, *Trouble in Store*, in 1953, Norman held residency at Pinewood Studios until 1966, scoring massive cinematic hits with such timeless film classics as *Man of the Moment*, *Just My Luck*, *The Early Bird* and *Up in the World*. Packed with pathos, pretty girls and self-penned songs – including the immortal 'Don't Laugh at Me 'cos I'm a Fool' – these films are priceless examples of variety clowning. A national treasure, Norman was welcomed for a very high-profile guest appearance in the 1995 *Summer Wine* New Year's Day Special, *The Man Who Nearly Knew Pavarotti*. His performance proved so popular that Norman's Billy Ingleton was hastily brought back for a cameo role in the Christmas show, *Extra! Extra!*, the following year. He was knighted in 2000.

Norman Wisdom is a legend of stage and screen whose beloved gump figure in the ill-fitting suit can have an audience in the palm of his hand with the merest cry of 'Mr Grimsdale'.

Eli Woods

With the immortal mutter of 'Are you putting it around that I'm stupid?', the gormless comic foil of Eli has played brilliantly opposite Jimmy James and his spiritual son, Jimmy Casey. Away from the immortal 'rustling box' routine, Eli has stooged for Des O'Connor, Paul Squires and Eric Sykes in the 1988 slapstick classic *Mr H Is Late*. In partnership with the equally drunk characterization of Jimmy Casey, Eli has notched up three memorable supporting turns in *Last of the Summer Wine* Christmas Specials – *Crums*, *Welcome to Earth* and *A Leg up for Christmas*.

'Mr Bell!'
Norman gets into character.

CHAPTER SEVEN

A BUMPER HARVEST

The Complete *Summer Wine* Episode Guide – from *First*... to *Last*...

'Nora, catching Compo in tears, takes pity on him and brings him home, where he tries to get too close to her heaving bosom and gets thrown out.'

GETTING ON SYDNEY'S WIRE, SERIES FOUR, EPISODE TWO

FIRST
OF THE SUMMER WINE
CAST LIST

Mr Clegg *Peter Sallis*
Mrs Clegg *Maggie Ollerenshaw*
Norman Clegg *David Fenwick*
Compo Simonite *Paul Wyett*
Foggy Dewhurst *Richard Lumsden*
Seymour Utterthwaite *Paul McLain*
Nora Batty *Helen Patrick*
Ivy *Sarah Dangerfield*
Wally Batty *Gary Whitaker*
Mr Scrimshaw *Derek Benfield*
Sherbet *Paul Oldham*
Dilys *Joanne Heywood*
Chunky Livesey *Tony Keetch* (Series One)
Jonathan Linsey (Series Two)
Mrs Dewhurst *Linda Beckett*
Mrs Norbury *Patricia England*
Lena *Judy Flynn*
Mexican Admiral *Joe Belcher*

Written by *Roy Clarke*

Pilot produced and directed by
Gareth Gwenlan

Series produced and directed by
Mike Stephens

PILOT EPISODE

FIRST OF THE SUMMER WINE

First transmitted: 3 January 1988

Clegg's day begins with a game of football with his cousin Brad, but he has to be helped home after getting injured. Seymour calls to take Miss Deborah Norbury out in his car, but they get only a few yards when she gets oil on her dress and runs home.

On Sunday, after church and tea, the lads go for a walk on the hills, where they find Foggy on guard duty with the territorials.

On Monday, Clegg has breakfast with his mum and dad. The room is full of Sunlight Soap fumes – it's washday. After work, the lads go to the cinema and then on to the local dance, where the topic of conversation turns to girls.

SERIES ONE
Six Episodes

EPISODE ONE

TALLER EXERCISES

First transmitted: 4 September 1988

Clegg bumps into Wally, who's determined he's going to make himself taller and has devised special exercises. One is to hang from things, such as the parapet of a bridge. He slips and falls into the river.

At work, everyone has a good laugh when Seymour almost runs down the boss, Mr Scrimshaw. Later that morning, in the cellar under the Co-op, Compo and Wally arrive through the grating. Wally wants to be measured to see if he's grown. After tea, Clegg and Compo call for Foggy, and it's on to the cinema, where they meet Wally and Seymour. They decide Wally needs to impress Nora, so they lower him upside down from the balcony. They soon get thrown out.

EPISODE TWO

THAT JUST DOESN'T SUIT

First transmitted: 11 September 1988

Seymour wants to get in touch with Miss Deborah Norbury, and when he finds out that Clegg and Sherbet are delivering a roll of lino to her home, he asks them to deliver a letter. The men have a run-in with Mrs Norbury, who insists they have brought the wrong lino, and they return it to the Co-op.

Wally is determined to make himself taller and has devised special exercises. One is to hang from things, such as the parapet of a bridge. He slips and falls into the river.

The boss, Mr Scrimshaw, has to go out on business and leaves Seymour in charge. He takes advantage of the situation by delivering the replacement roll of lino, but he, too, has a run-in with Deborah's mother. Clegg is in charge of the menswear department, where a customer wants a made-to-measure suit. Clegg has never measured anyone before, which becomes quite apparent when the customer returns for a fitting to find the suit two sizes too small.

Familiar old friends in an earlier time. Left to right: The young Norman Clegg (David Fenwick), the ever-military Foggy Dewhurst (Richard Lumsden) and the gormless Wally Batty (Gary Whitaker).

EPISODE THREE
THE WAY OF THE WARRIOR
First transmitted: 18 September 1988
Clegg's dad is in a panic because he has to go to the Co-op to get a new suit. Compo, meanwhile, has insulted Chunky Livesey and goes to Clegg, Seymour and Sherbet for advice. They tell him to keep his mouth shut. Mr Clegg goes for his suit measurement, and Mr Scrimshaw informs him that one shoulder is shorter than the other. Mr Clegg thinks that means an operation.

Compo is chased by Chunky Livesey but gets to the cinema, where he and the other lads see Foggy doing facial exercises. Foggy's preparing to become a total fighting machine. Compo thinks that's the answer to his problem and talks Foggy into fighting Chunky Livesey in the park. When Chunky arrives with a gang, Foggy and the others run off.

EPISODE FOUR
SNUFF AND STUFF
First transmitted: 25 September 1988
Mr Scrimshaw takes snuff, but where does he keep the tin, the lads wonder? They know it's somewhere in the gents' fitting room and they enlist the help of Wally, who pretends to be trying on some trousers. He bursts in on Mr Scrimshaw just as he's putting the tin inside a chair. The lads decide to add pepper to the snuff, but when Scrimshaw takes a pinch it has no effect. Next they try mouse droppings, but they have no effect either – until Scrimshaw gets home and he fails to understand why his cat keeps licking his moustache.

EPISODE FIVE
THE GREAT INDOORS
First transmitted: 2 October 1988
The lads have all decided to go camping. After half-day closing at the Co-op, they all go into the hills, where Foggy finds a place to put up the tent – in a disused barn. After lighting a fire, which fills the barn with smoke, the lads go off to the pub.

On their return, they find the barn is overrun by a herd of cows. They pack up and decide to go home. Instead of using the handcart they brought with them, they tow it on the back of Seymour's car. They can't all get in the car, so Compo and Sherbet sit on the cart, which tips up, throwing them and the camping gear all over the road. Seymour reverses to pick them up, but the brakes fail and the car ends up in a ditch.

EPISODE SIX
YOUTH WANTED
First transmitted: 9 October 1988
Compo's fed up with working for his mum and decides to apply for a vacancy at the Co-op. Mr Scrimshaw sends him on his way. Clegg says Compo needs to smarten up, and Mr Clegg lets him have one of his old suits. Wally has bought a large motorbike to try to impress Nora, but it falls over every time he gets off.

Scrimshaw still doesn't give in and won't offer Compo the job. The Co-op management committee visit the store enquiring about air-raid precautions. They visit the cellar, where the lads have been smoking. They say they were testing the cellar for leakage in case of gas attacks and that Compo was helping them. He gets the job, much to the disdain of Scrimshaw. That evening the lads go to the cinema, where Ivy and Dilys have put on some make-up – which runs after watching a weepy film.

Seymour asks Foggy what qualifications he would need to become a fighter pilot and is told that candidates are spun round in a chair to test for airsickness.

SERIES TWO
Six Episodes
EPISODE ONE
NOT THEE MISSUS
First transmitted: 3 September 1989
Compo has started taking an interest in girls. Clegg, Seymour and Sherbet play a trick on him while his attention is diverted by a passing lass. They substitute his bucket of clean water for a dirty one – which he only realizes when he starts to wash the Co-op windows.

Foggy needs new pyjamas, so his mother takes him to the Co-op, where Mr Scrimshaw recommends a pair with a stronger gusset.

Seymour is infatuated with Deborah Norbury, and Compo challenges him to go and ask her out – but he's told she's washing her hair. Compo comes up with an idea to help Seymour. He says he'll jump out at Deborah, allowing Seymour to come to her rescue. All goes wrong when Compo jumps out in front of Mrs Norbury by mistake.

EPISODE TWO
COMPO DROPS IN
First transmitted: 10 September 1989
The lads are talking about the Co-op dance the night before, after which Clegg was walked home by Anita Pilsworth. Compo's upset because he couldn't foxtrot and practises with a shop dummy, to the annoyance of Mr Scrimshaw.

Wally's still trying to impress Nora with his motorbike and failing miserably, and Seymour still lusts for the hand of Deborah Norbury. He says he's going to become a fighter pilot. Seymour asks Foggy what qualifications he would need and is told that candidates are spun round in a chair to test for airsickness. The lads spin him round at the Co-op and he gets very dizzy, just as he's supposed to measure up a customer for a suit. That evening, it's off to the cinema, but Compo has no money, so he climbs on to the roof to try to get in without paying. He's caught by the commissionaire when his legs dangle through the ceiling in front of the screen.

EPISODE THREE
THE GYPSY FIDDLER
First transmitted: 17 September 1989
The lads are feeling stiff after pushing a gypsy caravan belonging to Compo's mother.

At work, Clegg is still being pursued by Anita Pilsworth. Foggy, meanwhile, is practising camouflage techniques, and the lads get him to stand in the shop window dressed as a dummy, where he frightens Wally.

At the Co-op, Dilys and Ivy are talking about 'Mister Right' in Compo's hearing, and he gets an idea. He decides to dress as a fortune-teller and, to help Wally, plans to tell Nora that she will marry a 'short, miserable little nit in an LNER cap'. That should do the trick. Up in the hills, Compo tells the girls' fortunes, but while the lads are pushing the gypsy caravan, it runs away, dragging Compo past the girls, who discover the identity of the mysterious fortune-teller.

EPISODE FOUR
AIN'T LOVE DANGEROUS
First transmitted: 24 September 1989
Seymour hears that Deborah Norbury is under the weather and decides to take her some chocolates – but just how does he get past her dreaded mother? Clegg's mother is upset because Mr Clegg's Home Guard uniform has arrived, complete with steel helmet, armband and whistle. Seymour

Left to right: The younger versions of Ivy (Sarah Dangerfield) and Nora (Helen Patrick) gossip with their friend Dilys (Joanne Heywood) in wartime Yorkshire.

tries climbing up a ladder to Deborah's window after Foggy's scouted the ground. Seymour scares Deborah.

At the cinema, Compo is in trouble with Chunky Livesey again – he's been going out with Chunky's girlfriend. Compo manages to sneak past, with Wally sat on his shoulders wearing a long trench coat.

EPISODE FIVE

THE BODY SNATCHERS

First transmitted: 1 October 1989

Foggy's never seen a dead body, so the lads decide to play a trick on him. They pretend to have buried a body from the Co-op funeral service, but it's actually Wally wrapped in a sheet.

Mr Scrimshaw spends most of the day arranging a display of tins, but at closing time the pile collapses. Seymour is still infatuated with Deborah Norbury, and at the cinema he discovers she's upstairs in the circle. Going up to see her, he's tripped by Lena – a girl who's infatuated with Seymour – and he falls into Deborah's lap. She promptly walks out, leaving Lena to sit with him.

Compo has been thrown out of the cinema but sneaks in through the gents' lavatory window, pulling off a cistern in the process and soaking himself.

EPISODE SIX

QUIET WEDDING

First transmitted: 8 October 1989

Clegg's cousin Brad is marrying Dilys today, so the lads make their way to the register office on Compo's motorbike and sidecar, which keeps tipping over. Outside the register office, Seymour sees Lena all dressed up and is rather taken by her. At the reception, Compo has to sit with his trousers round his ankles because he's got oil on them. Mr Clegg reads out the telegrams, one of which is from Brad's air base, recalling him for duty.

Later, the lads are out walking and come across Foggy guarding a bridge. He shows them his bayonet, which drops into the river. They lower Compo over the bridge using Seymour's scarf to hold him. But it stretches with the weight, dropping him into the river.

LAST OF THE SUMMER WINE
CAST LIST

Compo Simonite *Bill Owen*
Norman Clegg *Peter Sallis*
Cyril Blamire *Michael Bates*
Nora Batty *Kathy Staff*
Ivy *Jane Freeman*
Sid *John Comer*
Mr Wainwright *Blake Butler*
Mrs Partridge *Rosemary Martin*
Wally Batty *Joe Gladwin*
Foggy Dewhurst *Brian Wilde*
Gordon Simonite *Philip Jackson*
Wesley Pegden *Gordon Wharmby*
Crusher Milburn *Jonathan Linsey*
Howard *Robert Fyfe*
Pearl *Juliette Kaplan*
Marina *Jean Fergusson*
Seymour Utterthwaite *Michael Aldridge*
Edie Pegden *Thora Hird*
Barry Wilkinson *Mike Grady*
Glenda Wilkinson *Sarah Thomas*
Eli Duckett *Danny O'Dea*
Clem 'Smiler' Hemingway *Stephen Lewis*
Auntie Wainwright *Jean Alexander*
Truly of the Yard *Frank Thornton*

with

Pub Landlords *James Duggan, Joe Marsden and Ron Backhouse*

Village Police Force *Tony Capstick, Kit Kitson and Louis Emerick*

Villagers *Tony Simon, Denis Mawn and Robin Banks*

Written by *Roy Clarke*

Pilot and Series One produced and directed by *Jimmy Gilbert*

Series Two produced and directed by *Bernard Thompson*

Series Three to Five and 1979 and 1981 Specials produced and directed by *Sydney Lotterby*

Series Six produced and directed by *Alan J. W. Bell*

Series Seven produced and directed by *Sydney Lotterby*

1983 Special and subsequent episodes to date produced and directed by *Alan J. W. Bell*

The Summer Wine *cast photo from 1998 – the last time that all the stars of the series got together for their annual picture, before the death of Bill Owen in July 1999.*

COMEDY PLAYHOUSE – THE LAST OF THE SUMMER WINE

OF FUNERALS AND FISH

First transmitted: 4 January 1973

The *Summer Wine* legend begins with Nora Batty hanging out her washing while Compo argues with the television rental man who's come to repossess his set.

Compo goes to meet Blamire, who's walking his neighbour's dog, and the two join Clegg at a church where a funeral is taking place.

After a chat in the old chapel, they move on to the library, where the chief librarian, Mr Wainwright, is making advances to his assistant, Mrs Partridge. The three are thrown out, thanks to Compo's eating, so it's on to Sid's Café, where the owner is arguing with his wife, Ivy, and then on to the pub for a swift pint. On their way home they catch a tiddler in the stream and keep it in a jam jar until they return it to the stream.

SERIES ONE

Six Episodes

EPISODE ONE

SHORT BACK AND PALAIS GLIDE

First transmitted: 12 November 1973

Blamire, needing a haircut, makes a trip to Judd the barber, who, as usual, is full of doom and gloom.

A trip to the library ends in disaster when Blamire and Clegg turn Compo upside down to rid him of evil spirits. They are swiftly ejected from the premises.

At the café, Compo thinks he's lost his key. They try the library, but it's shut. They discover that the librarian, Mr Wainwright, is at a buffet dance, but they are refused entry to the hall. Sid sneaks them in. While playing a game of cards in the back room, Compo realizes he doesn't need the key after all – he's left the back window open.

Clegg and Blamire see how the other half lives when visiting Upperdyke Hall in the third episode of Series One, Pâté and Chips *(1973).*

EPISODE TWO

INVENTOR OF THE 40-FOOT FERRET

First transmitted: 19 November 1973

Blamire feels it's high time that Compo saw the inside of a church. The trio stop off at a barn with their flasks of tea before retrieving a kite from a tree. Then it's off to the library where – as always – Wainwright is making advances to Mrs Partridge.

At the café, Ivy and Sid are arguing when the men arrive, and they finally persuade Compo to visit the church. Not exactly religiously enlightened, Compo claims the only thing he felt was an itchy nose.

EPISODE THREE

PÂTÉ AND CHIPS

First transmitted: 26 November 1973

The trio move up in the world with a visit to Upperdyke Hall with Compo's nephew Chip and his family. After a difficult trip in Chip's claustrophobic van, trapped by kids and a dog, the men enjoy their browse around the stately home until they are left to look after the children. Inside the mansion, the visitors are expecting the imminent arrival of the duke and duchess, only to be greeted by the regal entry of Compo and Chip's dog. The men are thrown out and stop off at the pub on the way home.

EPISODE FOUR

SPRING FEVER

First transmitted: 3 December 1973

Nora is panic-stricken to find Compo cleaning his home. Blamire can't understand why Compo is late at the library. Clegg blames it all on the onset of spring.

The next day Compo is caught buying a suit, and they soon discover he's advertised for a housekeeper. He meets her off the bus and treats her to a slap-up meal of mushy peas at Sid's Café. Realizing that Compo has nothing of interest to offer her, she leaves, allowing Compo to resume his pursuit of Nora Batty.

Episode Five
THE NEW MOBILE TRIO
First transmitted: 10 December 1973
A visit to a road safety exhibition prompts Clegg to buy a car from a man called Walter, whose advertisement he saw at the library. The men discover that Walter had tried to teach his dog to ride a bike. Clegg is equally unsuccessful with Walter's old banger and collides with a tractor when the brakes fail. Not one to give up, Clegg tries buying a car from a reputable dealer but, yes, while testing this one, they hit the tractor all over again.

Blamire gives instructions to Clegg, as Compo looks on with amusement in the Series One episode The New Mobile Trio *(1973).*

Episode Six
HAIL SMILING MORN OR THEREABOUTS
First transmitted: 17 December 1973
Pictures in the library attract Blamire to photography. Meeting up with Compo, they go to Clegg's house where he's sorting out his camping equipment. Armed with camera, Blamire snaps the others and suggests they take pictures of the beautiful sunrise by camping on the hills. A thunderstorm brings that dream to an end, and the trio spend the night in a barn. They oversleep and miss the sunrise.

SERIES TWO
Seven Episodes

Episode One
FORKED LIGHTNING
First transmitted: 5 March 1975
Various accidents on his bicycle prompt Clegg to get it repaired. At the café, Sid has a go but fails, so Clegg decides to take it back to the shop in Huddersfield where he bought it 30 years previously. Not allowed to take the bike on the bus, Clegg rides it there to discover that the shop closed down several years earlier. Sid has another go at fixing it and, proud of the job he's done, gives it a ride around outside

the café. He crashes. The trio run off into the distance, chasing Clegg's front wheel down the hill.

EPISODE TWO
WHO'S THAT DANCING WITH NORA BATTY THEN?
First transmitted: 12 March 1975

At the library, Compo tells Blamire and Clegg that his neighbour Gloria is returning to Australia. After being thrown out of the library by the new assistant, Miss Probert, they go for a stroll, during which they meet Shep the lollipop man, who hates children. They ask to borrow his piano for Gloria's farewell party at the café. Compo gets stuck up a tree as they transport the piano to the café. At the party, he manages to get a dance with Nora Batty, which comes to a swift end when he treads on her foot.

EPISODE THREE
THE CHANGING FACE OF RURAL BLAMIRE
First transmitted: 19 March 1975

Blamire decides it's time to find a job, and he joins ShinyGlow Products, which is run by a dubious Welshman called Oswald Green. Blamire takes the company's tatty old van to go to sell the ShinyGlow All-Purpose Cleaner with the help of Compo and Clegg. In the van, Blamire accidentally sprays himself in the face, which turns darker and darker. The others don't tell him. Blamire has trouble selling the product!

At the café he catches sight of his reflection in the mirror. Blamire gives up, but on seeing an advert for another job, he applies again, only to find that the company is also run by Oswald Green.

EPISODE FOUR
SOME ENCHANTED EVENING
First transmitted: 26 March 1975

'How much longer?' enquires Blamire as the men wait for Compo's television set to be returned. Compo gets thrown out of the library again – this time for playing a radio – so it's off to the café, where he moons over photos of his beloved Nora. That night, his request for 'Some Enchanted Evening' is played on the radio, dedicated to Nora. Compo thinks his luck has changed when there's a knock at the door, but it's only Wally Batty, who's decided to go home to his mam.

A week later, Blamire and Clegg are bored without Compo. They find him dressed up and clean-shaven and preparing to move in with Nora Batty. Compo's plan backfires when the two play a trick on him, pretending Wally has gone for good. The old Compo is soon back!

The original trio, Clegg (Peter Sallis), Blamire (Michael Bates) and Compo (Bill Owen), clown around by the water.

EPISODE FIVE
A QUIET DRINK
First transmitted: 2 April 1975

The trio pay a visit to the Clothier's Arms, where among the customers is 'Mouse' – a man renowned for never buying anyone a drink. The men take up the challenge to con Mouse into buying a round. They place Tina – a drunken lady whose husband is undertaking some dodgy deals in the pub – in Mouse's car. Returning to the bar, they challenge Mouse to see how long they can all sit with an empty glass before one of them stands up. Tina's husband comes running into the pub shouting that his wife is racing round the car park in Mouse's car. Mouse is up and out and loses the bet, much to the trio's delight.

At the party, Compo manages to get a dance with Nora Batty.

EPISODE SIX
BALLAD FOR WIND INSTRUMENTS AND CANOE
First transmitted: 9 April 1975

A quiet time by the river is disturbed by the arrival of Arnpepper – a man who's fallen out of his canoe. After retrieving it, they dry off in a barn and decide to buy the canoe.

Trying it out the next day, the canoe drifts away and the race is on to get it back. Hanging Compo over a bridge and dropping him into the canoe is one way to grab it back, but they miss and he ends up in the river.

Blamire suggests proper swimwear so their clothes don't get wet again. All is well until the canoe drifts off again, leaving them wondering how to get home in just their costumes. Things go well until a coachload of pensioners turns up.

EPISODE SEVEN
NORTHERN FLYING CIRCUS
First transmitted: 16 April 1975

At the library, the trio read of the death of a friend. Clegg decides they should go and buy his motorcycle and sidecar from his widow. But after buying it, getting it to work is not as easy as the men had hoped. Compo gets kitted out in the right gear but catches his shin on the starter and his nose starts bleeding from the pressure of the goggles. At last it's time for a ride, but they end up pushing the motorbike back to the pub with a puncture.

SERIES THREE

Seven Episodes

EPISODE ONE

THE MAN FROM OSWESTRY

First transmitted: 27 October 1976

'It's times like this when I'm getting low on fags that I miss Cyril Blamire.' Compo's comment is the first indication that Blamire's character has left the series, and heralds the arrival of Foggy Dewhurst. Blamire's departure is confirmed by a letter read out by Clegg in the café.

Compo remembers Foggy as having a blue uniform and a white face 'like a pencil with a rubber on the end'. They go off to meet him at the bus station. After dropping off some of his luggage, they end up at the local pub, where Foggy defends the honour of his regimental scarf and ends up with a nosebleed after Big Malcolm hits him. The scarf causes more problems when it gets entangled around the wheel of the trolley that the men are using to transport Foggy's luggage.

EPISODE TWO

MENDING STUART'S LEG

First transmitted: 3 November 1976

'Old Shagnasty', a.k.a. Mr Wainwright, throws the trio out of the library, so they're off to mend Stuart's leg at the café. Sid is in trouble with Ivy for not fixing the slates on the roof. Stuart says his knee clicks when he walks. All the men get on the floor and listen as he walks by. Foggy takes charge of the operation to fix the café roof. He attaches a rope to Compo and the other end to Sid's van to help pull him up. It all goes wrong when Sid loses control of the van and Compo ends up hanging from the roof.

EPISODE THREE

THE GREAT BOARDING HOUSE BATHROOM CAPER

First transmitted: 10 November 1976

It's off to Scarborough for the weekend in this two-parter, which concludes with the next episode. The men, joined by Sid and Ivy from the café, crowd into Gordon's van for their trip away. After lunch at their boarding house, it's time for a walk along the promenade.

Back at the boarding house, Foggy and Clegg can't understand why Compo keeps going to wash his feet in the bathroom. As luck would have it, Nora Batty's staying in the same house and Compo's trying to catch her in a state of undress. As the men go to bed, Foggy investigates the scratching noise coming from the cupboard, only to discover that Compo has brought his ferrets with him.

EPISODE FOUR

CHEERING UP GORDON

First transmitted: 17 November 1976

After an early morning swim in the sea – Foggy swims while the others laugh – the men have breakfast and go to visit a Scarborough church. They get kicked out when Compo's ferrets escape. Down on the beach, Foggy observes Gordon through his binoculars and decides he needs cheering up, but a ride on a donkey doesn't work. In a café, Compo tells Gordon that he'll teach him how to chat up women if Gordon teaches him how to fish. The weekend ends in disaster when the fishing line gets wrapped around a beach buggy and Compo picks up some women who frighten the men!

EPISODE FIVE

THE KINK IN FOGGY'S NIBLICK

First transmitted: 24 November 1976

A brief game of football ends in great pain for Foggy, who informs the men that his real forte is playing golf – though he hasn't actually played since 'that fool Hitler' invaded Poland in 1939. Goaded by the others, he challenges Sid to a round but finds that his clubs have warped. Unperturbed, they make their way to the course, where Compo embarrasses the others by being the loudest and scruffiest person in the clubhouse bar.

Foggy has a few problems with his clubs – he can't actually hit the ball – and Compo disappears when he discovers that the club pays for balls that are found on the course. Compo earns himself some money by collecting balls and undercutting the club prices. Meanwhile, Foggy's game goes on so long that he has to finish it by gaslight!

EPISODE SIX

GOING TO GORDON'S WEDDING

First transmitted:1 December 1976

The trio are going to nephew Gordon's wedding. Compo has bought an alarm clock as a present but has no wrapping paper. Foggy attempts to borrow some from Nora but instead ends up with a yard brush in his face. At the church, Foggy tries his hand at photography, while Compo is having problems with his buttonhole. He throws the flower on to the floor, the best man slips on it, breaks his leg and ends up in hospital.

Compo is appointed the new best man, to the chagrin of

Horsey, horsey don't you stop... Foggy and Compo go clippity-clop in Isometrics and After *(1976).*

the others. During the ceremony they realize the ring has gone to the hospital with the best man, so they go and collect it. All then appears to be going well until Compo's alarm clock goes off.

EPISODE SEVEN
ISOMETRICS AND AFTER
First transmitted: 8 December 1976
'We are all unfit,' proclaims Foggy, and decides on a fitness regime for them all. He introduces them to isometrics – the method of exercising without taking your vest off!

The first lesson is to lift a table off the floor by one leg. They try it at the library, where the tables are actually screwed to the floor. They manage to lift one and are promptly thrown out. After some jogging, it's down to the café, before Foggy decides that the men should try horse-riding – an excellent idea if only the creatures would stop!

SERIES FOUR
Eight Episodes

EPISODE ONE
FERRET COME HOME
First transmitted: 9 November 1977
Compo's lost a ferret and thinks it might have got into Nora's house via her washing basket. His entry to her house is barred by the customary yard brush up the hooter.

After a visit to the café with the others, it's back home, where Compo tries to contact Wally Batty by tapping on the wall. Wally arrives and informs them that the ferret is upstairs, but they'll have to wait until he gives the sign before they can retrieve it. To avoid looking suspicious, Foggy suggests they all walk around pretending to look for a contact lens. Soon a crowd has gathered, all looking for the non-existent lens, including Nora, whose attention is diverted long enough to retrieve the rodent.

EPISODE TWO
GETTING ON SIDNEY'S WIRE
First transmitted: 16 November 1977
Sitting by a stream, the trio can't remember what day it is. For a man of Foggy's military precision, this is too distressing, and he goes off to check on the fish life to take his mind off it. He ends up in the water. At the café, Sid is trying to install a doorbell. The boys try to take over. Foggy uses what he thinks is a salt cellar to unravel the wire, but it turns out to be pepper and soon all eyes are watering. Ivy chucks them out.

Nora, catching Compo in tears, takes pity on him and brings him home, where he tries to get too close to her heaving bosom and gets thrown out. The men return to the café, the doorbell finally gets fixed but the noise startles Ivy and they get evicted all over again.

EPISODE THREE
JUBILEE
First transmitted: 23 November 1977
Patriotic as ever, Foggy wants to do something for the Queen's Silver Jubilee celebrations and goes to see the vicar, who's in charge of local events. The men are promptly enrolled in the pageant. At the café, Ivy has been drilling holes in Sid's golf clubs. The men arrive, and Sid informs them that Ivy wants him to take her dancing. The trio get him to help with the pageant preparations instead, though when he discovers they have to dress up as sailors and stand on the back of the float driven by the vicar's wife, he wishes he hadn't got involved in the first place.

EPISODE FOUR
FLOWER POWER CUT
First transmitted: 30 November 1977
Foggy falls off a wall and Clegg almost gets run over by a hearse carrying former lollipop man and friend Murdoch. The trio pay their respects to Murdoch by visiting his open coffin and later attending his funeral.

Clegg seems to have taken an interest in flowers and says that they have feelings. Later, at the café, he explains that plants react to music, so off they all go into the woods with recorders, where the only things that move are some worried ramblers in the bushes. At the café again, Clegg offers the other two and Sid a pound each if they play to some flowers without seeing a reaction. A poor rendition of 'Greensleeves' gets a reaction all right – from Ivy, who kicks them all out.

EPISODE FIVE
WHO'S MADE A BIT OF A SPLASH IN WALES THEN?
First transmitted: 7 December 1977
Foggy is having a dalliance with a lady in Wales – too much for the men, who want to find out what's going on. Sid decides to take Ivy to see her sister and then to offer Foggy a ride back with them. Sid fancies a drink, so Clegg has to drive. Not the most confident of drivers, Clegg has problems reversing the car into a

Having a wonderful Christmas time! The trio visit their old chum Edgar in hospital, in Small Tune on a Penny Wassail. *Opposite: The three stars pose for a publicity photograph for this classic 1978 Christmas Special.*

parking space on arrival in Wales. Eventually, he parks it... on Foggy's foot. One visit to the hospital later and Foggy finds himself being pushed around a park in a wheelchair, which goes out of control – but he has the last laugh as Clegg and Compo end up in the pond!

EPISODE SIX
GREENFINGERS
First transmitted: 14 December 1977
It's Saturday morning and time for a visit to the market, where Foggy expresses his disbelief at the size of the vegetables on sale. Clegg suggests a visit to Lewis Bickerdyke, who's renowned for his fresh veg. An encounter with Bickerdyke's dog makes the visit impossible.

Walking past a vegetable wholesaler, the men catch sight of a huge carrot that acts as a sign hanging up outside the store. Clegg suggests borrowing it and walking past Bickerdyke's to make him think they're growing bigger vegetables than he is. Later, they come across Wally Batty at the pub. He's drunk but quickly sobers up when he sees the huge carrot.

CHRISTMAS SPECIAL 1978
SMALL TUNE ON A PENNY WASSAIL
First transmitted: 26 December 1978
It's Christmas Day. Compo is bored and Clegg doesn't like Christmas anyway. Foggy takes them to the hospital to visit Edgar. Compo draws attention to himself when he demonstrates his new digital watch which lights up in the dark – he gets under Edgar's bed to prove it.

Back at Clegg's, Christmas dinner is eaten before the presents are handed out. Foggy and Clegg have bought each other the same jumper. Compo has bought them both a watch. Sid and Wally have managed to escape for a while but nearly get run down by Compo, who comes tearing down the road on a skateboard, colliding with the Salvation Army band.

EPISODE SEVEN
A MERRY HEATWAVE
First transmitted: 1 January 1978
Compo thinks that Nora Batty resembles Dorothy Lamour. It must be the heat.

Pondering the mysteries of the universe and cold tea – the ever-cheerful Ivy (Jane Freeman) continues to make life a bundle of fun for her poor husband Sid (John Comer).

At the café, the men hear that Nora's brother in Australia is unlikely to see another Christmas, so Foggy has an idea to make a film of an old-fashioned Christmas to send to him. The snag is that it's midsummer and they're in the middle of a heatwave, and just where do you find holly at this time of year?

Filming begins and Clegg creates snow by pouring soap flakes out of the window above the café. He gets trapped, and Compo tries to rescue him with a ladder.

In the middle of this fiasco the postman arrives with a telegram for Nora, informing her that her brother has made a startling recovery and has run off with his nurse!

EPISODE EIGHT
THE BANDIT FROM STOKE-ON-TRENT
First transmitted: 4 January 1978
The trio are wary of Amos Hames when they see him coming out of the police station. Amos informs the men he's only around for the day and asks for directions to the bank. They think he intends to rob it, and Foggy decides to protect innocent bystanders from getting hurt by directing the traffic away from the bank. They end up getting chased into a chip shop by a learner driver.

Outside again, they try to stop a security van delivering to the bank. Foggy gets arrested before finding out that all Amos wanted was to cash a cheque.

SERIES FIVE
Seven Episodes

EPISODE ONE
FULL STEAM BEHIND
First transmitted: 18 September 1979
Clegg's ironing when Foggy comes in blowing a whistle and waving a flag – excitedly explaining that the railway line

between Keighley and Oxenhope is about to be reopened. He duly marches the men off to witness the event. On the way they study a train as it passes them under a bridge and duly covers them in dirty steam.

At the station, they find the railway engine and Compo accidentally starts it up, jumping off as it moves away – driverless. Foggy takes charge and he and Clegg hang Compo over a bridge to try to drop him on to the train. He misses! They manage to board the train and eventually stop it, but as they walk away up the line, it starts to chase them.

Episode Two
THE FLAG AND ITS SNAGS
First transmitted: 25 September 1979

Foggy has a vision. The others wish he didn't have to drag them up a hill to tell them what it is. He wants a flag to hang from a post at the top of the hill, to put pride back into the countryside. Finding the flagpole isn't a problem – there's one behind the bicycle shed. Getting it up the hill is another matter. Mules are the answer and Willis is the man who's got them. He may have them, but trying to round them up is another thing altogether.

Episode Three
THE FLAG AND FURTHER SNAGS
First transmitted: 2 October 1979

Foggy collects his flag from the railway station, but when Compo tries to open it, the string gets caught in his zip. At the café, Ivy and Sid are having a private party upstairs for The Royal and Ancient Order of Bullocks – of which Wally Batty is a member.

Foggy takes the others to meet the commodore – who used to be in charge of the sea cadets – and asks to borrow their flagpole. Aided by Wally and the Bullocks, they raise the flag and all appears well until the flagpole collapses and all Foggy can see is a banner held by Compo and Clegg with the word 'bullocks' written across it.

Episode Four
DEEP IN THE HEART OF YORKSHIRE
First transmitted: 9 October 1979

Foggy, Clegg and Compo are in the woods when they catch sight of café owner Sid heading towards the hills with a bedding roll under his arm. At the pub, they meet Nora Batty, who can't find her Wally – he's also been seen heading towards the hills with a bedding roll.

From a distance the trio see signs of a fire burning, and they come across Sid and Wally dressed as cowboys. Sid insists it's all part of a planned pageant. Some of the volunteers have gone home, so Foggy, Clegg and Compo take their places as Big Chief Corporal Signwriter, Mrs Chief Corporal Signwriter and Little Gaping Fly. (Guess who's who!)

Episode Five
EARNSHAW STRIKES BACK
First transmitted 16 October 1979

Not for the first time, our trio are bored, and at Compo's house Foggy decides it's time to go swimming. But at the pool all the water has dried up. Foggy upsets the others by berating Yorkshire in general, and local mythical god Earnshaw in particular. They try to help a man in a plaster cast repair his car – with the usual disastrous results.

Back at Compo's, Foggy still can't be persuaded that there are any Yorkshire gods. His disbelief is brought to an abrupt conclusion when, thanks to Wally hitting a nail through a pipe on the other side of the wall, Foggy gets soaked through.

Episode Six
HERE WE GO INTO THE WIDE BLUE YONDER
First transmitted: 23 October 1979

Compo decides he wants to try his hand at hang-gliding. At the café, the men bump into Wally, who's been told he has to take his wife Nora out more. Sid is trying to mend a microwave oven. Compo asks Wally if he can build him a hang-glider, but Foggy insists that what's called for is getting practice at being high up. He marches the men off to a viaduct, but they escape to a pub first. After a couple of pints, Compo challenges Foggy to see who can climb highest up a tree. A few minutes later Clegg has to call the fire brigade to rescue them.

Episode Seven
HERE WE GO AGAIN INTO THE WIDE BLUE YONDER
First transmitted: 30 October 1979

The second half of this two-parter sees Foggy showing the men the spot he's picked for Compo's flight, down at the reservoir. While waiting for Wally and Sid, Foggy takes Compo and Clegg for some limbering-up exercises.

Wally and Sid arrive with their flying machine, which resembles a giant pigeon. The first flight, from the roof of the barn, is unsuccessful, with the only thing taking off being Compo's trousers. After two further attempts, and with Sid and Wally falling out of the rescue boat, Foggy gets Compo on top of Sid's van to help him build up speed. Disaster beckons.

Christmas Special 1979
AND A DEWHURST UP A FIR TREE
First transmitted: 27 December 1979

Foggy decides to do his Christmas shopping early this year – in the middle of the summer! The trio are soon thrown out of the shops. At the café, Foggy shows off his military prowess and challenges Compo to come at him with a knife. Ivy comes at Compo with a metal tray.

Listen to the banned! Clegg and Foggy are less than impressed with Compo's musical talents.

At the pub Foggy meets a man called Big Eric who claims to work for the Forestry Commission, who sells him 100 Christmas trees cheap. The only snag is that they have to go and collect them from the forest. Meanwhile, Nora and Ivy are trying to devise a way of dealing with Compo's amorous advances. The men find the trees but they are crawling with insects. Back at the café, Nora and Ivy ambush Compo with passionate advances, which, for once, leave him screaming.

CHRISTMAS SPECIAL 1981
WHOOPS
First transmitted: 25 December 1981
After a two year gap the trio return for this festive episode, which begins with Compo reminding the others that Christmas is fast approaching – but they just can't seem to get into the spirit of it all. The men go off to find two old friends, Chuffer Enright and Splutter Lippinscale. Chuffer was renowned throughout the Dales for his duck impressions, but after seeing his dodgy knee, they give up on him. They leave a message for Splutter to meet up for a drink.

Christmas Eve arrives and Compo is depressed because Nora is ignoring him.

Sid and Wally arrive with Chuffer and Splutter, and off they go climbing up lampposts in the pub car park. Christmas arrives with the trio jumping off a moving bus like they used to when they were younger.

SERIES SIX
Seven Episodes

EPISODE ONE
IN THE SERVICE OF HUMANITY
First transmitted: 4 January 1982
A pile of clothes at the river bank sparks off fears among the men of a suicide attempt. Foggy pushes Compo and Clegg into the river to take a look, but a man in a canoe turns up to reclaim his garments. Foggy thinks that forming a rescue party for such eventualities is what's called for, and the men go off to look for equipment they can use in future rescues. Hearing a large crash, the men go to see if they can help, but Foggy gets a bloody nose for interfering.

Wally needs help to rescue Nora from under a bed, which

Foggy, Compo and Clegg take refuge in a barn. This set was often used as a back-up, studio-like location if the Holmfirth weather turned nasty and held up filming.

collapses when they lift it and she chases them out of the house. After removing the ladder from the side of a house – not noticing a man is now stranded on the roof – it's back to the river, where this time Foggy and Clegg end up in the water.

Episode Two
CAR AND GARTER
First transmitted: 11 January 1982

'How do you get marmalade off a ferret?' asks Compo, as another day begins with our lovable trio.

New character Wesley Pegden is introduced, as the men meet this man in greasy overalls who spends most of his time in a shed tinkering with cars. Taking Wesley to the café does nothing to cheer up Ivy, who's fed up with dirty and scruffy men frequenting her establishment. The men try to think of a way to lift Ivy's opinion of Wesley. Back at his shed, Sid gets dressed up in leathers to test-drive Wesley's car, which never starts. When Ivy sees Sid, she belts him, so Compo ends up giving Nora a garter and undertaking the test-run himself. The car starts, but after a few feet the engine blows up.

Episode Three
THE ODD DOG MEN
First transmitted: 18 January 1982

Observing a man taking his dog for a walk, Foggy hits on the idea of making money by walking people's canine friends. He gets a shock at one house, where he is mistaken for the owner's wife's lover. The men meet Wally, who – as always – is depressed. He invites them back to his house, but Nora kicks them out.

The dog-walking business turns more sour when the trio find themselves being chased by an Old English sheepdog. They take refuge in the back of a horsebox – but so does the dog!

Episode Four
A BICYCLE MADE FOR THREE
First transmitted: 25 January 1982

A bicycle is not made for three to ride on, as the men discover when they try riding on Clegg's bike down a hill – and fall off. When they hear the prices that local shopkeeper Percy wants for three second-hand bikes, they take up his offer of building their own from spares in his garage. Calling at the café, they discover it has been decorated and, because of their oily clothes, Ivy makes them eat outside.

The bikes are finally finished. Compo's saddle is too high, and Foggy's wheel is off-balance, making him look like a funfair carousel horse as he bobs along the countryside. Foggy builds a three-seater, six-wheel bicycle on which the men can sit next to each other as they ride. All goes well until they are riding down a hill at speed and hit the brakes at the same time. Ouch!

EPISODE FIVE
ONE OF THE LAST FEW PLACES UNEXPLORED BY MAN
First transmitted: 1 February 1982
Compo wants to know what life is like in Nora Batty's bedroom. On a visit to the café, the men meet Wally Batty, who's off to the auction rooms. At home, Compo is getting smartened up because – the men discover – he wants his photograph taken in Nora's boudoir. Wally buys a wardrobe at the auction, and Compo hides inside to sneak his way into the house. Nora doesn't like the wardrobe and pushes it down the stairs, leaving Compo all shook up.

EPISODE SIX
SERENADE FOR TIGHT JEANS AND METAL DETECTOR
First transmitted: 8 February 1982
Compo's wearing new trousers – a pair of tight jeans, to be precise. Foggy made him buy them from Duggie's second-hand shop, where Clegg got talked into purchasing an old metal detector.

At the café, Foggy offers to find a missing screw from Ivy's hair dryer, which Sid is trying to repair, but she sends them out to test the metal detector. Up on the hills, Foggy gives Compo some money to hide to see if they can locate it with the detector, but Compo pockets it. Back at the café, Sid is happy to use the detector to find the screw until it gives out a high-pitched deafening squeal and he smashes a load of crockery.

EPISODE SEVEN
FROM WELLIES TO WET SUIT
First transmitted: 15 February 1982
In Bill Owen's favourite episode – shown again after his death in July 1999 – the day begins with our trio coming across Sid at the river, where he's swimming under water in a wet suit. Compo buys it off him and practises walking about in it with a pair of flippers on. He jumps off a bridge, but the water underneath is only a foot deep.

After causing havoc at the café and the newsagent's, Foggy persuades Compo to try water-skiing. Wally makes the skis and Sid uses his motorbike to pull him along the water – which doesn't go according to plan, with Compo spending more time in the water than on it.

CHRISTMAS SPECIAL 1982
ALL MOD CONNED
First transmitted: 25 December 1982
Our trio are going away this Christmas to a cottage with all modern conveniences. Everything is going to be fine. After all, Foggy's organized the trip. While at the station, Foggy becomes entangled with the newspapers of a group of men and he's thrown out of the waiting-room.

After the train journey and a lift on the back of an old tractor, they come across the cottage, which turns out to be a tatty old caravan. They can't find the key and push Compo through the window. They try to light a fire to warm themselves, but end up setting the caravan alight. They decide to try to get home by boat, but finally have to use an upside-down portable lavatory to take them down the river.

SERIES SEVEN
Six Programmes
EPISODE ONE
THE FROZEN TURKEY MAN
First transmitted: 30 January 1983
'What exactly is it we're looking for?' asks Foggy, as the men make their way up into the Yorkshire hills. The answer is an old treacle tin that Compo buried back in 1932.

After the customary eviction from the café, the trio make their way to the pub, where Compo and Clegg decide to find Foggy a woman, although he's not aware of their plan. They approach the barmaid and inform her that Foggy is an eccentric millionaire who made his money from frozen turkeys. As Foggy approaches the bar, he comes across a man with a Rubik's Cube. Interfering as always, he takes over the game but drops it when the barmaid tries to chat him up.

Back on the hills, Foggy is determined to find Compo's old can. Compo informs the men that when he buried it half a century ago, he was on roller skates. Foggy borrows two scooters to try to reproduce the scene, but Compo loses control and ends up in a field full of manure.

EPISODE TWO
THE WHITE MAN'S GRAVE
First transmitted: 6 February 1983
Sid's mending a mixer (no, not Ivy) at the café when the men arrive, this time followed shortly afterwards by Wally, who's sneaked away from Nora. Wally's depressed. Foggy decides that Wally should get out more, but on approaching Nora, ends up with a face full of mop. Compo has the idea of replacing Wally with Clegg – after all, Nora takes little notice of her husband anyway. The swap is done outside the

house, where Clegg takes over the cleaning of a carpet. All is well until Nora needs a hand moving some steps upstairs, and that's when she discovers Clegg. The men try to sneak Wally back by hiding him in a pram, but it runs away!

EPISODE THREE
THE WAIST LAND
First transmitted: 13 February 1983

Before a trip out for the day on their bikes, Compo is hungry, so the men stop off at a barn for a snack. While there, Foggy hears noises and believes the barn is haunted – but it turns out to be a group from the local health farm sneaking out for something to eat. Realizing the financial potential in selling them illicit food, they take them to the café, where Nora has started working as a waitress.

The trio escort the others back to the health farm with their ill-gotten gains and Compo is thrown over the wall to unlock the back gate of the establishment. The trio are discovered selling food at the health farm and have to pretend to be slimmers – they escape eventually by pretending to be joggers.

EPISODE FOUR
CHEERING UP LUDOVIC
First transmitted: 20 February 1983

After a stroll through the fields, the trio come across their old friend Ludovic, who's had rather too much to drink. On enquiring why he's so miserable, he shows them that he's bought a tatty old van. Compo drops them in it when he asks for a lift and, because Ludovic is drunk, Clegg has to drive.

On the move, Ludovic shows them how the van divides in two with a partition, but without realizing, he inadvertently knocks Clegg out of the vehicle and on to the road. Clegg bumps into Wally and Nora, who give him a lift on their motorbike, and when they catch up with the van, panic has set in as the others have realized that no one is driving it!

EPISODE FIVE
THE THREE ASTAIRES
First transmitted: 27 February 1983

The vicar is looking for volunteers for a concert party, and Foggy drags Compo and Clegg along to audition. Their first challenge is to get past the vicar's wife – a nervous lady who wants nothing to do with the concert. Once in the hall and after demolishing most of the scenery, Foggy tells the vicar that the men are going to perform a hat and cane dance. Compo finds a box of costumes but becomes trapped in a suit of armour.

To try to get him home without drawing attention to themselves, they wrap his head in bandages, disguising the helmet. Nora sees them and thinks Compo is hurt. He tries to take advantage and goes into her house. When the bandages come off, Compo is kicked out. Getting the helmet off doesn't prove easy. The only thing left is to ram it into a telegraph pole, which seems to do the trick.

EPISODE SIX
THE ARTS OF CONCEALMENT
First transmitted: 6 March 1983

With his military prowess, Foggy tries to teach the men to blend into backgrounds without being noticed. To prove the point, he gets dressed up as a bush but walks in front of a group of cyclists.

At the café, the men aren't welcome as Ivy's expecting a large group of visitors. Foggy's determined to stay. The special party turns out to be the group of cyclists!

Up on the hills, the men come across a couple whose car has broken down. They help by giving it a push, but Compo's trousers get caught and the car departs, taking Compo's lower garments with it. They meet Wally and Nora out on their motorbike. Wally is wearing a long overcoat, so they borrow his trousers which, unfortunately for Compo, are far too small.

The men decide to try to get home by boat, but finally have to use an upside-down portable lavatory to take them down the river.

CHRISTMAS SPECIAL 1983
GETTING SAM HOME
First transmitted: 27 December 1983

While resting in the hills, the trio talk about Sam, a friend who's in hospital. Their attention is distracted by Mr Fairburn from Co-op Tailoring and his lady friend from the bacon counter. On the way to the hospital they call to see Lily Bless 'er – a lady friend of Sam's – who gives them some buns for him. They arrive at Sam's bed to find the other woman in his life – his wife Sybil – who becomes suspicious when she sees the buns. Sam knows his time is short and asks the men to sneak him to Lily's one last time. He arrives in Sid's old fish and chip van. While at Lily's, Sam dies – with a large smile on his face! Now they have to get him home without Sybil finding out.

The next day the men go to pay their respects to Sybil and find that Sam is laid out in the garden. That night Lily says Sam should be laid out with dignity in her front room. They go to collect him and leave Foggy in the coffin while they borrow a shop dummy so that Sybil doesn't catch on. A neighbour's dog runs into Sam's garden. Its sniffing around the coffin causes Foggy to sit up. The dog's owner faints.

The next night they need to get Sam back home but can't get Sid's van to work. The funeral is brought forward an hour, and the men try to explain to Sybil what's happened. She's too busy to listen. Ivy collars them and says that she and Sid swapped the bodies back.

Lily Bless 'er goes to the church but waits outside. After the funeral, Sybil sees her and invites her back for tea. The trio go to scatter the ashes on the hills. Foggy takes charge of the proceedings and manages to throw himself over the edge.

SEASONAL SPECIAL 1984
THE LOXLEY LOZENGE
First transmitted: 30 December 1984
Wesley is in need of some help, and after approaching the three men, he's likely to need some more. He informs the trio that he's found a rare Loxley Lozenge. Foggy tries to use his powers of deduction to establish exactly what a Loxley Lozenge is. His final conclusion of a medieval cough sweet is blown to pieces by Wesley, who takes them to an old barn and shows them what's left of a once-classic car. With just the chassis in place, an old sofa is fixed on for seating to allow the men to 'steer' the vehicle while Wesley tows it to his garage. The first attempt fails when the towrope snaps. All appears well on the second attempt, until the sofa parts company with the chassis and rolls off down the hill.

SERIES EIGHT
Six Episodes

EPISODE ONE
THE MYSTERIOUS FEET OF NORA BATTY
First transmitted: 10 March 1985
Foggy thinks Nora has big feet; Compo disagrees. An expert witness is required. The men kidnap Wally but he gets the wrong idea, thinking they are after his pigeons. Back at Nora's house, Foggy tries to make Wally imagine what Nora looks like at night, but not only can he not remember her feet, but Compo starts getting over-excited.

Foggy decides the only thing left is to try to compare their feet with Nora's, but she catches on that something isn't right and has a go at Wally. Finally, Foggy gets a shoe sizer from the shoe shop, which the men attach to long poles so that they can reach Nora's feet without her knowing. But when she steps on it, they all fall in the river.

EPISODE TWO
KEEPING BRITAIN TIDY
First transmitted: 17 March 1985
An old dumped mattress on the roadside prompts Foggy to set up The Dewhurst Campaign for a Cleaner Countryside. Compo gets stuck under the mattress when they try to remove it and almost gets run over by demon insurance salesman Ogden Butterclough. While helping the men, Butterclough's car suffers a puncture. He's left his spare with 'a certain lady at No. 22, The Crescent', so the men have to take him to get the puncture mended.

At the café, they're introduced to Ivy's nephew, Milburn, who likes to be called Crusher. The spare tyre is left on the café floor, where Ivy promptly falls over it.

Opposite: Feet and inches – the familiar trio want to know Nora's shoe size in The Mysterious Feet of Nora Batty *(1985). Right: On your bike! Wally and Nora Batty 'enjoying' a day out.*

Back at the car the men find that the spare tyre was there all along and affix the mattress to the roof rack. On the move, the mattress flops over the windscreen and, as Compo climbs on to fix it back in position, the car runs away. When it comes to a stop, Compo is up a tree and the car is in a ditch.

Episode Three
ENTER THE PHANTOM
First transmitted: 24 March 1985

After being knocked down by a group of hoodlums on track bikes, the men decide to fight back. Foggy comes up with the idea of changing Compo's image and turning him into The Phantom. They start the transition by doing up an old moped and then taking Compo to borrow some racing leathers from Crusher.

Compo wants to impress Nora with his new guise and asks Wally when he's next taking her out. First, though, Compo must learn to ride his new racing machine.

First he ends up driving straight into a barn; next he practises wheelies and ends up on top of Foggy. The time finally arrives for Compo's big moment. Nora is picnicking by a lake. But he wets her through and ends up in the water with the bike.

Episode Four
CATCHING DIGBY'S DONKEY
First transmitted: 31 March 1985

While out on the hills, Foggy spots Digby trying – in vain – to catch his donkey. At the pub, the men meet Ormeroyd, a man renowned for fighting anybody for a quid! Unfortunately, Digby accepts the challenge. After a scuffle outside, Foggy tells Digby that the men will catch his donkey for him. Foggy tempts the creature with a carrot and ends up with his fingers bitten. While crawling through the grass, the men come upon Howard and Marina doing a tango. In a final attempt to snare the animal, the men try lassooing it while riding a bike, but Foggy ends up being dragged through a field.

Episode Five
THE WOOLLEN MILLS OF YOUR MIND
First transmitted: 7 April 1985

Compo is worried about Nora. He thinks that she's a neglected woman, and to cheer her up he intends to enter the local marathon. Foggy is all for the idea and decides that some rigorous training is needed. A planned run up into the hills is called off when Compo's knees give way, so they decide to hang him from a tree.

On the way home from having a drink, the trio run into Howard and Marina down an alley. Calling at Nora's house, Compo breaks the news that he won't be running the marathon after all. He sings her a song instead and gets a bucket of water over the head for his troubles.

Episode Six
WHO'S LOOKING AFTER THE CAFÉ THEN?
First transmitted: 14 April 1985

Wesley gives the men a lift to town. Arriving at the café, they find Ivy very agitated. She needs to go out and is waiting for a Mr Crabtree to come to look after the café. Unfortunately, he gets knocked down crossing the road, so Foggy volunteers to take charge of the premises. Ivy refuses. When she leaves, he takes over nevertheless. The first customer arrives, and Foggy and Compo fight over who will serve him. They go to prepare a ham salad complete with thumb print and caterpillar.

While Ivy's away, Crusher is supposed to clean the paintwork over the shop window. Foggy decides to help and borrows Wesley's Land Rover for Clegg and Compo to stand on. Wesley drives off and leaves Compo on the roof of the vehicle. The loud radio drowns out Compo's calls for help. The Land Rover passes Nora Batty's, where Compo catches sight of her in her nightie. Compo finally falls off and lands in a field between the unsuspecting Howard and Marina.

New Year's Special
UNCLE OF THE BRIDE
First transmitted: 1 January 1986

Rosemary, the post lady with the biggest round, delivers parcels to Compo and Clegg. They contain decorated eggs from Foggy, who's gone to Bridlington to inherit his uncle's business.

The two remaining men decide to give the eggs to Wesley's and Edie's daughter Glenda for her wedding present, so they go to deliver them. Wesley is just off to take his brother-in-law's washing back, so they go along for the ride. The brother-in-law turns out to be Seymour Utterthwaite, an eccentric inventor who used to be a headmaster. Their introduction to this new third man – played by Michael Aldridge – is as batty as you'd expect, with the men almost run over by Seymour's self-propelled wheelbarrow.

At Edie's house the women are putting the finishing touches to Glenda's wedding dress when Marina arrives with her present – a frilly garter.

Barry's stag night takes place at the White Horse, where all the guests get drunk. Seymour gives Barry a present of an electronic remote control which puts out all the lights in the pub. Howard is caught in the car park showing Marina the difference between cross-ply and radial tyres! Barry declares his ambition to run across the moors barefoot, so off the men go.

Seymour Utterthwaite (Michael Aldridge, centre) made his first appearance in the 1986 New Year's Special, Uncle of the Bride. *Replacing Brian Wilde as the 'third man' for the rest of the 1980s, Clegg and Compo's lives were never going to be quite the same again!*

The big day arrives and Barry is missing – stuck down a pothole from his midnight tryst. He's rescued but has hurt his leg, so Clegg has to drive his car and reverses into a duck pond. With little choice left and with the guests gathered at the church, our trio finally arrive with the groom in Seymour's wheelbarrow. It crashes into the churchyard wall and, during the ceremony, explodes, which brings out the fire brigade.

SERIES NINE
12 Episodes

EPISODE ONE

WHY DOES NORMAN CLEGG BUY LADIES' ELASTIC STOCKINGS?

First transmitted: 4 January 1986

Howard wants Clegg to deliver a note to Marina at the supermarket, which doesn't prove as easy as it sounds. While trying not to arouse suspicion, he ends up buying all sorts of things he doesn't need, including ladies' elastic stockings.

Compo and Clegg arrive at Seymour's and discover he's invented a multipurpose, all-powerful drill that needs to be tested. Convinced that there's oil locally after seeing some floating on his duck pond, he persuades the men to drill for more. The only thing they strike is a water main.

EPISODE TWO

THE HEAVILY REINFORCED BOTTOM

First transmitted: 11 January 1986

Seymour decides Compo needs to get fit after hearing him wheezing while out walking. At the café, they see Crusher with a canoe, which gives Seymour an idea.

A jogging trip is short-lived when Compo tires quickly and hitches a lift on the back of a passing truck. Compo

Compo, right, seems suitably unimpressed with Seymour's latest invention, but having experienced everything from falling through a canoe to being ejected from a motor car, it's hardly surprising!

gets taken down to the canal to make his first attempt at canoeing – but he drops straight through the bottom of the canoe. It is repaired with a reinforced bottom to stop him falling through. This time both he and the canoe are carefully lowered into the river by a crane. But the boat is now too heavy, and both it and Compo sink without trace.

EPISODE THREE
DRIED DATES AND CODFANGLERS
First transmitted: 18 January 1986
Crusher's bragging about fixing his Auntie Ivy's mixer, but she switches it on and gets covered in batter. Seymour offers to fix it instead. Nora loses her rag with Wally for taking their carpet shampooer to be fixed by Seymour.

Arriving at Seymour's, the men find he's invented a new doorlock, and he asks them to show him their keys. Compo finds something in his pocket, doesn't recognize it and throws it in the pond. Then he remembers it's an old dried date that Nora once threw at him and he wants it back. Their search is interrupted by Howard and Marina, who've got their bicycles entwined.

Seymour demonstrates his new door device, but even on uttering the codeword 'Codfanglers', it refuses to budge.

Crusher and Wally turn up asking for their mixer and carpet shampooer, and Howard and Marina want to know how they're going to get home. They all squeeze into Crusher's car, except Compo, who's towed behind riding the two bikes.

EPISODE FOUR
THE REALLY MASCULINE PURSE
First transmitted: 25 January 1986
It's Compo's belief that any man who uses a purse is a 'right Mildred'! Seymour decides to invent a masculine purse. He's still having problems with his voice-operated doorlock, even though he's changed the password to Marjorie (hence the phrase 'Marjorie door!'), so Compo gets shoved through the pantry window.

The purse is ready for testing, but since it has to be strapped to the ankle it won't fit over Compo's wellies. They go to see Wally Batty to borrow his squeaky boots. Having to raise a leg to get at the purse, the men are thrown off a bus when Compo accidentally kicks the conductor in an unauthorized place.

Episode Five
WHO'S FEELING EJECTED THEN?
First transmitted: 1 February 1986
Seymour tries his hand at motor safety and builds an ejector seat. The men need a lift from Wesley to get to Seymour's house, but because there's not enough room in his car, they strap the ejector seat to the roof and put Compo in it. His journey is short-lived when the car goes over a pothole and Compo finds himself ejected.

To prevent him from hurting himself further every time he tries out the seat, the men stuff Compo's clothes with foam rubber. This time when they try to eject him, the seat goes with him and they end up in a field, while Barry, who is driving, disappears through a hole in the wall.

Episode Six
THE ICE-CREAM MAN COMETH
First transmitted: 8 February 1986
After their usual deep discussions – this time on the subject of ice-cream – the men go to the café, where Compo complains of back pains. Seymour has the answer – the Utterthwaite Back Support – which turns out to be a bit of old rubber tubing that needs inflating. Compo tries it on, but it leaks, so they go to Wesley to get it mended. On the way they meet Barry and Glenda, who are out for a picnic and who offer them a lift in their car. Compo's support starts leaking again, and Barry and Glenda wonder where the noise is coming from! On reaching Wesley's, the trio find he's built them a mobile ice-cream business – a bicycle with a fridge attachment. Their attempts at selling are doomed when the brakes fail on the machine and Compo collides with Howard and Marina on their own bicycles.

Episode Seven
SET THE PEOPLE FREE
First transmitted: 15 February 1986
Howard and Wally have been confined to their houses – Howard must clean the windows while Wally must decorate. Seymour reckons he can get them both out of their homes, though he still can't get into his, and Compo has to enter through the pantry window yet again.

Seymour thinks the best way to release Howard is simply to call on him for assistance. Pearl thinks otherwise, and Seymour departs with a face full of emulsion.

Next they try using a ladder attached to Wesley's Land Rover. Pearl catches them again. They've no better luck rescuing Wally. Compo distracts Nora, and they get Wally into a dinghy, but it springs a leak and they all end up in the river.

Episode Eight
GO WITH THE FLOW
First transmitted: 22 February 1986
Clegg has a religious experience with two young missionaries. Seymour takes two other missionaries to the vicarage to prove that religion is part of everyday life. While there, he volunteers help and ends up selling tickets for the local production of *The Tales of Beatrix Potter*. Seymour's attempts at selling tickets are not wholly successful, and he ends up being ejected from the pub. Compo tells him not to worry and to go with the flow. Back at the vicarage, Ivy and Nora are making costumes, and in order to impress them, Compo dresses up as a mouse to sell tickets instead.

Episode Nine
JAWS
First transmitted: 1 March 1986
The men visit a local engineer's to pick up Seymour's latest invention – a waste-disposal unit for Edie, which Wesley has to install. Stopping on the way back for a drink, they encounter Eli Duckett for the first time. He's having trouble playing darts; being blind as a bat doesn't help. The trio decide it's safer to drink outside.

Wally has a new washing line for Nora, and Compo volunteers to take it home for him. The new waste-disposal unit is fitted, and to everyone's surprise...it works. Compo – disguised as Wally – helps Nora put out the washing, but when they go inside, she soon discovers the swap!

The joy over the waste-disposal unit is short-lived – it soon backfires and splatters rubbish over Edie's windows.

Episode Ten
EDIE AND THE AUTOMOBILE
First transmitted: 8 March 1986
The town is on alert – Edie is having a driving lesson with Wesley! The trio are almost knocked down by her on their way to the café. Wesley soon follows them in, dazed and confused after the lesson. Glenda volunteers Barry to take over, but he ends up as shaken as Wesley. Seymour decides to take charge, but he can't actually drive, so they call on Wally for assistance.

When eventually they find Wally, who's gone missing, his help also proves useless, so it's time for one last attempt using Clegg. His nerves, though, get the better of him and they all decide to walk home instead.

Episode 11
WIND POWER
First transmitted: 15 March 1986
Life is all about mind over matter – that's the message Seymour decides to teach Compo and Clegg. To demonstrate, he sits by the riverside in just his shirtsleeves,

concentrating heavily. The duo take Seymour to the café to thaw out!

Seymour wants to test his theories of wind power and volunteers Compo to try his ideas. On go the roller skates and off goes Compo, first into a group of cyclists and then into the midst of a herd of cows. Later, they try fixing a sail on to Compo's back and set him off down the road on the skates again. Nora and Wally, out on their motorbike and sidecar, are overtaken by Compo, who's trying to impress Nora. His joy is short-lived when he runs off the road.

Episode 12
WHEN YOU TAKE A GOOD BITE OF YORKSHIRE, IT TASTES TERRIBLE

First transmitted: 22 March 1986

Clegg receives some bad news – an old friend, Bill Henry, has died in America.

The men break the news around the town, and while at Wesley's, they decide to pay their own tribute by doing 'the three pubs'. This entails cycling 12 miles and drinking nine pints.

On their way to the first pub, Clegg tells Compo that he and Bill Henry used to walk along a gate when they were younger. Clegg tries it again and falls off! On the way to the next pub, Seymour suggests they drive in formation. They crash into each other and Clegg is convinced that Bill Henry's ghost is behind the mishaps.

Clegg's one last attempt to rekindle his youth with Bill Henry is to try climbing a tree. After several attempts the men all end up on a high branch. Unfortunately, their rope ladder ends up on the ground.

Compo tries to bite off more than he can chew with Nora in a scene from Big Day at Dream Acres *(1987).*

Christmas Special 1986
MERRY CHRISTMAS, FATHER CHRISTMAS

First transmitted: 28 December 1986

Marina asks Clegg to deliver a Christmas present to Howard without Pearl finding out. Easier said than done. On the way to the pub, the trio see a man dressed as Santa Claus riding a bike. This upsets Seymour, who likes the traditional sighting of Father Christmas on a roof. Compo is soon volunteered for the position. Enlisting the help of Wesley and Barry, they have a first attempt at getting Compo on the roof. They try to keep him balanced with a 'thingummy' – a long pole with padding at one end. But he slips and slides down. The ladies are talking outside Nora Batty's house when Compo reappears on the roof. To impress her he does a song and dance routine but slips again, and as he falls he takes a chimneypot with him.

New Year's Special 1987
BIG DAY AT DREAM ACRES

First transmitted: 31 December 1987

Everyone's invited to a party at Dream Acres. Ivy's in charge of the catering, Seymour's providing the public-address system and Compo has had his trousers mended.

A tramp steals Clegg's bicycle but gets knocked off it by a trilby hat driving a motor car! The tramp claims he was taking the bike to the police station, and the trio fall for his story. They take him to the pub to recover.

Nora's lift to Dream Acres, where she's due to act as waitress, is interrupted when Crusher's car suffers a puncture. He's left covered in oil.

The tramp spins the trio a yarn about coming from a wealthy family and shows them where he used to live – Dream Acres. He says he's returned to visit his childhood pet donkey, Heathcliffe. He persuades the men to swap Heathcliffe for another donkey – not telling the men that it's favourite in the donkey derby and he'll make money betting against it! The men recruit Howard, who has a new van, to help them smuggle out the donkey. It won't budge, so Crusher is called in to carry it.

Pearl comes looking for Howard, and after hearing a noise from the van, assumes he's with Marina.

The trio find out what the tramp is up to and attempt to swap donkeys back again. Compo dresses up as a jockey to allay suspicion. Eli tries to help, but the donkey strays into a house and wrecks the rooms. Seymour gets Compo and Clegg to dress up as a pantomime horse in order to lure the donkey away. It runs off, dragging Compo behind it.

The favourite wins the race after all – Crusher moved the wrong donkey!

A moment of contemplation for Michael Aldridge on the set of Seymour Utterthwaite's house. Note the microphone in the top right-hand corner.

SERIES TEN
Six Episodes

EPISODE ONE

THE EXPERIMENT

First transmitted: 16 October 1988

After being held upside down by Seymour and Clegg, Compo wants to know why the blood is rushing to his head. Meanwhile, Nora is working part-time at the café with Ivy. To show Compo how the blood moves about the body, Seymour straps him to a ladder, but when it's hoisted up, he slides down. Seymour decides to show them himself how the experiment works and gets Compo and Clegg to hang him upside down. The rope lifting him slips, and he's left hanging high in the air.

EPISODE TWO

THE TREASURE OF THE DEEP

First transmitted: 23 October 1988

A practical joke backfires and Compo falls into the canal. The trio go to dry out Compo's clothes at the launderette. When the machine makes a noise, they discover what Seymour thinks is a piece of Georgian silver.

Back at the canal, Seymour tells the others it could be part of the proceeds of a burglary dumped in the water and that in order to look for it, they need Wesley to help them build a glass-bottomed underwater exploration vehicle (two old oil drums welded together). Setting off to explore, Compo comes across Howard and Marina in a rowing boat. Howard sees the periscope, thinks it's Pearl, starts rocking the boat, and both he and Marina end up in the canal.

Seymour shows Wesley what they found in Compo's clothes. He tells them it's only part of a lavatory ball-cock.

EPISODE THREE

DANCING FEET

First transmitted: 30 October 1988

The men are helping Wesley with his car – pushing it, to be more precise. During a break in their exercise, Compo muses as to where hard skin comes from. Pushing the car again, they come across a tractor in the road. Seymour connects a towrope to it. After turning into a field, the driver doesn't hear the men calling, and he turns on his crop sprayer, covering the trio in something rather nasty.

After getting cleaned up, they visit Charlie's shop to see

if he has anything for Compo's hard skin. Charlie advises them to see Betsy Trumfleet – a gypsy healer. She fills Compo's boots with herbal jelly, which soon melts. They go on to the church social for a meal, but when Compo goes to collect his raffle prize, his wellies start steaming.

Episode Four
THAT CERTAIN SMILE
First transmitted: 6 November 1988

A visit to the hospital to see Clem Hemingway (Smiler) is on the cards. Clem, in his usual miserable state, tells the trio that he's missing his dog Bess. They decide to try to smuggle it into the hospital to cheer Clem up. The dog snaps at everyone, so Seymour goes to Barry to borrow a sedative. After sedating it, Compo sticks the dog up his jumper and takes it into the hospital.

Clem cheers up, but Marina, who overhears them from behind the screen, is shocked, thinking a birth is taking place! Smuggling the dog out again, they meet Nora and Edie, who get a surprise when they see a dog's tail appearing through Compo's trousers. On the bus home, the dog wakes up and chases off all the passengers.

Episode Five
DOWNHILL RACER
First transmitted: 13 November 1988

Seymour announces that skiing is excellent exercise for the legs and insists that Compo and Clegg give it a try – though in place of skis they have to use trays.

Up in the hills, Howard and Marina, having a quiet liaison, are disturbed by the men clumping past with trays on their feet looking for a steep slope. Their first attempt at skiing ends with them in a heap at the bottom of the hill. So Seymour sets about making the Utterthwaite Ski – an old bicycle frame fitted with skis and attached by rope to Wesley's Land Rover. Seymour insists that Nora will be impressed if Compo's seen on it, so off he goes down the hill dressed in red long-johns and a lady's corset. When the rope tightens, Compo shoots off and lands in Nora's arms.

Episode Six
THE DAY OF THE WELSH FERRET
First transmitted: 20 November 1988

Both Seymour and Clegg are surprised when they arrive at Compo's house and find him wearing a suit. He's off to Old Jonesy's funeral, so they go with him and on the way Compo calls at the allotments to pick up Taffy – Jonesy's Welsh ferret.

The men arrive at Jonesy's house to pay their respects. With the ferret under his hat, Compo looks for a place to keep it until after the funeral. But it escapes, and the men are convinced it's got into the coffin. They spot it on the bookshelf, and Compo puts it in his pocket. At the service, the ferret tries to get away again. At the pub afterwards, it makes one last bid for freedom and hides in the pool table.

Christmas Special 1988
CRUMS
First transmitted: 24 December 1988

Seymour, Compo and Clegg are dressed as Father Christmases to collect money for charity. They come across Wesley and Barry, who are moving Glenda's present – a water bed. Out collecting again, they find there is a bogus Santa Claus going around. It's Howard, trying to see Marina, who's dressed up as the Good Fairy at the Christmas Grotto. His excuse to Pearl is that he's helping a relative – Auntie Wainwright – who has had a premonition that her shop is to be burgled.

Calling at her shop, they meet the infamous Auntie Wainwright, who sells a stuffed parrot to Compo, a toy train to Clegg and a doll to Seymour. She gives them tea (10p each!) and enlists their help with her broken window blind.

Christmas Eve arrives and Nora and Ivy are both reminiscing about their late husbands.

The trio arrive at Auntie Wainwright's for their night vigil. She offers them a drink, which turns out to be castor oil. Barry and Wesley ask the men for help with the water bed. They sit on it in the back of Wesley's Land Rover and feel seasick. Returning to Auntie's, they find the place in darkness. On entering, all the ladies are there with a surprise Christmas party. Outside the shop, Marina wants Howard to kiss her and make the earth move and the bells ring – which they do when the shop blind falls on them and the church bells start up. Finally, Glenda asks Barry what he's bought her for Christmas, and as he looks up at her he sees a damp patch on the ceiling. Water starts to drip on his glasses!

SERIES 11
Seven Episodes

Episode One
COME BACK, JACK HARRY TEESDALE
First transmitted: 15 October 1989

While out walking, our trio get a lift from Jack Harry Teesdale and his wife – an emotional woman who seems to spend most of her time chomping on a handkerchief.

They can't work out the reason for her permanent state of distress. Later, they ask and she tells them that she gets upset every time they come back from a caravanning trip

The Yorkshire equivalent of the nutty professor! Seymour Utterthwaite (Michael Aldridge) with Clegg and Compo outside his house of fun.

because she can't guide the van into the driveway without angering her husband.

Finding Jack Harry at the pub, Seymour insists he can help get the caravan into the drive. After extensive calculation of angles, the caravan ends up in the drive next door! After Seymour almost gets run over, they give up. Jack Harry decides to return to the pub, narrowly missing Nora and Ivy on the way.

EPISODE TWO
THE KISS AND MAVIS POSKITT
First transmitted: 22 October 1989

Compo announces that he's going to give Nora a great big kiss. While at the café, he decides to practise on Ivy, who hits him on the head with her tray. They meet Nora, who's with Edie and Glenda. The women drag off Clegg, leaving Compo and Seymour wondering what's going on. At his house, Clegg explains that the ladies are trying to fix him up with a timid woman he once knew at school, Mavis Poskitt. He says Nora will be round imminently to pick him up. This gives Compo an idea.

Forcing her way into Clegg's house, Nora thinks he's cowering in bed but gets a shock when she finds Compo there instead. The trio enlist the help of Marina, who pretends that Clegg has left his boxer shorts at her house!

EPISODE THREE
OH SHUT UP AND EAT YOUR CHOC ICE
First transmitted: 29 October 1989

Up in the hills, Compo is convinced he can smell a rat in a bale of hay. The men all climb on the bale and are observed by a minibus of Japanese tourists. Seymour says the bale is in a dangerous place, but when they try to move it, it runs away and narrowly misses Wesley and Barry. They can't carry it up the hill, so they borrow Wesley's three-wheeler and some rope and try to pull the bale. Shortsighted Eli sees Clegg sitting on Seymour's knee and, thinking he's a child, gives him some money for a choc ice.

Back in the hills, Howard and Marina just miss being hit by the bale as it drags the car back down the slope. It's not all bad news, though: Nora thinks Compo is injured and administers first aid.

EPISODE FOUR
WHO'S THAT BLOKE WITH NORA BATTY THEN?
First transmitted: 5 November 1989

Nora's out on a Wednesday night without a wrinkled stocking in sight. Compo's worried. Spying Nora with a man, Compo decides it's time to impress her. Seymour suggests taking up sport. First, he tries dressing up in a bathing costume, but when Nora sees him, she thinks he looks ridiculous. Next, Seymour suggests windsurfing, though they don't have a surfboard and end up using an ironing-board being pulled across the water by a tow rope on Wesley's vehicle. Barry tells them the man Nora has been seeing is his Uncle Eric, who's trying to enlist agents to sell Christmas hampers.

EPISODE FIVE
HAPPY ANNIVERSARY GOUGH AND JESSIE
First transmitted: 12 November 1989

The men are off to a golden wedding anniversary, but what is Compo to wear? At the pub, Eli offers a suit, which turns out to be bright blue. At the party, the men decide that after 50 years of marriage, Gough deserves a break, so they smuggle him out and take him for a drink. Unused to drinking, Gough gets drunk. At the next pub, they decide it will be safer to leave Gough in the skip outside while they pop in for a quick one. Unfortunately, the skip gets collected.

Back at the party, the ladies are wondering where the men are. Gough goes past the house in the skip with a traffic cone on his head singing 'The Little Yorkshire Rose'. The men are running behind but beat a hasty retreat when they see the women.

EPISODE SIX
GETTING BARRY HIGHER IN THE WORLD
First transmitted: 19 November 1989

Out walking, the men reminisce about the games they used to play. They see a kite, and Compo says he'd like to fly one again. The one they build doesn't fly, so Seymour asks Wesley to make one, which he does – but he makes it in metres instead of feet and inches!

At the ladies' coffee morning, they are talking about Barry. Edie says he needs more drive and asks Seymour to have a word with him. But Barry gets preoccupied with flying the huge kite. 'We need more speed,' declares Wesley, and he uses his Land Rover to pull the kite along. It shoots up in the air with Barry still holding on. He flies through the air above the ladies, who are driving by.

EPISODE SEVEN
THREE MEN AND A MANGLE
First transmitted: 26 November 1989

Compo thinks it's his birthday when Nora invites him into her bedroom. He soon discovers that all she wants is for him to move an old mangle to Sammy Peters' place.

Seymour declares he'll have nothing to do with moving the object but, witnessing Compo and Clegg 'making a bog of it', he goes to help, only to get his tie caught in the rollers.

Needing a rope, Compo pinches Nora's washing line, which she discovers when she goes to hang out the clothes

A touching farewell as Michael Aldridge (left) leaves his two friends after five years with Summer Wine. *Here he makes a brief appearance in the first episode of Series 12,* Return of the Warrior.

and falls flat on her face. The trio haul the mangle up on to a viaduct, but when the police arrive, they let go of the rope and the mangle crashes through the roof of the panda car. Eli and his brother tow the men and the mangle, but when the rope snaps, they end up in a ditch and Seymour's tie gets caught once again.

CHRISTMAS SPECIAL 1989
WHAT'S SANTA BROUGHT FOR NORA THEN?
First transmitted: 23 December 1989
Compo's trying something that he hasn't done for a while – working! He's trying to earn some money to buy Nora a Christmas present by putting on a show with his 'performing ferrets'. As he's dressed as a jockey, Ivy bans him from bringing his ferrets into the café. At Compo's show, pandemonium erupts when the ferrets escape, leaving the audience standing nervously on their seats.

Christmas Eve arrives, and on their way to Clegg's house Compo and Seymour see Howard decorating his tree. Compo taps on the window and Howard falls into the branches. Clegg tells Compo there's still one place open where he can buy a present for Nora – Auntie Wainwright's. Auntie sells him a fancy hat that gets mistaken for a vase of flowers at the pub and gets watered by the landlady. They try to dry it out in Clegg's oven.

Howard tries to get a present to Marina by hanging it on a fishing line out of an upstairs window. Pearl surprises him, so he asks Clegg to look after it for him.

Meanwhile, the hat has burned.

At the Christmas party, Compo gives Nora the present that Howard had bought for Marina. It turns out to be fancy underwear and earns Compo a bang on the head with a tray!

SERIES 12
Ten Episodes

EPISODE ONE
RETURN OF THE WARRIOR
First transmitted: 2 September 1990
Compo and Clegg are helping Seymour with his luggage. He's off to take up the post of a relief headmaster. Seymour leaves on the bus as Foggy returns on a different one, though he just misses Compo and Clegg. They all meet at the station, and soon it's like old times. After a drink at the pub, where a man falls over Foggy's luggage, they borrow Eli's bike to try to make things easier.

Foggy decides that riding the bike is the best way forward, and off they all go, complete with luggage. Unfortunately, the bike goes out of control and ends up on the back of a removal van.

EPISODE TWO
COME IN, SUNRAY MAJOR
First transmitted: 9 September 1990
As the men walk through the hills, Compo and Clegg get bored with Foggy's incessant talking and sneak away, leaving him to march on his own. Eventually he catches up with them in the pub and comes up with the idea of using portable radios to stay in touch if the men get lost. Up in the hills, the men test the radios, but Compo falls down a hill and crushes his. Howard and Marina appear and with Compo and Clegg convince Foggy that the radio got damaged when Compo threw himself in front of Marina's runaway bicycle.

EPISODE THREE
THE CHARITY BALLS
First transmitted: 16 September 1990
Compo, Clegg and Foggy can't understand why Jack Harry Teesdale is wearing a pair of shorts. In the café, he explains that he's taking part in a sponsored dribble for charity. Foggy decides that the others should do it too, but practice is cut short when he gets hit by Compo's welly.

The duo are kitted out in football gear, and it's off to the sponsored dribble. Foggy's walking-stick gets savaged by a dog when he tries to retrieve a ball from a garden. Jack and his partner Howard are dribbling a ball when Howard pretends to twist an ankle so that he can go to the first-aid caravan which is manned (or womanned) by Marina. When Pearl and the other ladies turn up, he makes a miraculous recovery.

EPISODE FOUR
WALKING STIFF CAN MAKE YOU FAMOUS
First transmitted: 23 September 1990
Foggy yearns to be remembered as somebody famous, and he thinks this time he's come up with the idea to ensure that – bicycle polo. The trio go to Wesley and ask him to make them some polo mallets, then it's off to Foggy's house where he changes into a pair of jodhpurs, which amuses Compo and Clegg.

During a practice session, the men collide with each other. Wesley provides them with some foam rubber for protection and off they go again. On the way to the event, they manage to avoid Eli by walking in the road, and Foggy ends up getting soaked through by a sprinkler at the local garden centre.

EPISODE FIVE
THAT'S NOT CAPTAIN ZERO
First transmitted: 30 September 1990
The men are talking about the garden party they are going to when they meet the main attraction – Captain Zero, the human cannonball, whose van has broken down.

While waiting for Wesley to arrive, they take Captain Zero (real name Clutterbuck) to the pub. After rehearsing his act by standing on the tables, they're thrown out. They return to the cannon, but Captain Zero gets arrested for being drunk.

Foggy volunteers Compo to take his place, which he enjoys at the start when all the women allow him to kiss them. But being fired out of a cannon is another thing and Compo's left with his underwear smouldering.

EPISODE SIX
DAS WELLY BOOT
First transmitted: 7 October 1990
Ivy's toaster has packed up at the café and, much to everyone's surprise, Foggy fixes it. Out walking, the men come across an old boat that Foggy decides he'll restore – though Wesley ends up doing all the work. Meanwhile, back at the café, the toaster blows up!

Wesley has fitted the boat with an engine he's taken out of Barry's car, but when they put it in the water, the boat sinks. Eventually, the boat is on the water and Compo says he'd like to get Nora aboard. Foggy suggests that if he pretends to be ill when Nora's on the boat, Compo can save her by jumping on and rescuing her. But while practising, he goes straight through the bottom of the boat and it sinks once again.

EPISODE SEVEN
THE EMPIRE THAT FOGGY NEARLY BUILT
First transmitted: 14 October 1990
On their way to the café, the trio see two motorists arguing over a parking space. Foggy decides to intervene and promptly finds himself being dumped in a litter bin. Wesley has to cut him free.

Foggy realizes there's money to be made out of parking spaces, so enlisting Wesley's help once again, the men go looking for them. Eventually, they find a place and come across Howard and Marina, who insist they're looking at industrial ruins. The problem with the space is that it's too far from town, so Foggy suggests valet parking. They get a customer, but all goes wrong when Clegg – who doesn't like driving – ends up running the car into the back of a bus.

EPISODE EIGHT
THE LAST SURVIVING MAURICE CHEVALIER IMPRESSION
First transmitted: 21 October 1990
Compo is depressed because he thinks he's lost his sexual magnetism. Foggy decides to make him famous after Compo says he can do impressions of Maurice Chevalier. Collecting a suit from the local charity shop, Foggy says he'll get Compo on television to impress Nora.

At the studios, Compo sends Foggy and Clegg back to ensure that Nora is watching. All goes well with the impression, but as Compo sings 'You Must Have Been a Beautiful Baby', his lucky ferret pops out of his trousers and causes uproar in the studio.

Foggy yearns to be remembered as somebody famous, and he thinks this time he's come up with the idea to ensure that – bicycle polo.

EPISODE NINE
ROLL ON
First transmitted: 28 October 1990
It's just a normal day in Yorkshire – Nora's putting out the milk bottles, Compo's out in his underwear mending his trousers and Clegg finds Howard struggling with a double bass.

At the café, Ivy's annoyed that she's not doing the catering for the barrel-rolling event. Foggy volunteers the three of them to take part but insists they train first. They start jogging, but that doesn't last long and they soon stop for a drink. After a test-run in their barrels, the men realize they need padding, so they cover themselves in old inner tubes. This time they almost collide with Howard as he plays his double bass to Marina.

EPISODE TEN
A LANDLADY FOR SMILER
First transmitted: 4 November 1990
After Pearl catches Clegg and Howard looking at a weevil, the trio go off to the café, where they find Smiler. He tells them that his wife has left and gone off to Australia and that he's looking for somewhere to stay.

On a walk, they meet Howard, who's depressed because Marina has told him she wants a full-time lover and not somebody who spends the whole time sneaking around the countryside. Compo takes charge of the situation and tells Howard to ignore her and that she will come running back to him. Next, he turns his attentions to Smiler's problem He spins a sob story at the café and hopes to get Smiler lodging with Marina. But his plan backfires, and Smiler ends up at Nora Batty's instead.

CHRISTMAS SPECIAL 1990
BARRY'S CHRISTMAS
First transmitted: 27 December 1990
It's Boxing Day, and on his way to meet Compo and Clegg, Foggy aggravates a man on a bus by constantly talking to him when he's trying to read a book. They meet Wesley, who's bought himself a hearse for Christmas, and he gives them a lift to the pub. Under their table they find Barry dressed as Santa Claus, waking up after a party from the previous night.

The ladies are trying to comfort Glenda, who's upset because Barry didn't come home the night before. Foggy phones Glenda and tells her that Barry has lost his memory. To contact him, she can call Foggy's pager, which he bought himself for Christmas.

They fetch Barry a drink, then try to sober him up by taking him for a walk in the hills, where Foggy decides that, rather than carry him, a horse can pull Barry instead. Unfortunately, Foggy's pager starts bleeping and the horse bolts!

SERIES 13
Six Episodes

EPISODE ONE
QUICK, QUICK, SLOW
First transmitted: 18 October 1991
Compo's depressed. Nora's taken in Smiler as her lodger, and to make things worse she's washing his long-johns for him! Smiler insists that he has no amorous intentions towards Nora, but Compo remains unconvinced.

While out for a walk, the men meet Wesley, who's supposed to be cleaning up his shed. They take him for a drink. While at the pub, Foggy says he has an idea to cheer up Compo, which he first saw practised by the natives in the jungle – a mystical dance around the person who's depressed. Compo can't help but cheer up when the ladies

Edie Pegden (Thora Hird) looks suitably shocked by the arrival of the town's new courier service in this scene from the 1991 Christmas Special, Situations Vacant.

– who are out looking for Wesley – see Foggy and Clegg performing the tango together.

EPISODE TWO

GIVE US A LIFT

First transmitted: 25 October 1991

Compo wakes up to the dulcet tones of Nora sending off Smiler with a wheelbarrow to fetch a sack of King Edwards. The trio go walking in the hills, which Compo is convinced are getting steeper. They meet Smiler and con him into giving Compo a lift in the barrow. Foggy decides it's time for a chair lift, so it's off to Wesley's, where he fits four pram wheels on to an old armchair.

Up in the hills Howard and Marina are bird-watching. Compo tries out the chair lift but gets tipped out, so they try bigger wheels. This time it works, so they all climb on board, but the rope pulling them up the hill snaps and they plunge down the hill, running over the roof of a police car.

EPISODE THREE

WAS THAT NORA BATTY SINGING?

First transmitted: 1 November 1991

Foggy asks for books on methods for silent killing and promptly gets kicked out of the library. He meets Clegg and they go to Compo's house, where they find him listening at Nora's door. He's convinced he could hear her singing.

Up in the hills, Compo believes that Nora and Smiler are having an affair, so they go to have it out with him. Compo is distraught when he sees Nora and Smiler getting on a bus together, so the men pinch Howard's and Marina's bikes and follow them to the church. Compo cheers up when he discovers that all Nora needs Smiler for is to do some dusting.

EPISODE FOUR

CASH FLOW PROBLEMS

First transmitted: 8 November 1991

Compo has a problem…he's skint! After finding some old

coins in a fountain, Compo remembers he's owed some money by Biff Hemingway. Unfortunately, the debt goes back to their schooldays! The men try to trace Biff's whereabouts. They try his old address, only to find new houses built on it. Clegg suggests they try the electoral register at the police station.

The men visit several Hemingways, including one who runs a tailor's shop. They come to the last one on the list, who turns out to be a big man with an even bigger temper. So Compo gives up and returns to the fountain in a hurry, soaking Nora as she walks past.

EPISODE FIVE
PASSING THE EARRING
First transmitted: 15 November 1991
Howard asks Clegg to do him a favour and return one of Marina's earrings. Clegg's problems are doubled when at the café he learns that Howard has found the other earring but can't get it past Pearl. Foggy decides a fishing rod out of Clegg's window is the best way to catch it, but Pearl catches them! Next, he phones Howard and tells him he'll keep her talking while Howard slips the earring to Clegg – but he passes it to Pearl instead. Finally, the men try to help Smiler get back into Nora's house by using a ladder. Compo takes advantage of the situation and is caught trying to climb into her bedroom.

EPISODE SIX
POLE STAR
First transmitted: 29 November 1991
Nora asks Compo to put up her washing line. He can't reach, so she gets Smiler to help instead. Compo is now really fed up. Foggy insists that Nora would be impressed if Compo could vault up on to the wall. Hand-vaulting brings tears to his eyes, so next it's time to try a pole – which lands Compo among some oil drums.

While the ladies discuss the contents of men's pockets at their tea morning, Compo practises. Finally, he's confident enough to try vaulting in front of Nora. It's on to the wall – nimbly and gracefully – then off again, into the river and landing on Howard and Marina!

CHRISTMAS SPECIAL 1991
SITUATIONS VACANT
First transmitted: 22 December 1991
Howard is in the park, privately practising excuses for Pearl. Foggy, meanwhile, says Compo needs a new pair of trousers, which he stresses can often be given free as part of uniforms for jobs. After nearly getting knocked over by a motorbike, Foggy decides to start up a courier service. They get some motorbike leathers from Wesley – which he insists must be kept clean. They also borrow his motorbike, but while taking a promotional photograph, Wesley gets covered in oil. They go to explain to Edie that it wasn't his fault. The courier idea is abandoned after Compo gets stuck under the motorbike when it falls on him.

SERIES 14
Nine Episodes

EPISODE ONE
BY THE MAGNIFICENT THIGHS OF ERNIE BURNISTON
First transmitted: 25 October 1992
Clegg discovers Howard inside a wheelie bin. Howard asks him to deliver a birthday card to Marina.

Foggy thinks that nobody their age is fit enough any more – until he sees Ernie Burniston cycling and jogging. His view is reinforced when Nora tells Compo he's too old to be climbing walls. It's time to get fit.

At Clegg's house, Howard bursts in wearing Pearl's nightgown – she's hidden his clothes. Foggy suggests Howard dresses up as a woman, then he can deliver Marina's card without Pearl recognizing him. Howard bottles out and Clegg delivers it instead, receiving a big kiss from Marina, who thinks the card is from him. Compo's back goes during training, and the men push him home on a trolley. He makes a miraculous recovery when he hears that Ernie Burniston has been rushed to hospital with a hernia.

EPISODE TWO
ERROL FLYNN USED TO HAVE A PAIR LIKE THAT
First transmitted: 1 November 1992
Compo overhears Nora extolling the virtues of men in riding gear, so he puts on motorcycling leathers, only to be scoffed at by Nora, who tells him it's horse-riding gear she's into. Meanwhile, Foggy pays a visit to Auntie Wainwright's, where he buys an old pair of military riding breeches which he lends to Compo. Unfortunately, Nora tells Compo that she can't wait to see him ride a horse. Enter Smiler – dressed as Mr Muscle, the Oven Cleaner – to stamp about inside a horsebox. The ladies are impressed when Compo emerges unscathed – until the door opens, revealing Mr Muscle in all his glory.

EPISODE THREE
THE PHANTOM OF THE GRAVEYARD
First transmitted: 8 November 1992
Old 'Slasher' Sylvester – a schoolteacher of the men – has passed away, and the trio are off to his funeral. While walking, they meet Howard dressed in bright shirt and shorts – a plot by Pearl to embarrass him and keep him in the house away from Marina. After a pint, they escort him home but are met on the way by Marina, who thinks Howard is dressed up for a younger woman.

MORRIS BRIGHT AND ROBERT ROSS'S TOP TEN EPISODES

BALLAD FOR WIND INSTRUMENT AND CANOE (1975)
For the elongated vowels of Michael Bates and the spectre of things to come.

THE KINK IN FOGGY'S NIBLICK (1976)
For Compo's trousers, which brought a whole new meaning to the phrase 'British Open'!

GREENFINGERS (1977)
For the definitive representation of old men behaving as children and Joe Gladwin's drunk scene.

FROM WELLIES TO WET SUIT (1982)
For the opportunity to witness one of the country's greatest performers indulging his love for physical clowning.

SET THE PEOPLE FREE (1986)
For the avuncular charm of Michael Aldridge and the essence of patriotic cameraderie.

RETURN OF THE WARRIOR (1990)
For the much-welcome reappearance of everybody's favourite third man.

THE MAN WHO NEARLY KNEW PAVAROTTI (1995)
For the sheer pleasure of a great British comic institution joining a great British comedy institution.

CAPTAIN CLUTTERBUCK'S TREASURE (1995)
For proving that almost 40 years on, Fagin could still pick a pocket or two!

WHO'S THROWN HER TOM CRUISE PHOTOS AWAY? (1999)
For being the funniest *Summer Wine* episode in the world…ever!

MILLENNIUM SPECIAL: LAST POST AND PIGEON (2000)
For the obvious reason…

Foggy takes Compo to Auntie Wainwright's to get him a suit for the funeral. Howard decides to attend the funeral so he can put on a dark suit and meet Marina in the church porch. The men go to the wrong church, leaving Howard cuddling the vicar. Meanwhile, Marina, bedecked in black and veils, bumps into Eli, who runs away, thinking he's seen the phantom of the graveyard.

EPISODE FOUR
THE SELF-PROPELLED SALAD STRAINER
First transmitted: 15 November 1992
Nora is going out and Compo wants to know where. Meanwhile, Wesley calls at Auntie Wainwright's, where she sells him a ride-on lawnmower, which he intends to adapt for the job of cleaning house windows.

The trio see smoke coming from Nora's kitchen window and throw a bucket of water through. It soaks Smiler, who's burned the toast. He tells them that Nora has gone off to look after a sick cousin.

Wesley tries out his new machine and has to be rescued off the roof by the fire brigade. Compo decides to get Nora some flowers but can't afford to buy them. He goes to pick some wild ones and comes across Howard and Marina, to whom he claims to be teaching botany. Wesley gives the men a lift to Nora's cousin on his machine, but it goes awry again and this time Compo needs rescuing.

EPISODE FIVE
ORDEAL BY TROUSERS
First transmitted: 22 November 1992
Ivy and Nora are looking for volunteers for the church concert. Foggy suggests that he could tell the audience war stories. Compo accuses him of making them up, and an old school challenge for rooting out liars is invoked. It's Ordeal by Trousers – too gruesome to print here, but suffice it to say it involves a beetle being dropped down the front of the aforesaid garment.

The ladies, meanwhile, are still looking for volunteers for the concert, and other than Mr McIntyre and his pipes, there's not much doing. The trio get conscripted for a song and dance routine. Calling themselves The Blue Mountain Boys, they sing 'I'm Gonna Sit Right Down and Write Myself a Letter'.

Episode Six
HAPPY BIRTHDAY, HOWARD
First transmitted: 29 November 1992
Marina asks Clegg to deliver a birthday present to Howard without Pearl noticing – a job that would be easier if she hadn't chosen to buy him a giant cuddly panda! After carrying it through the streets, they meet Howard, who refuses to take it in case his wife finds out. To make transporting the cuddly toy easier, the men place it in a wheelchair, which gives Compo an idea. He pretends to be ill so that Nora takes him home with her. Once inside the house, he recovers quickly but she throws him out. Pearl sees the panda sitting outside her house and, thinking quickly, Howard says he's bought it for her.

Episode Seven
WHO'S GOT RHYTHM?
First transmitted: 6 December 1992
Compo complains to the others that, as usual, he's got no money. Foggy says he should get a part-time job. They call on Smiler, who's working for 'Uncle Henry Ltd' – alias Auntie Wainwright – to see if he knows of any spare work that might be available.

After a visit to Nora's, the trio come across a marching band – with two musicians who bear an uncanny resemblance to Howard and Marina – and Foggy has an idea. It's back to Auntie Wainwright's, where Compo acquires a one-man band. He tries to impress Nora with his musical aptitude but ends up tumbling down the steps.

Episode Eight
CAMERA SHY
First transmitted: 13 December 1992
On the way to Auntie Wainwright, the men meet Smiler, who's trying to sell some black ice-cream. Auntie sells Compo a stuffed owl, Clegg an old cup and Foggy a camcorder. While practising filming in the hills, Howard becomes convinced that Foggy has caught him on tape with Marina. Back at Clegg's, Foggy wants to watch his film, but there's no video recorder. They ask Howard if they can borrow his, but Pearl suggests they watch it in her house – with all the ladies present for one of their coffee mornings. Howard pays Compo to cause a distraction while the film is being shown. Did he have anything to worry about? You'll have to watch and see!

Episode Nine
WHEELIES
First transmitted: 20 December 1992
Foggy has hit on a new idea and, after showing a drawing to Wesley, the trio go to Auntie Wainwright's to buy some bicycle wheels – only to come away with a giant wheel and a lady's foundation garment. Back at Wesley's, the invention is complete. It's a 'wheel-on-wheels', and Compo has to test it. The first attempt ends swiftly when he crashes into a wall. The second attempt is no better when the rope that's towing it snaps, sending the wheel and Compo careering out of control. He hits a barn, knocking Howard and Marina off the roof, and carries on, eventually entering an indoor go-kart track, before coming to an abrupt halt in the local pond.

Christmas Special 1992
STOP THAT CASTLE
First transmitted: 26 December 1992
Foggy is chatting with a man down a manhole, while Clegg is at home doing the ironing. The trio visit Auntie Wainwright's to borrow an inflatable castle for a seasonal parade – hire charge £34, blowing up extra! The castle is too heavy to carry, so they employ the services of a pram, whose wheels promptly fall off. They take the castle to Wesley to inflate, but he puts too much air in it and his shed is demolished. They have to get the castle to Smiler, who, dressed as Noddy, is driving the car that is pulling the trailer which is to carry the castle. (Are you following this?) They drop the castle from a bridge to get it on to the trailer but it hits a police car instead.

The day of the parade arrives. Everyone is in costume: the trio are medieval soldiers, Pearl is the wicked witch, Marina is Snow White with Edie as Dick Whittington and Glenda as the cat. Ivy is a fairy, Nora is Bo-Peep and Howard (thinking Marina is going to be Bo-Peep) is dressed as a sheep! The parade starts well until Foggy catches the castle with his pikestaff and deflates it with the ladies inside.

SERIES 15
Nine Episodes

Episode One
HOW TO CLEAR YOUR PIPES
First transmitted: 24 October 1993
Compo wants to sweep Nora Batty into his muscular arms. Unfortunately, he's not quite up to the task, and Foggy suggests a fitness regime revolving around an assault course.

After an attempt at tree-climbing and dangling from the rafters of a barn, Foggy gets the other two men crawling through sewer pipes. When they get stuck inside one, Wesley has to come and cut them free.

Howard is out displaying posters for a bicycle race. He drops one off at Auntie Wainwright's, who promptly sells him a combined coat rack and umbrella stand.

When Howard and Marina turn up for the start of the race, they find dozens of other people have turned up to take part too. Worse still, as they set off, Pearl passes by on the top deck of a double-decker bus.

EPISODE TWO
WHERE THERE'S SMOKE, THERE'S BARBECUE
First transmitted: 31 October 1993

Howard's behaving more oddly than usual. He turns up at Clegg's house with a pocket full of nails and is later seen at the café with wood down his trouser leg.

Auntie Wainwright cons Foggy into buying a telescope and Clegg a portable barbecue. They go off into the hills to try out the barbecue, but it explodes. Wesley is called upon to fix it.

Back at Clegg's house, Foggy attempts to open a jar of beetroot and spills it on his shirt. Borrowing one of Howard's, the men go back to the hills to retry the barbie. They find Howard and Marina sitting on a love seat that Howard has made from the wood and nails. But when the boys light the barbecue, it almost destroys the seat, leaving Howard and Marina to walk off into the sunset with the charred remains.

EPISODE THREE
THE BLACK WIDOW
First transmitted: 7 November 1993

Both Foggy and Compo are suffering the after-effects of the home brew they drank at the funeral tea of Ernie Mordue the night before. Howard informs them that Clegg has been abducted by Mrs Jack Attercliffe after complimenting her on her buns! They find Clegg at home, where he tells them he's about to be whisked off to the over-60s' tea dance. Compo suggests finding a replacement widower, so they enlist Smiler and take him to Auntie Wainwright's for a new suit. At the dance, Compo tells Widow Attercliffe that Smiler has fancied her for years. He points him out, but she picks the wrong man and ends up with Foggy.

EPISODE FOUR
HAVE YOU GOT A LIGHT MATE?
First transmitted: 14 November 1993

Howard wants Clegg to buy a china doll from Auntie Wainwright's to give to Marina. First, though, Clegg and Compo have to go to the police station to bail out Foggy, who's been arrested for lurking in the bushes.

Smiler has been conscripted by Auntie Wainwright to sell security lights, which explode every time they're switched on. Meanwhile, the ladies are at the church hall going through men's trouser pockets in time for the jumble sale.

The trio call at Auntie's for the china doll, but she also manages to sell Foggy a set of the dodgy security lights, which Foggy manages to sell on to Howard. Later, up in the hills, Howard hands Marina the china doll, but when she gives him a thank-you cuddle, he goes up in smoke as the lights he has hidden under his jumper explode.

EPISODE FIVE
STOP THAT BATH
First transmitted: 21 November 1993

Howard wants the trio to meet him at Auntie Wainwright's to collect a present for Marina. The problem now is how to get the cast-iron bath that Auntie has managed to sell to Howard to Marina's. Foggy borrows a trolley from Auntie (for a fee, of course), and she also sells him a stag's head and Clegg an old mop.

As they push the bath through the town, it suddenly runs away with Compo in it. It comes to a halt against a drainpipe, which it fractures, sending water cascading over Compo. They try carrying it over their heads next, across the fields, but meet the ladies having a picnic, and when Howard hears Pearl's voice, they beat a hasty retreat.

EPISODE SIX
SPRINGING SMILER
First transmitted: 28 November 1993

Nora Batty has thrown Smiler out of the house. Now he's offering £50 to anyone who can get him thrown out for good. Foggy hits on the idea of Smiler becoming a paramour so that when he makes a pass at Nora, she'll get rid of him. They ask the great lover of the Dales, Howard, his advice on lovemaking. He suggests a present. They go off to Auntie Wainwright's, who sells the men a pair of antique earrings.

Now comes Smiler's big chance. He goes to tell Nora that he's in love with her. For a change, Foggy's plan actually works and Nora throws Smiler out.

EPISODE SEVEN
CONCERTO FOR SOLO BICYCLE
First transmitted: 5 December 1993

Compo decides to give his bicycle an airing, and after running into Foggy (literally!) they visit Clegg. Howard has told Clegg that Marina has left him for a taller man (Smiler), so he's decided to try 'taller' exercises – one of which includes dangling from the banisters.

Auntie Wainwright gets Smiler to deliver a small chest of drawers to a customer, whom she is shocked to discover is Marina.

As a result of their earlier collision, Foggy decides bicycle safety wear is what's called for. Compo is covered in foam rubber, and while testing it out demolishes Wesley's shed. Next he has an old inner tube shoved up his jumper. This time he ends up riding straight through the ladies' picnic.

Outside the public library, Clegg (Peter Sallis) is wondering exactly what Marina (Jean Fergusson) would like to borrow from him. He certainly appears to be praying for early closing!

PUBLIC
OPENING
MONDAY
TUESDAY
A Charming Couple
ELIZABETH FORD

EPISODE EIGHT
THERE ARE GYPSIES AT THE BOTTOM OF OUR GARDEN

First transmitted: 12 December 1993

Auntie Wainwright is visited by a gypsy but manages to sell her a set of garden furniture. When the gypsy's husband arrives to bring the set back, she sells him a set as well. Compo, meanwhile, is worrying about his animal magnetism following further rejection from Nora.

While walking in the woods, the men hear a knocking sound, which Foggy assures them is a giant spotted woodpecker. It's actually Howard and Marina building a tree house. Foggy, not realizing that, organizes a nature tour and enlists Wesley to drive the ladies in a minibus. They all arrive at the spot where the woodpecker is supposed to hang out, but the only wildlife they see is Pearl chasing Howard after he falls out of the tree house.

Not even being covered from head to toe in foam rubber can save Compo (Bill Owen) from wreaking more havoc – as Wesley's shed is about to find out in the episode Concerto for Solo Bicycle *(1993).*

EPISODE NINE
ALADDIN GETS ON YOUR WICK

First transmitted: 19 December 1993

Foggy is inspired to create a three-man sailboard after he sees a man windsurfing.

Auntie Wainwright, meanwhile, has gone upwardly mobile, dressing Smiler up as Aladdin and getting him to drive a mobile emporium. At the shop, Auntie sells the trio an old cupboard and, while testing it to see if it can float, they meet Howard and Marina in frogmen suits. Smiler threatens to tell Pearl unless Howard buys something. Howard returns home to Pearl that night with 15 rolls of vinyl wallpaper.

Using Edie's damask tablecloth as a sail, the men launch themselves out on the lake. Compo finds a key that unlocks the doors to the cupboard and they promptly fall through the bottom into the water.

CHRISTMAS SPECIAL 1993
WELCOME TO EARTH

First transmitted: 27 December 1993

Clegg takes his bike to Wesley to have it repaired, because the brakes failed, causing a collision with Howard. While it's being repaired, the men go for a walk and come across an old stone circle and a member of the Heckmondwyke Extra-Terrestrial Club. He tells them that he believes an alien spaceship will land there shortly and that he's ready with an early warning device – a bleeper.

Howard has bought Marina a bleeper so that she can contact him, but trying it that night sets off the other one. The trio race up the hill, joined by the rest of the pub. At the stone circle, Foggy organizes a joint turning-on of torches and lights – which reveals not aliens but Howard and Marina.

NEW YEAR'S SPECIAL 1995
THE MAN WHO NEARLY KNEW PAVAROTTI

First transmitted: 1 January 1995

Wesley calls at the café to ask the trio to help him move a piano to Auntie Wainwright's. On the way, they almost run over an old mate, Billy Ingleton – a mate of Pavarotti – who claims he's set to be a world-famous pianist. He offers to buy the piano.

Auntie Wainwright, meanwhile, is fretting over the whereabouts of the instrument and sends Smiler to locate it.

Trying to find the name of the piano's maker, Billy gets stuck in the piano. On his release, he tells the men he needs an audience for his playing, so Foggy sets out to organize a concert. The day of the concert arrives, but Billy loses his bottle and tries to run away. The men catch him at the railway station. He's fortified with whisky and goes on stage in front of the band conducted by Eli. After all the build-up, Billy can play only the introduction to a piece and so he pretends to faint, leaving Compo to entertain the audience with a rendition of 'Nora's Back in Town'.

SERIES 16
Eight Episodes

EPISODE ONE

THE GLORY HOLE

First transmitted: 8 January 1995

Foggy drags Compo and Clegg up a hill to examine a hole in the road. On the way, they meet Howard, who's suffering from a bout of indigestion after eating several scented notes sent by Marina.

Back at Compo's house, the men look for a photograph of an old chum but find only an old hand-winding siren from the war. Compo tries it out, and Wesley – who is painting Nora's kitchen – drops emulsion over her in surprise. They take the siren to Auntie Wainwright, who swaps it for a genuine flagpole (with a certificate to prove it), which they take up to Foggy's hole in the road. Edie and Glenda are out driving and, narrowly missing Howard and Marina on their bikes, swerve the car and end up on top of the mound of earth overlooking the glory hole.

EPISODE TWO

ADOPTED BY A STRAY

First transmitted: 15 January 1995

While sitting in the pub, the trio are approached by a Mr Broadbent, who asks for directions to 'the wilderness'. Foggy thinks he's after money, and they leave him, but up in the hills they meet the man again, and this time he says he's searching for wisdom. He leaves the men his van, which they discover comes complete with Mrs Broadbent in the back. They try to lose her, but she keeps turning up again.

Meeting up with Smiler, they swap the van for a 'thingummy' that Auntie sold him. Mr Broadbent returns, saying that he misses his wife. The feelings aren't mutual, and she sets about him with her handbag.

EPISODE THREE

THE DEFEAT OF THE STONEWORM

First transmitted: 22 January 1995

Howard asks Clegg to come to look at his cellar. While down there, he tells Clegg that he'll be able to communicate with him by tapping on the stone wall. When he tries it out, Pearl catches him and Howard insists he's looking for stoneworm! To try to help Howard, the men start to spread rumours about the existence of stoneworm.

Passing the tailor's shop in town, the trio see the owner running around his premises – a mouse is loose, which Foggy plans to catch. He gets Compo to stand still in the shop window, but the mouse runs up his trouser leg.

Howard returns home with a milking machine Auntie Wainwright has sold him. Pearl tells him she's phoned the council and that there's no such thing as stoneworm.

EPISODE FOUR

ONCE IN A MOONLIT JUNKYARD

First transmitted: 29 January 1995

Somebody dressed in motorcycle gear is looking for Compo. First the stranger calls at his house, then nearly runs him over when the men are talking to Howard, who's out jogging. Then the men see the motorcyclist outside the pub talking to Nora Batty. Compo sends Foggy to find out who it is. It turns out to be one of Compo's old girlfriends called Babs.

As the ladies discuss the motorcyclist, they remember one of Compo's other old flames – called Grace. She was a dumper-truck driver!

Dressed in racing leathers, Compo takes the men to the place where he used to court Babs. She arrives suddenly and whisks Compo away on the back of her bike. Compo decides he's too old for that sort of game and resolves to stick with Nora.

Auntie Wainwright is visited by a gypsy but manages to sell her a set of garden furniture. When the gypsy's husband arrives to bring the set back, she sells him a set as well.

EPISODE FIVE

THE SPACE ACE

First transmitted: 5 February 1995

In the hills, the men see a man climb into a wheelie bin and launch himself down the slope. The man – Stanley Pocklington – tells them he's training to be an astronaut. Howard and Marina are at Auntie Wainwright's to buy some backpacking gear – Howard has declared himself an 'outside man'.

The trio take Stanley to the pub, where he has too much to drink. He ends up being towed in his wheelie bin by Wesley, who is on his way to Auntie Wainwright's with a load of paint. Wanting to help, Foggy talks Compo into doing tests in deceleration – first on a bike, then in a chair on Wesley's trailer. Compo crashes with the wheelie bin and jumps on board to stop it moving, but runs into the paint tins, which open and cover Howard and Marina. The space ace comes round, sees them and thinks he's on another planet.

EPISODE SIX

THE MOST POWERFUL EYEBALLS IN WEST YORKSHIRE

First transmitted: 12 February 1995

Howard's decided to take up hypnotism. Foggy claims he can already do that and to prove it, he tells Compo and Clegg that he will hypnotize the first person they meet – which happens to be Eli! At the pub, Compo challenges Foggy to hypnotize the barmaid, but he gets thrown out when caught by the landlord.

Next Foggy tries to hypnotize a man at the bus stop but instead hypnotizes himself. He ends up on the bus, which is transporting a group of people to demonstrate against the building of a motorway. Still under the spell, Foggy gets off the bus when told to and is given a placard to carry. On the march, a man clicks his fingers, which wakes up Foggy, who, seeing the placard, tosses it over a wall – hitting Howard, who's secretly meeting Marina.

EPISODE SEVEN

THE DEWHURSTS OF OGLEBY HALL

First transmitted: 19 February 1995

Foggy has received a letter which he believes may prove he's related to the Dewhursts of Ogleby Hall. He calls the Royal College of Heralds to enquire about the coat of arms with the motto 'Loyal, Silent and Deadly'.

Wondering how to meet Lord Ogleby by accident, Foggy comes up with the plan of catching Compo poaching. Compo agrees to the task, but only if Foggy buys a hat for Compo to give to Nora. The shops are too expensive, so the men try Auntie Wainwright's, who ends up selling them one each. In Lord Ogleby's grounds, the men are chased out by a dog, which savages the hat that Compo wanted to give Nora.

EPISODE EIGHT

THE SWEET SMELL OF EXCESS

First transmitted: 26 February 1995

Compo uses his bed as a trampoline to catch a glimpse of Nora through her bedroom window. He gets stuck in the springs and needs Foggy and Clegg to free him. They push him to Wesley's to cut him out. On the way, the bed rolls down a hill and comes to a stop over an open manhole. As Wesley cuts him free, Compo disappears down the manhole. The ensuing smell makes Compo exceptionally unpopular in the town.

Deciding to blow the smell away, Compo stands on the back of Wesley's open Land Rover but almost freezes solid. After thawing him out, they stand him at the back of the vehicle again and take him through the car wash. A final attempt at trampolining outside Nora's almost works, but Compo bounces too high and is left hanging off the guttering.

SERIES 17
Ten Episodes

EPISODE ONE

LEAVING HOME FOR EVER OR TILL TEATIME

First transmitted: 3 September 1995

Howard arrives at Clegg's house with two suitcases – Pearl has thrown him out after finding lipstick on his collar. Foggy takes charge and says they must play on Pearl's sympathy. They place Howard on a park bench, looking forlorn, and write a note to Pearl telling her to be there at 15.45.

Auntie Wainwright sells them a combined hat rack and umbrella stand with free bonnet, which they deliver to Pearl with the letter.

Unknown to our trio, Marina has turned up and is sitting with Howard. Foggy distracts Pearl, while Compo and Clegg try to hide Marina. Clegg ends up in the bushes, with Compo and Marina falling in the pond with Howard. Howard claims he was saving Compo, and Pearl believes him and allows him back home.

EPISODE TWO

BICYCLE BONANZA

First transmitted: 10 September 1995

Foggy decides the men need to get 'off-road' more, and fortunately (or unfortunately) Auntie Wainwright is holding a bicycle sale. After collecting the cycles, the trio go to Clegg's to make sandwiches before going off-road cycling. En route, Foggy discovers that his brakes are faulty and he disappears over a wall.

At the ladies' coffee morning, Glenda informs them that Barry is taking up body building – much to the disgust of Edie.

Back in the hills, the men are stuck in a bog. Wesley tries to pull them out with his Land Rover, which also manages to get stuck, but not before the rear wheels have sprayed the trio with mud.

EPISODE THREE

THE GLAMOUR OF THE UNIFORM

First transmitted: 17 September 1995

Howard announces that Marina has left him again. This time she's gone off with a traffic warden called Cyril Gridley, who used to bend your thumb back until you said 'Czechoslovakia'! Feeling depressed, Howard tells Pearl that he's off to join the Foreign Legion. On his way to France, he bumps into the trio, who tell him that what Marina is impressed by is the uniform. They all go to Auntie Wainwright, who's now selling fancy dress. Howard gets kitted out in Foreign Legion garb, and they make for the supermarket to tell Marina that Howard will enlist if she stays with Cyril.

Pearl sees Howard and believes he has signed up, but she

When will Howard (Robert Fyfe) ever learn that you can't ask Auntie Wainwright (Jean Alexander) a question without ending up buying something you never wanted?

also sees him later with Marina on the back of his bicycle. Foggy gets Compo dressed up to make Pearl think it was him with Marina, but Cyril gets the wrong idea and Compo is soon running away shouting 'Czechoslovakia'!

Episode Four
THE FIRST HUMAN BEING TO RIDE A HILL
First transmitted: 24 September 1995

After a kiss, cuddle and a clip round the lug 'ole from Nora, Compo meets Foggy and they call at Clegg's, where Howard informs them that Pearl has confiscated his bicycle. Foggy commands Howard to be more decisive, so off he goes to get his bike, only to return with an inner tube wrapped round his neck. The only solution is a bicycle disguised as something else to put Pearl off the scent. Wesley invents one – a cycle disguised as a small, landscaped hillock! Giving it a test-drive, Compo surprises two policemen when he stops alongside their car and then runs Howard and Marina – who are travelling on her bike – off the road. They decide to dump the bike, but bearing in mind its design, they place it in the middle of a traffic island.

Episode Five
CAPTAIN CLUTTERBUCK'S TREASURE
First transmitted: 1 October 1995

At the pub, the men meet Lieutenant-Commander Willoughby RN (Retired) who is being thrown out by the landlord. At the café, he cons Foggy into buying a map that's supposed to show where famous Yorkshire pirate Captain Clutterbuck hid his treasure. Meanwhile, Howard and Marina are digging a hole in a field, following Foggy's discussion on sniper trenches providing good cover. After Foggy hands over £30 for the map, the men visit Auntie Wainwright's to buy a metal detector and go off to find the treasure. Dozens of other people are out looking for it too. Trying to escape from two angry men to whom he's sold a map, Willoughby falls into the trench, enabling Foggy to get his money back.

Episode Six
DESPERATE FOR A DUFFIELD
First transmitted: 8 October 1995

Compo has decided that as he's not making any progress

with Nora, it's time to find his first love – 'big' Audrey Mottershaw. He shows Foggy and Clegg a school photo. Foggy points out that the one he thinks is Audrey is actually Billy Cinders. Nobody knows where Audrey lives, though Nora knows she married a Duffield from Hedley Terrace, but it's been pulled down. And there are eight Duffields in the phone book.

Howard lends Compo a teddy boy suit complete with velvet collar and off they go in search of Audrey. Wesley gives them a lift to the last Duffield on the list, though as he's also delivering furniture Compo ends up inside a wardrobe. Swerving to avoid Edie, the wardrobe shoots off into the road. Edie informs everyone that they needn't have bothered looking for Audrey because she moved to Canada. So Compo decides it's back to Nora again.

EPISODE SEVEN
THE SUIT THAT TURNED LEFT
First transmitted: 15 October 1995
While out walking, the trio come across a man acting suspiciously. He tells them he's invented a magnetometer to find the hidden forces of nature. Wesley, meanwhile, has been told he has to drive the bus for the church outing. The stranger tells the men that when the power is found, you must stand in a circle holding hands.

Howard is in for a surprise when Pearl appears dressed like Marina – in a low-cut top and short skirt – and he has to go out holding hands with her. The trio are also holding hands and get thrown out of the pub. In the hills, the stranger finds a large power source which needs vast numbers of people to hold hands. The church outing helps out, but the only hidden force of nature that's discovered is Howard and Marina.

EPISODE EIGHT
BEWARE OF THE ELBOW
First transmitted: 22 October 1995
Compo is hearing voices while sitting on Nora's steps. In the hills, Compo sees a fat lady rise up in the air and then disappear. Foggy and Clegg think he's losing his mind. They take him for a pint, but while at the pub he sees the fat lady again passing the window.

The fat lady turns out to be a giant inflatable balloon being used by a man who wishes to protest about people being thin. His wife reminds him of a picklefork and she keeps jabbing him with her elbow. The trio decide to help the man on his crusade. They surprise Wesley and Smiler, who are shifting some furniture for Auntie Wainwright, and then Howard and Marina, who are performing a tango in a field. The balloon springs a leak and lands on top of the ladies, who are in Edie's car. She swerves and drives into a car transporter.

EPISODE NINE
THE THING IN WESLEY'S SHED
First transmitted: 29 October 1995
After a fairly wet morning – Eli gets soaked when he holds up a sign for Compo by Nora's kitchen and Foggy tells a war story to a man at the canal, who throws himself in to get away – the trio take a stroll and see Wesley acting suspiciously. They help him carry some motor parts, but he won't let them in his shed. When he takes his invention for a test-run, they follow him. The men cadge a lift with Eli, but his driving is worse than his eyesight and he drives into a haystack which has been hiding Howard and Marina. Wesley's invention turns out to be a car you can drive on land or in water. When Compo test-drives it to impress the ladies, it sinks. But he pretends to be injured and Nora gives him the kiss of life.

EPISODE TEN
BRUSHES AT DAWN
First transmitted: 5 November 1995
Foggy comes away from the barber's smelling of sweet jasmine, which gets him a kiss from Marina. He meets up with the others, and while passing a graveyard, Compo thinks he's seen a dead vicar. The vicar gets them to carry some armour into the church hall, where Nora Batty is found in a cupboard with Billy Chislehurst. Compo is depressed and decides to challenge Billy to a duel. So it's back to the church, where he slaps Billy across the face with a racing paper, and then it's off to train for the fight.

The duel is to be fought in armour, on bikes, using yard brushes. After several attempts at jousting, the men fall off and become entangled. Compo has his elbow uncomfortably positioned for Billy, who gives up. Nora rewards the victor with a kiss.

CHRISTMAS SPECIAL 1995
A LEG UP FOR CHRISTMAS
First transmitted: 24 December 1995
Howard's depressed. He says he feels inadequate after watching a film starring Arnold Schwarzenegger (or, as Compo refers to him, Arnold Schwarz'n'vinegar!).

Smiler is test-driving a large motorbike for Auntie Wainwright. When he doesn't return, she calls the police,

The ladies' coffee mornings, and their chats about all things male, have become a favourite part of the show over the years. Hence the smiles from (top left, clockwise) Juliette Kaplan, Jane Freeman, Kathy Staff, Sarah Thomas and Thora Hird.

who come round to investigate and end up buying a stuffed white owl for £17.50.

Foggy decides to build Howard up and gets him jogging, then doing press-ups. The men have to take Howard home in a wheelbarrow. Wesley is showing Glenda his new vehicle – a hearse. Howard is up and running again and shows Foggy that he's fit enough to jump a wall – which he does, and lands on a chicken coop, breaking his leg at the same time. The first vehicle to pass is Wesley in his hearse. They pass Smiler on the motorbike, who, seeing Howard sitting up in the back, swerves off the road.

On Christmas Eve, to try to cheer Howard up, the men invite him to Clegg's house for a drink. They invite Marina too. But how do they get her past Pearl without her noticing? They borrow the motorbike and leathers from Smiler, which Compo wears and turns up at Clegg's house in, while Pearl is around. He sneaks out the back of the house and Marina dresses in the leathers so that Pearl will still think it's Compo.

The other ladies turn up to wish Howard a merry Christmas and to give him his presents. Compo and Marina have to swap clothes back as the ladies decide to stay and have a party at Clegg's. Marina is stranded on the roof on her own...until Santa turns up!

CHRISTMAS SPECIAL 1996
EXTRA! EXTRA!
First transmitted: 29 December 1996
There are strangers in the area looking for directions. Unfortunately, they first ask Clegg and then Eli. The trio stumble on a film crew and get roped in as extras. At the café, Pearl shows the ladies an electronic tag she has attached to Howard's bike to keep tabs on him.

At the film set, Compo is dressed as a hussar and is expected to ride a horse, so he rides off on Howard's bike. The ladies discover him in a barn. Nora thinks he looks magnificent in the costume, so Compo decides to ride the horse after all. Unfortunately, it throws him off. The director tells him he only wanted Compo to conduct the band and choir.

Barry arrives on the film set on a scooter that Auntie Wainwright sold him, but it frightens the horse, causing it to bolt while the film director is sitting on it. Nora thinks that it's Compo on the horse and is pleased to see he's all right.

SERIES 18
Ten Episodes

EPISODE ONE
THE LOVE-MOBILE
First transmitted: 20 April 1997
At Auntie Wainwright's, Smiler gets conned into buying a tandem, so he tries to resell it. He gives a lift to Compo, but they both end up in a hedge. Foggy and Clegg turn up with Wesley and pick up Compo, leaving Smiler and the tandem in the hedge. Up on the moors, they meet Lance and Ethel, a couple who run a dating agency and who never stop arguing with each other. Their car has broken down, so Wesley offers to help. Smiler arrives on his tandem and decides to give the agency a go. He ends up with Ethel. Barry, meanwhile, has his own problems – he has to kiss Glenda in public!

Back at the agency, Ethel returns to Lance. Not even she can put up with Smiler.

Foggy helps Barry by getting Compo to teach him how to kiss in public. Arriving at Edie's, Barry tries it out with Glenda, while Compo tries it on with Nora.

EPISODE TWO
A CLEAN SWEEP
First transmitted: 27 April 1997
Outside a church, the ladies are watching a wedding when a man wearing a large plastic chimney walks past. He meets the trio, who help him on to a bridge, not realizing he's depressed – through lack of business – and intends to throw himself off.

Saving him in the nick of time and taking him to the café, Foggy says he needs to look more like a sweep to attract clients. So it's off to Auntie Wainwright's to get him some brushes. Finding an old house, the sweep tries his brushes up a chimney, but they get stuck, so Compo has to go on to the roof to free them. He gets covered in soot. However, it's not all bad news: as he walks back to town, Compo receives a kiss and a £10 note from a bride in a passing Rolls-Royce.

EPISODE THREE
THE MYSTERIOUS C. W. NORTHROP
First transmitted: 4 May 1997
Smiler asks Clegg for advice on love. Not for himself, of course, but for a friend – C. W. Northrop. Compo, meanwhile, is outside Nora's, standing on his head as he tells her he's having a mid-life crisis. Smiler admits to Clegg and Howard that he's attracted to Ivy and has written to her using the alias C. W. Northrop. Seeing Ivy outside the café, Smiler realizes he's not left her a love note but his dry-cleaning ticket. At the ladies' coffee morning, Ivy's secret paramour is the topic of conversation. They try to trace Mr Northrop in the phone book and on finding an address go to warn him off – only to find they've got a complete stranger into trouble with his wife.

EPISODE FOUR
A DOUBLE FOR HOWARD
First transmitted: 11 May 1997
Howard's looking for someone the same size as him, for

reasons as yet unknown. He approaches the men for help. He tries Wesley, also to no avail. While helping a magazine salesman, the trio meet up with Howard again at Auntie Wainwright's, where he's bought a shop window dummy. Howard explains that he needs someone his size so that at a distance it looks like him and when Pearl catches his double with Marina, she'll be embarrassed. They decide Eli will fit the bill.

They take Marina to Eli, and all goes well until Eli mistakes a policeman for her and gives him a kiss, which leads to his arrest. The magazine salesman, meanwhile, ends up selling nothing, but buying a wheelbarrow of rubbish from Auntie Wainwright.

Episode Five
HOW TO CREATE A MONSTER
First transmitted: 18 May 1997

On his way back from the library, Clegg is startled by Howard, who wants to borrow his bike – Pearl has confiscated his own one again. Foggy gets thrown out of the Adult Education Centre after asking one of the assistants if her father was ever a Japanese sniper. Smiler has got a job as a lollipop man but can't control the children. Auntie Wainwright sells him some armour to protect himself.

Foggy assures Compo he can train anybody to do anything and tries ridding Clegg of his fear of going into Auntie's shop. She ends up selling them two wardrobes. Foggy turns his attentions to Smiler, and they march him to a barn where he attacks a scarecrow. His confidence now built up, Smiler kisses Marina, tries to throttle Barry in his car and attacks the trio with his lollipop.

Episode Six
DEVIATIONS WITH DAVENPORT
First transmitted: 25 May 1997

Up in the hills, the trio meet Davenport, a man who writes guidebooks. He accepts help from Foggy, who insists he knows the area backwards and promptly gets them all lost.

Edie tells Wesley that the ladies need a lift, so he designs a trailer with revolving seats.

Foggy persuades Davenport to climb a tree to look for a road, but the branch snaps and he falls to the ground.

Wesley takes the ladies out, but the spinning makes them dizzy and Edie orders him to phone for a minibus.

The trio hitch a lift on Howard's and Marina's bikes but end up in a ditch. Wesley offers them a lift on his trailer. They, too, get dizzy.

Finally, an attempt by Compo to look through Nora's windows ends in disaster when he gets stuck hanging upside down from the rope he borrowed from Smiler.

Episode Seven
ACCORDING TO THE PROPHET BICKERDYKE
First transmitted: 1 June 1997

The men meet a stranger, who believes the world is on fire. Wesley, meanwhile, couldn't be happier when Barry and Glenda turn up in their new car, which is making a slight noise and needs looking at. Barry is apprehensive, particularly when Wesley takes the engine out.

The stranger, called Gunnershaw, tells the men over a drink about the prophet Bickerdyke – a man who used to work on the railway and just before dying told Gunnershaw when the world would end. Up in the hills, Gunnershaw predicts that the world will end on a Wednesday at 2.17 p.m. – the time which it happens to be. They hear a loud bang and see smoke and think the end of the world has arrived. But it's just Barry's car, which Wesley is supposed to have fixed.

Episode Eight
NEXT KISS PLEASE
First transmitted: 8 June 1997

Howard is confined to barracks and needs to get a message to Marina. Clegg refuses, so he gets Eli to do it instead. Compo bets Foggy that he can get Nora to kiss him. He cons his way into her house by saying one of his ferrets is loose and comes out bragging to Foggy that he got the kiss. Foggy doesn't believe him, so they go to Auntie Wainwright's to buy a camera for future proof.

Eli's search for Marina ends in disaster when he sees her and falls into a hedge. Auntie sells the men a camera and a sign on which Compo writes that he needs the kiss of life. But when the sign is turned the other way, it reads: 'Come in and browse without obligation'. Compo makes one final attempt at getting a kiss from Nora. Dressed in a suit, he tells her they're being filmed for a kind neighbour's programme, which he's put her name down for, and this, at last, earns him the kiss he's been waiting for.

Episode Nine
DESTINY AND SIX BANANAS
First transmitted: 15 June 1997

Compo asks Nora to accompany him to the Citizens' Advice Bureau. She finds it's all a ruse when he asks the adviser if living next door to Nora for 40 years constitutes a common-law relationship.

The trio are out walking when a man runs up and claims there are giant apes in the woods. Foggy is in his element as a so-called jungle fighter. Compo and Clegg pick up six bananas and meet up at Auntie Wainwright's with Foggy, dressed in a safari suit, and Wesley, with his all-terrain vehicle. Foggy explains how he'll capture the apes using a blowpipe and darts with anaesthetic on them – well,

Horlicks, actually, which Foggy insists always gets him off to sleep. After hitting one of the apes in the rear, they discover it's Howard and Marina in black tracksuits.

EPISODE TEN
A SIDECAR NAMED DESIRE
First transmitted: 22 June 1997
Clegg gets a surprise from Howard when a hole appears in his wall. He tells Clegg that he's heard a rumour about Marina and the undermanager of the supermarket. Discussing this with Foggy and Compo, they meet Smiler, who's pushing a motorbike and sidecar.

Compo has an idea to use them to take Nora out, as her late husband Wally used to do. Howard is determined to find out if the rumours about Marina are true. When he meets her she says she wasn't offered marriage but a garage for her new convertible.

Compo gives a lift to Nora, Ivy and Pearl. They see Howard and Marina out together and give chase, but the motorbike goes out of control and stops in a ditch.

CHRISTMAS SPECIAL 1997
THERE GOES THE GROOM
First transmitted: 29 December 1997
Compo and Clegg are off to a stag night where they meet Truly, an old friend, who's retired from the police force. The men, including the groom, Ronnie, and Barry, have had too much to drink and Truly rings Wesley for a lift. At Clegg's house, Truly recalls his married life to the former Mrs Truelove. The picture being far from rosy puts Ronnie off getting married, and the next morning he does a bunk in a milk float. Foggy, meanwhile, still worse for wear from the stag night, has been taken in by the post lady, who offers to look after him. Smiler can't work out what to buy for a wedding present and ends up with a vase from Auntie Wainwright's – which he promptly gets his hand stuck in.

The trio eventually catch up with Ronnie, who's chained himself to a road sign in the hills. They carry him and the sign into Wesley's Land Rover but are stopped by the police for stealing the sign. Barry's in a panic because he can't find the wedding ring. He remembers giving it to Foggy, but he's disappeared. A neighbour tells him the post lady took Foggy away in her car. Collecting Ronnie from the police station, Truly handcuffs him to himself and they go to Compo's to show him what a bachelor pad can look like in the hope it will encourage him to get married. Ronnie rather likes it!

Next they enlist the help of Marina, who poses as a gypsy and warns Ronnie of the bad life he'll have if he doesn't get married. He finally succumbs. As the ceremony is about to begin, Clegg gets a phone call from Foggy saying that he's been kidnapped by the post lady and taken to Blackpool.

SERIES 19
Ten Episodes

EPISODE ONE
BEWARE THE OGLETHORPE
First transmitted: 4 January 1998
Compo, Clegg and their new-found friend Truly take a walk in the hills. They call at the café, where they find Nora – with no wrinkles in her stockings – and a depressed-looking man whom they discover to be an old school chum called 'Coggy'.

Wesley has invented another machine – a heavy-duty sucker/blower – and he needs someone to test it. Glenda volunteers Barry, but after several explosions, she changes her mind. Wesley tries Howard, who decides it would be safer at home doing the housework. Wesley meets the trio, and Compo, not wanting to end up like Coggy, volunteers to help. He soon wishes he hadn't, when he gets blown down the hill.

EPISODE TWO
TARZAN OF THE TOWPATH
First transmitted: 11 January 1998
Compo suggests that the men try rolling down the hills as they did when they were nine years old. They soon make their way to the café to recover! Howard asks Barry to take a note to Marina, but he chickens out, so Eli takes it instead. He gives it to the wrong woman at the supermarket.

Following the hill-rolling, Ivy tells the men that the Chinese used to walk on people's backs to cure their pain. Nora tries it on Compo and frightens off two customers.

By the canal, Compo remembers the days when horses pulled boats, and the others get him to pull them along.

Barry agrees to take a new note to Marina for Howard, but Glenda finds out and thinks Barry's after Marina. Compo is now pulling Foggy and Clegg along in a boat using a tricycle. At the top of a bridge, the rope tightens and pulls the bike and Compo over the top, into the canal.

EPISODE THREE
TRULY AND THE WHOLE TRUTH
First transmitted: 18 January 1998
Truly wants his face in the papers, so he tells Compo and Clegg he'll try to rescue somebody. He starts with Howard, whom he tries to knock off a bicycle in order to save him. Out on the road they see a hole that Truly thinks a workman may have fallen down. He leans over to look but falls in himself.

Summer Wine *guest star Tony Millan makes a picturesque appearance in the episode* According to the Prophet Bickerdyke *(1997).*

Compo finds an old life-jacket at home, which prompts Truly to perform a rescue at the river. At the riverside, a dog is running around. Truly says he'll wait for it to jump in, then he'll rescue it. To ensure the newspapers are there, he phones them anonymously. While trying to catch the dog, though, Truly falls in the water and ends up being rescued by Howard and Marina, who are doing a bit of fishing.

Episode Four

OH HOWARD, WE SHOULD GET ONE OF THOSE

First transmitted: 25 January 1998

Wesley is entering the Smedley Mad Machine Competition but is keeping his invention a secret. He's even got a guard dog, which Barry discovers to his peril when delivering Wesley's breakfast. The café is closed today, and the men wonder where the ladies are going, when they spy Ivy and Nora walking with tins of buns. The ladies get stuck in a ditch in the hills, thanks to Edie's driving, and the men help get them out. Wesley drives past with his invention, and the trio follow him. It turns out he's created a motorized bed.

The ladies deliver the buns to old Granny Bassenthwaite, but on the way back, Edie swerves to miss Eli and ends up in the ditch again. While climbing out of the car, Nora hurts her foot, so Compo gives her a lift home on the motorized bed.

Episode Five

THE SUIT THAT ATTRACTS BLONDES

First transmitted: 1 February 1998

Compo again realizes that he's getting nowhere with Nora and decides to look for one of his old girlfriends, Phoebe Smethers. At the café, he buys a suit that's meant for the jumble. It has a good history for attracting the women. It used to belong to Barry, who wore it when he dated a girl with blonde hair – which is why Glenda wanted shot of it.

When Compo calls at Phoebe's house, the door gets slammed in his face, so he goes in search of another former love, Babs. She's all over him when they meet, and he runs off.

Howard decides to dress as a woman, allowing him to meet Marina in broad daylight without being recognized. Compo tries to make Nora jealous by walking around the jumble sale with this 'new woman', but Pearl recognizes Howard, leaving Compo to try the full in-your-face approach again. Nora chases him away.

Episode Six

THE ONLY DIESEL IN CAPTIVITY

First transmitted: 8 February 1998

Compo has received some startling news – an old schooldays rival is calling to see Nora. It's Goatie Hellowell, who wants Nora to join the church cleaning team. Compo decides to challenge Goatie to a series of tests – which Compo always lost at school. First they run round the block, which ends in a draw.

Barry buys a saxophone with a carrying case in the shape of a cuddly ostrich from Auntie Wainwright. Wesley sees the ostrich and thinks he is to become a granddad and goes to build a go-kart for his grandchild.

Compo and Goatie, meanwhile, try tree-climbing and have to be rescued by the fire brigade. The final challenge is trolley-racing. They swerve off the road when they hear a lorry coming – but it's Barry trying to play the saxophone.

Barry (Mike Grady, second left) seems to be enjoying the ordeal as he and the other men land in a flowerbed during the filming of What's Happened to Barry's Nose? *(1999).*

Episode Seven
PERFECTION – THY NAME IS RIDLEY
First transmitted: 15 February 1998
Who is this Mr Ridley that all the ladies are going off to clean for today? Even Howard has volunteered to take him for a bicycle ride. The men find Barry all upset because Edie has borrowed his car to take the ladies to Mr Ridley's, as her vehicle is out of action. Compo fixes Edie's car, and they go off to the pub, where Auntie Wainwright arrives with Eli, who's wheeling a wardrobe for her. Howard arrives with Mr Ridley and Compo introduces him to Marina. When the ladies turn up after their cleaning duties, they witness their Mr Ridley dancing on a table with Marina, outside the pub.

Episode Eight
NOWHERE PARTICULAR
First transmitted: 22 February 1998
Howard has bought a van, which he wants to keep secret. Meanwhile, Compo has conned Nora into believing he has a dog, and the other two men are all dressed up, as Truly is taking Clegg to the town hall to sort out his council tax.

Compo needs to find something to do, so he calls on Nora, who clouts him with her yard brush, then he tries to help Barry clean his car, but ends up covering it in feathers from a torn pillow, and goes to aid Smiler, who's delivering things for Auntie Wainwright on a handcart, which he wrecks. Next he moves on to Wesley just as he's about to test Howard's new van. Along the way they pick up Marina, who sits on Compo's knee. When the van goes up a steep hill, Compo and Marina fly out of the back in the chair, which runs down the hill and comes to rest next to Truly and Clegg.

Episode Nine
FROM AUDREY NASH TO THE WIDOW DILHOOLEY
First transmitted: 1 March 1998
Nora's expecting a visitor, which gets Compo wondering. And Howard, calling to see Marina at the supermarket, discovers she's been writing to another man. At the café, Compo discovers that Nora's visitor is the Widow Dilhooley, who used to be Audrey Nash. Truly remembers dancing with Audrey many years before and decides to invite her again.

Wesley has invented a motorized rickshaw, which he gets Barry to test with unfortunate consequences. Howard is determined to find out who Marina is writing to, so he follows her and discovers that it's Smiler.

Truly buys an old-fashioned suit from Auntie Wainwright in the style he wore when he first danced with Audrey Nash. He's shocked to discover she's now a rather large woman who doesn't remember him at all. And she ends up dancing with Compo.

Episode Ten
SUPPORT YOUR LOCAL SKYDIVER
First transmitted: 8 March 1998
After Nora receives a postcard from the Canary Islands, Compo decides he has to impress her. He serenades her outside her kitchen window and is rewarded with a bowl of water over his head. At Auntie Wainwright's, Smiler is dressed in an airman's outfit complete with a parachute. This gives Truly an idea of how Compo can impress Nora.

At the café, Compo is now dressed in the airman's outfit. Truly tells Ivy and Nora that he's going to undertake a parachute jump. Later, Truly calls them to come and watch. To make it look like Compo has jumped, Truly gets him to sit in a tree and fall out when Nora arrives. He thinks they are arriving – but it's only Barry on Wesley's new remote-controlled vehicle. But it's too late: Compo jumps and ends up dangling from the branches.

SERIES 20
Ten Episodes

Episode One
THE PONY SET
First transmitted: 18 April 1999
Our trio meet a stranger – Mr Lucy – waiting for a bus. They see him later running away from his wife and standing on a bridge. Compo startles him and he falls in the water. On the way home, the men see Marina dressed in riding gear that she's bought from Auntie Wainwright.

At the ladies' coffee morning, Glenda tells the others that Barry is thinking of taking up horse-riding. They think he's up to something, and so does Glenda when Marina cycles past in her riding gear. Overhearing that Nora is attracted to men in riding gear, the men go to Auntie's to buy Compo an outfit. She talks Compo into trying out her riding simulator – a wooden horse on wheels attached to Wesley's Land Rover. But when Wesley stops suddenly, the wooden horse continues, rolling straight past the ladies in Edie's car.

Episode Two
HOW ERROL FLYNN DISCOVERED THE SECRET SCAR OF NORA BATTY
First transmitted: 25 April 1999
Nora has a scar on her leg, but Compo wants to know which one. He ponders the question up in the hills with the men, when they come across Billy Hardcastle – a man dressed as Robin Hood. He tells them he's a direct descendant of Robin Hood and that he will live in the woods once he gets a band of merrie men together. Nora thinks Billy Hardcastle looks like her screen hero Errol Flynn, so Compo decides to dress up like Robin Hood. Smiler, Marina and Howard turn up in the forest dressed as merrie men. Compo, meanwhile, is up a tree so that he can

jump down dressed as Robin Hood. It all goes wrong and he's left dangling from the branches. At least he gets to discover which leg Nora's scar is on!

Episode Three

WHO'S THROWN HER TOM CRUISE PHOTOS AWAY?

First transmitted: 2 May 1999

Marina has finished with men. To prove it, she's thrown her Tom Cruise photos away.

After meeting Smiler dressed as a woman to promote Auntie Wainwright's ladies department, the trio find Howard sitting by a stream feeling sorry for himself.

Truly decides to make Marina jealous by using Smiler in drag to join Howard while he drives around town. Barry turns up, so they get him dressed as a woman too. Marina sees Howard driving past with two women in a car and follows him in Wesley's Land Rover.

Unfortunately, Howard drives past Edie's house as the ladies come out from their coffee morning. Pearl sees Howard, Glenda sees Barry and then Edie sees Wesley.

Compo sells Howard the Tom Cruise photos he rescued from the bin, which Howard duly gives to Marina. She hits Howard over the head with them.

Episode Four

WHAT'S HAPPENED TO BARRY'S NOSE?

First transmitted: 16 May 1999

Howard has a delivery of weight-lifting equipment sent to Clegg's house so as not to arouse Pearl's suspicions.

Barry wants to be more assertive and asks Truly for help. Barry soon gets thrown out of the pub and ends up being hit on the nose by a disgruntled driver. Helping Barry back to Clegg's house, the men find that Howard has hurt his back using the weight-lifting equipment. Just how are these injuries going to be explained to Pearl and Glenda? Smiler turns up on roller skates and Truly suggests they all say they were hurt skating. They go off to the café and end up in a heap in the flowerbed outside. Wesley gives Howard a lift home and all is well until Pearl hears Marina call for Howard on a megaphone she bought from Auntie Wainwright's.

Episode Five

OPTIMISM IN THE HOUSING MARKET

First transmitted: 23 May 1999

Smiler is selling door to door from two heavy suitcases. Wesley and the men offer him a lift and drop a case on Smiler's foot. They rush to Auntie Wainwright's to pick up a wheelchair.

On the way to pick up Smiler from the hospital, Compo cadges a lift in the wheelchair and abuses the sympathy of Nora – who thinks he's ill – by stealing a kiss. As the men push Smiler around, they keep banging his foot, so Wesley designs a bumper by using half a car tyre on the front of the wheelchair. Compo gives it a test-run, but it gathers speed downhill and Barry chases after him on a kid's scooter, passing his manager, whom Glenda is trying to talk into giving him a promotion. The wheelchair stops when it hits a wall, throwing Compo into the river.

Episode Six

WILL BARRY GO SEPTIC DESPITE LISTENING TO CLASSICAL MUSIC?

First transmitted: 30 May 1999

Compo decides to impress Nora by tightrope-walking. To steady himself he borrows a clothes prop from Howard, delivering a message for Marina in return.

Barry grazes his knuckle while fixing the sink for Glenda at home.

After Compo tries out walking on a gate, and falling off, the trio meet Lester Coalville, a man testing for earthquakes. Giving the men a lift in his van, they meet Wesley and Barry with his arm in a sling. He claims he injured it when he fell off a roof! Lester's wife Maud thinks he's out with another woman and enlists the help of Smiler to find out what he's up to. Lester thinks he's discovered an earthquake, but it's Howard and Marina using a Morse code machine. Howard runs off when Pearl arrives on the scene and Maud marches Lester off when she discovers him with Marina.

Episode Seven

BEWARE THE VANILLA SLICE

First transmitted: 6 June 1999

Howard has come up with a plan to confuse Pearl. He gets Clegg to call for him and then refuses to go out, saying he'd rather be at home with his wife. Out walking, Compo asks Clegg and Truly if they remember a game they played as kids called 'Thumpy Dub', which involved standing on a bridge trying to knock each other off using poles with padding on the end. Eli remembers the game and practises walking on a bridge until Barry and Glenda surprise him and he falls off.

Howard's plan works. Pearl gets fed up with him at home and throws him out.

At their coffee morning, the ladies are wondering why Marina is buying vanilla slices.

Compo meets an old adversary – Doggie Barnes – who challenges him to a game of Thumpy Dub. They both end up in the river!

A rare shot of Bill Owen with his stand-in, Robin Banks, here relinquishing his wellies for a moment to play the bookseller Mr Heptinstall in Welcome to Earth *(1993).*

DAISY
ANE
KS

Howard (Robert Fyfe) thinks driving these two 'ladies' (Mike Grady and Stephen Lewis) will make his mistress, Marina, jealous in the uproarious episode Who's Thrown Her Tom Cruise Photos Away? *(1999). Wouldn't you be?*

EPISODE EIGHT
HOWARD THROWS A WOBBLER
First transmitted: 13 June 1999
Howard wonders why Pearl is laughing on the phone. Truly volunteers the men to follow Pearl to see what she's up to, and Compo volunteers to meet Marina on Howard's behalf. Pearl leaves the house all dressed up, and the men stay close behind. Compo, meanwhile, meets up with Marina to escort her home, but coming to a huge puddle, has to carry her across. Pearl arrives at Edie's and tells the women that her plan to get Howard to notice her appears to be working. Pearl makes her way to a pub, where she's meeting a relative, whom she kisses. Howard thinks it's her fancy man and storms off without believing it was all innocent.

EPISODE NINE
THE PHANTOM NUMBER 14 BUS
First transmitted: 20 June 1999
A stranger – Mr Bramwell – is in town asking people about a number 14 bus which used to run 50 years ago. Auntie Wainwright sells him a lamp, saying it came from that very bus! He meets the trio and tells them the history of the bus.

Pearl is fed up with Howard buying tubes of glue from the supermarket and sets up a stall outside the house to sell them. To ensure Howard stays there, she glues his shoes to the ground.

Up in the hills at 4.27 p.m. – the time that Mr Bramwell claims the number 14 bus mysteriously disappeared – everyone thinks the phantom has returned with a ghostly figure at the wheel. It turns out to be Wesley, covered in dust, driving one of his weird inventions.

EPISODE TEN
IRONING DAY
First transmitted: 27 June 1999
Auntie Wainwright is having a sales promotion – a free bottle of home-made wine with every purchase. It's strong stuff – just two glasses get Smiler drunk. The men try to sober him up, but he sees Eli's bike and rides off on it. Barry is walking a neighbour's dog, and as Smiler passes on the bike, he grabs the lead and makes off with the dog. Smiler sees Marina, who needs help getting a drunk Howard

(he's also had some of Auntie's wine) off a bridge. The rescue attempt sees both men land in the water.

Compo and Truly arrive and take Howard and Smiler to Clegg's to dry them out. Compo creates a diversion so that Howard can sneak past Pearl to change his clothes. He pretends to be looking at something over a wall. Pearl looks too, and they both end up tumbling over it.

MILLENNIUM SPECIAL

LAST POST AND PIGEON

First transmitted: 2 January 2000

Billy Hardcastle appears in a Stone Age outfit. It's early in the morning, and the vicar's filming Billy for a local record of the new millennium. The trio come riding past on their bikes, Billy steps out in the road and off they fall. They tell him that Compo is off to France with a local group to visit the war graves at Dunkirk.

Later, Nora signs for a package for Compo, which turns out to be his passport.

At the café, Nora enters with a letter for Compo. It tells him he can't go to France after all. Compo is heartbroken. The ladies are chatting about Compo's cancelled trip. Howard appears dressed in beret and dark glasses – he's off to do some assistant directing on the vicar's millennium film. Compo's still gloomy, trying to work out why he isn't allowed to go to France.

The ladies turn up in Edie's car, and Nora tells him they've had a collection and he will go after all, and that Truly and Clegg are going with him.

Wesley is tinkering outside his shed when Edie's long-since-seen sister Ros arrives and tells him she's coming home for good.

The trio board a motorbike and sidecar and start their long journey. They meet Billy, who asks them to take his pigeon, Gladys, to France and release her. The men are soon on the ferry leaving the white cliffs of Dover. They arrive at Dunkirk and almost bump into a French version of Compo! They get to their hotel and try to work out how to smuggle in the pigeon. During the evening the men get quite tipsy and Compo blows a loud blast on his bugle.

Later, the pigeon hides on top of the wardrobe in the men's bedroom. When they try to rescue it, the wardrobe crashes to the ground.

The sun rises on a new day. The trio are sleeping on the beach!

In England, rehearsals for the church pageant continue apace, and Glenda tries to get Ros and Edie to patch up their old differences.

Compo, Truly and Clegg get to some French woodland and arrive at a pond, which Compo stares at because it brings back memories.

At the church, spectators are watching the filming of the historical pageant. Marina appears as Nell Gwynn!

Ros is pushing Edie in a wheelchair. They approach Wesley and Edie's house and see a banner reading 'Welcome Home Ros'. There are hugs and kisses all round.

In the woodlands of France, Compo gets a wreath and bugle out of the sidecar. He hangs the wreath on one of the trees. He then plays the Last Post on his bugle and Clegg releases the pigeon.

SERIES 21

Ten Episodes

These episodes appear in order of production.

EPISODE ONE

LIPSTICK AND OTHER PROBLEMS

Howard's waiting anxiously by a phone box to make a personal call. Compo says that if the person using the phone doesn't come out quickly, they'll chuck him out. They don't see a much larger man take his place!

Marina gives up waiting for the call, rides off on her bike and falls in a ditch. Barry drives up and Marina kisses him for looking after her. When he later arrives at Wesley's garage, he's seen with lipstick on his face. Glenda's not pleased!

The three men almost get run over by a lunatic motorbike rider, who turns out to be Auntie Wainwright road-testing her stock.

The trio decide to tell Glenda that Barry was kissing for charity, and to make it more believable they borrow Nora's lipstick and apply it to each other. Two policemen wheel Auntie's bike past a bus shelter and see the three men wearing lipstick!

EPISODE TWO

UNDER THE RUG

Truly tells Barry that to get to managerial positions one has to be master of one's own home. Howard, meanwhile, is awaiting a package, which is to be delivered to Clegg's.

Glenda is vacuuming when Barry arrives and calls to her. He startles her, she breaks a vase and he's thrown out of the house.

Howard's parcel arrives. It contains a wig. They all poke fun at Clegg.

Auntie's doctor has told her to get out and spend more. She goes to the café and reluctantly buys half a cup of tea.

The men want Howard to wear the wig and think that if they can persuade Smiler to put it on, Howard will get jealous. Marina helps by grabbing Smiler at the supermarket and kissing him with the wig on. Howard decides to wear it. Pearl's not impressed, and the wig gets posted back through Clegg's letterbox.

EPISODE THREE
MAGIC AND THE MORRIS MINOR

A middle-aged couple, Stanley and Belle, are driving a Morris Minor along a country road.

At home, Clegg hears a tinny voice. It's Howard on a mobile radio.

Later, the trio meet the couple with the car, who claim to have been beckoned to the field by an ancient civilization.

In the park, Howard meets Marina and explains how the mobile radios work. He dashes behind a bush. Eli walks past, hears a squawk from the radio, mistakes Marina for a duck and throws bread at her.

Belle sees Barry and says he's the Chosen One. She says he must take her for his bride. Barry flees. Edie is driving the ladies when they see Barry run past being chased by Belle. The car ends up in a ditch.

Stanley prises Belle away from Barry. Edie rams her car into Wesley's Land Rover. Glenda turns on the radio and they all hear Howard's and Marina's voices.

EPISODE FOUR
ELEGY FOR FALLEN WELLIES

(Original working title: Black Tights)

Nora, Ivy and several ladies are performing a chorus girl number. A police car delivers an unclaimed crate to Truly's house. Walking home in their costumes, Ivy encourages Nora to give Compo a surprise in her sexy outfit.

An ambulance rushes through the street. Clegg, Truly, Nora and Ivy are at the hospital. The doctor approaches and his face says it all.

At home, Truly and Clegg drink a toast to their dear friend. In Nora's kitchen, she reminisces with Ivy, and Edie and Wesley discuss Compo's ferrets. A new day dawns and Truly and Clegg go for a walk. In the hills the men shout their goodbyes to Compo.

Truly's crate finally gets opened. It contains 200 pairs of painters' white overalls. The crate is loaded on to Wesley's Land Rover, and the men and women make their way into the hills. From the top and across the valley a message has been written on the hill. Made up of painters' white overalls, it reads: See Ya Compo.

EPISODE FIVE
SURPRISE AT THROSTLENEST

(Original working title: Preparations)

Nora hands a letter to Clegg and Truly, containing Compo's last wishes. He asks his friends to take a souvenir from his house and to deliver his ferrets to an old friend, Reggie Unsworth. He signs off by wishing his mates good luck.

Howard, who's been thinking about life and death, decides it's time to take Marina further than they've ever been. Barry, who's been looking after the ferrets, carries a wounded finger from one of them. Taking the ferrets to their new home, they overtake a burly cyclist, who sees Barry and thinks he's given him the finger!

Howard and Marina are out with their bikes. They move towards an embrace but are sent sprawling by the angry cyclist.

The Land Rover arrives at its destination. Truly, Clegg, Wesley and Barry stare as they encounter a scantily clad middle-aged woman tending the garden. It's Reggie Unsworth.

EPISODE SIX
JUST A SMALL FUNERAL

(Original working title: Funeral)

It's the day of Compo's funeral. Truly and Clegg are reminiscing; Nora and Ivy are making sandwiches. Nora's worried that Compo died with a smile on his face and people will want to know why. They all visit the chapel of rest.

Auntie Wainwright closes the shop for the funeral but leaves a mobile number in case of emergency sales.

Reggie needs something suitable to wear and grabs Howard to help her. Marina spots them together and crashes her cycle. Reggie wants somewhere cheaper to buy her clothes. They suggest Auntie's.

In the church the congregation are holding a funeral rehearsal. Auntie's mobile rings. She answers it and leaves in a hurry.

All the characters prepare themselves for the funeral.

The church is now full. The door slams and Reggie makes a grand appearance. She walks up to the coffin, touches it, then sits between Truly and Clegg. The coffin is put into the hearse and the funeral cortège passes through the hills with hearse, limos, private cars and Reggie on her tractor.

EPISODE SEVEN
FROM HERE TO PATERNITY

(Original working title: Newcomers)

Clegg finds it strange walking through the hills without Compo. Truly tries to imitate their old friend, stands on a wall and falls off.

A letter arrives for Compo. It's from his son – a big surprise to the men – and it says he's arriving in town that day.

The town is full of talk about Compo's son. The two men try to work out how to break the news of his father's death. At the pub a huge crowd has gathered. An old transit van arrives. The driver emerges, producing a ventriloquist's dummy dog. Nora sees the family resemblance and hugs the newcomer. It falls to Clegg to divulge Compo's death.

The newcomers seem to have brought several animals with them, including a chicken and goat, which keep escaping. Tom's daughter Babs and their friend Mrs Avery make up the new family, who announce they are coming to live in the area.

Episode Eight

SOME VANS CAN MAKE YOU DEAF

(Original working title: Exhausted)

Howard's enjoying breakfast on his terrace, much to the amusement of Clegg and Pearl. Tom roars up in his van and distributes Mrs Avery's business cards.

Howard suggests that Marina make an appointment to see Mrs Avery. Newcomer Tom, meanwhile, has problems with his van's exhaust – Wesley suggests they try the scrapyard.

Howard watches Marina having her palm read by Mrs Avery, but hides as Tom and Barry drive up. Barry's been looking for an antique for Glenda, and Tom persuades him that his old washtub would be ideal.

In the hills the ladies need a lift – Edie's car is back in a ditch. Tom stops and offers them one. Howard, who's hiding in the back of the van, is worried when he hears Pearl's voice. The van travels along merrily until the exhaust gives up. The jolting causes Howard to be revealed, much to Pearl's annoyance.

Episode Nine

FOLLOW THAT ORGAN

Tom's in an old armchair conducting daughter Babs through some physical exercises.

Later, Babs goes out jogging with Mrs Avery, and Tom follows them in his van with Truly and Clegg in the back. Tom asks if they would like to back Babs financially as she wants to get into show business.

Howard approaches Smiler and asks how he got to be so tall. Auntie insists she can put inches on Howard. He ends up wearing high heels!

Barry's in the back of Wesley's Land Rover brushing the cream suit that Glenda's bought him. The men bring out a musical organ. It's on wheels, so they tow it back home with Barry on the seat. As the car turns a corner, the organ comes loose and shoots off down the road. Barry gathers speed, and the Land Rover chases him in hot pursuit. Tom's instructing Babs and Mrs Avery in some physical exercises as Barry and his organ demolish the washing line.

Episode Ten

WAGGONERS' ROLL

Howard asks Clegg to recommend a quiet pub, which he does – the Waggoners.

Tom gets worried when Babs disappears. The two men meet Barry, who's out in his golfing gear. Tom asks for their help to find Babs.

Smiler's been helping Auntie Wainwright with a sofa which has a life of its own and starts rolling down the street on its casters.

The men find Babs at a rough-looking pub. Tom decides to give Barry a present for helping. Barry emerges wearing heavy metal gear and a ponytail. Howard and Marina arrive at the pub. They think they're alone, but Edie's car turns up with the ladies. The couple leave hastily.

By the roadside, the men are waiting for Wesley to fix Tom's vehicle. Edie drives past, and the car comes to a screeching halt as Barry's spotted. Glenda's not happy, as Barry certainly doesn't look as if he's been playing golf!

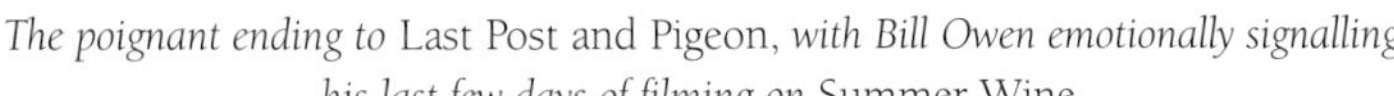
The poignant ending to Last Post and Pigeon, *with Bill Owen emotionally signalling his last few days of filming on* Summer Wine.

ACKNOWLEDGEMENTS

With huge thanks to *Summer Wine* creator and script writer of every word of every show, Roy Clarke, and to respected producer/director since 1981 and dear friend since 1998, Alan J. W. Bell, who not only gave this project his wholehearted support from the beginning but also gave us our BBC comedy acting break as Men at Bar!

To *Summer Wine* stars Jean Alexander, Jean Fergusson, Jane Freeman, Robert Fyfe, Mike Grady, Dame Thora Hird, Juliette Kaplan, Stephen Lewis, Danny O'Dea, Kathy Staff, Sarah Thomas, Frank Thornton and Gordon Wharmby for tirelessly supporting this book and making two outsiders feel very welcome.

To *Summer Wine* producers Jimmy Gilbert and Sydney Lotterby for invaluable insights into the show's history, and the late Duncan Wood for revealing how it all started.

To Ronnie Hazlehurst for allowing us to hear the beauty of Yorkshire.

Then there are the unsung heroes – the team that put the programme together. Our grateful thanks are extended to Bernadette Darnell, Francis Gilson, Christine Mellor and Tracie Wright who ensure that ten weeks on location run as smoothly as possible, and our friends on the set – Biff, Bob, Duggie, Jean, Keith and Pat – whose dedication makes hard work seem light. To the man who creates a little bit of Yorkshire within a bigger bit of Yorkshire, and for proving that being a set designer does not preclude being chased by admiring groupies – our thanks for the former and immense respect for the latter goes to Stefan Paczai. To the men who are anonymously credited as cast stand-ins but whom we look upon as stars in their own right, Robin Banks, Denis Mawn and Tony Simon – a bit of nosh, a crossword and a music hall comedy quiz with those three form unforgettable memories of our days on location. And special thanks too must go to the man whose daily quips always made us feel welcome on set – 'Morris and Robert are here, it must be lunchtime!' – thanks to our good pal, assistant director Phil Hartley.

Our thanks also to Ron Backhouse of the White Horse pub who gave us a big welcome and an even bigger breakfast; to all the staff of the Huddersfield Hotel, especially Paul Pierce, who if he ever retired would have no problem finding his own place on the show!! And to the good people of Holmfirth who were happy to embrace us with renowned Northern hospitality.

Thanks to those dedicated and helpful folk at the BBC – Ben Dunn, Charlotte Heathcote and Lara Speicher – for all their efforts; to Clive Eardley, Margaret Tilletson and Tony Burton of the *Summer Wine* Appreciation Society for their invaluable assistance and research. To Malcolm Haworth whose photographic passion for the

Peter Sallis with the authors – Morris Bright (left) and Robert Ross.

series over the past two decades has produced a wealth of stunning images, some of which we are proud to reproduce in this book.

A very special thank you to Peter Sallis – the only actor to appear in every episode of *First of…* and *Last of the Summer Wine*, for his precious time and dry humour. An extra special thank you to Brian Wilde who happily returned to talking about his *Summer Wine* days especially for this book, and finally our deepest thanks to the late Bill Owen who gave invaluable time during the last few weeks of recording his final shows. Professional to the last and very supportive of all that was *Summer Wine*, being in his presence was a rare privilege and one we will long cherish.

INDEX

Titles in bold refer to episode names. Page numbers in italics refer to illustrations.

PETER SALLIS
FRANK
THORNTON
BILL OWEN